365 Great
20-Minute Recipes

Beverly Cox

A JOHN BOSWELL ASSOCIATES BOOK

■ HarperCollins*Publishers*

HarperCollins books may be purchased for educational, business, or sales promotional use. For information, please write: Special Markets Department, HarperCollins Publishers, Inc., 10 East 53rd Street, New York, NY 10022.

Series Editor: Susan Wyler
Design: Nigel Rollings
Index: Maro Riofrancos

Library of Congress Cataloging-in-Publication Data
Cox, Beverly, 1945–
    365 great 20-minute recipes / Beverly Cox. — 1st ed.
        p.   cm.
    "A John Boswell Associates book."
    Includes index.
    ISBN 0-06-016962-1
    1. Quick and easy cookery.   I. Title.   II. Title: Three hundred sixty-five great twenty-minute recipes.
TX833.5.C68   1995
841.5′55—dc20   94-23886

96   97   98   99   DT/HC   10   9   8   7   6   5   4   3

Contents

Homemade in minutes, these hearty meals in a bowl include Light Chicken Noodle Soup with Spring Vegetables, New England Clam Chowder, Cheddar and Corn Soup, and Pinto Bean Skillet Chili.

Tuscan Tuna Salad, Sesame Beef and Broccoli Salad, Santa Fe Chicken Salad, and Grilled Lamb and White Bean Salad are a sampling of the tempting tosses offered here for a big lunch or light, cool supper.

Variety and flavor pair with quick cooking to produce a fabulous assortment of pasta favorites: Spaghettini with Quick Tomato Sauce, Pasta Puttanesca, Garlic Shrimp Linguine, and Ravioli with Spinach-Pecan Pesto, to name a few.

From Breakfast Burritos and Baked Eggs Florentine to a Bacon and Wild Mushroom Omelet or Asparagus and Scallion Frittata, this assortment of quick dishes can carry you through the entire day.

Bread, tortillas, muffins, and biscuits are all used here to create a truly tempting assortment of finger and knife-and-fork sandwiches, such as Ham and Cheddar Rarebit, Swiss Turkey Burgers, Sausage and Pepper Subs, Texas Pinto Bean Tostadas, and Pizza Margharita.

Side dishes as well as main-course vegetarian delights include Goat Cheese Potato Cakes with Smoked Salmon, Havana Black Beans and Rice, Broiled Cheese Polenta with Tomato-Mushroom Sauce, Carrot and Raisin Slaw, and Garlic-Roasted Broccoli with Balsamic Vinegar.

Introduction

Modern cooks are usually busy cooks. Except for an occasional lazy weekend or special occasion, we are often hard-pressed to prepare elaborate, time-consuming meals. This is a dilemma for many of us, because at the same time, our tastes are more sophisticated than they have ever been, we demand high quality in our food, and we are interested in good nutrition.

In developing the recipes for this book I have discovered many interesting convenience products that help keep preparation and cooking times to a minimum without sacrificing flavor. I have also taken advantage of time-saving devices, such as the food processor and microwave oven, when appropriate, to stay within a 20-minute limit. Wherever possible, chop onions and fresh herbs in the processor; use the pulse button, or turn quickly on and off, to chop without pureeing. If by chance you do not have this equipment, your preparation time may be a bit longer, but the work will still be quick.

Many of the dishes featured in the book are substantial enough to stand on their own, with perhaps just the addition of good bread or a salad. I have also tried to include recipes to suit many different occasions. I hope that you will enjoy this collection, and that it will help to simplify your life in the kitchen.

The 20-Minute Pantry

New, time-saving food products have played an important role in this book. Many good-quality products that do not compromise the flavor of finished dishes are now available. High-tech packaging—such as airtight plastic wrapping—is one reason why fresh products with a minimum of adulteration (and therefore better taste) now have a longer shelf life. Some of the best convenience foods include canned broth (beef, chicken, and vegetable), both regular and reduced-sodium; canned stewed tomatoes in many flavor varieties; canned, diced "pasta-ready" or "recipe-ready" tomatoes; canned cooked beans, such as kidney and pinto beans; canned reduced-sodium cream soups to use as sauces; ready-made pizza dough and Boboli-type crusts; Swedish pancake mix for easy crepes, and Bird's Imported English Dessert Mix for good, quick, crème brûlée; refrigerated ready-to-bake biscuits in a tube; grated cheeses; some of the better-quality bottled salad dressings and salsas; refrigerated and frozen sauces, such as pesto and marinara; better-quality bottled pasta sauces, with innovations like sun-dried tomato paste and puree; frozen vegetables, particularly combinations such as "stew vegetables"; frozen mashed and hash brown potatoes;

quick-cooking brown, white, or wild rice; ready-cut fresh vegetables such as broccoli florets and sliced carrots; washed and packaged mixed salad greens and sliced fresh fruit.

The well-stocked pantry of the "20-minute cook" should also include such staples as good olive oil and vinegars; Dijon mustard (both plain and grainy); dried pastas in different shapes; canned tuna, salmon, and crabmeat; olives, pickles, anchovies, green chiles, artichoke hearts, roasted red peppers, capers, jalapeño peppers, maple syrup, chocolate, and of course a well-stocked shelf of dried herbs and spices.

The 20-Minute Kitchen

The recipes in this book are streamlined to use a minimum number of cooking utensils, cutting down on preparation and cleanup time. Many recipes are prepared in one pot or skillet. The following list of recommended equipment can help make the "20-minute kitchen" a reality:

1. One large, thin-walled or lightweight aluminum pot with strainer insert for cooking pasta. Thin walls boil water faster—for boiling you don't need a heavy pot because food does not touch the bottom. The strainer-steamer basket insert makes draining the pasta a snap and is also handy for steaming vegetables.

2. One large (10- to 13-inch), heavy nonstick skillet with ovenproof handle and lid. A heavy skillet conducts heat more evenly, and a good nonstick surface cuts down on fat and avoids the mess of sticking. Size is important for quick-cooking because more food can be cooked at one time without crowding. An ovenproof handle allows you to save time by finishing cooking or browning in the oven or under the broiler. A lid allows the skillet to double as a casserole for making stews and braises.

3. One heavy 3-quart saucepan with lid for a variety of uses including cooking vegetables, rice, and sauces.

4. Well-made heavy, sharp knives: an 8- to 10-inch chef's knife, a small paring knife, a serrated knife for slicing bread and tomatoes.

5. At least two or three wooden and/or plastic spoons and spatulas to stir and turn food without scratching pans.

6. A food processor for chopping and pureeing.

7. A microwave oven for melting butter and chocolate, cooking bacon, steaming small quantities of vegetables, and thawing and reheating foods.

8. One good can opener, either manual or electric. If manual, buy one with plastic-coated cushioned handles for much easier use.

Chapter 1

Speedy Soups, Chowders, and Chilies

In days' past, most soups were long-simmering affairs, practical only for the cook who was home full time, with plenty of hours to devote to the pot on the back burner. Fortunately, the food industry has come to our rescue, and now even those of us with only 20 minutes to get a meal together can make a substantial soup. Good-quality canned chicken and beef broth—both regular and reduced-sodium—can now become the basis for a really tasty soup, and canned stewed tomatoes with a variety of seasonings add flavor, color, and texture to both soups and chilies. Additionally, canned beans, frozen and canned cut-up vegetable mixtures and purees, and quick-cooking rice and small pasta shapes all make for practically "instant" soup ingredients.

When making soup, it's usually best to use a large, thin-walled pot because it will bring liquids to a boil much faster than a heavy pot. Covering the pot also speeds the boiling process. Most soups lend themselves to doubling or tripling without much additional preparation or cooking time. Many of them make great make-ahead one-dish meals for informal entertaining, and most freeze well, too.

This soup collection offers something for all seasons and occasions, from the fancy and upscale to the more humble and everyday. Seafood, which makes a wonderfully flavorful soup, appears in various guises: Charleston She-Crab Soup, New England Clam Chowder, and Oyster Stew. Nutritious canned beans make for such satisfyingly hearty soups as White Bean and Sausage Soup and Quick Cuban Black Bean Soup. The new frozen mashed potatoes lend a smooth body and richness to Leek and Potato Soup and Acorn Squash Buttermilk Soup. And because we all love a bowl of steaming spicy chili, several recipes are provided, including Incendiary El Paso Chili, Pinto Bean Skillet Chili, and Quick Pork Chili Verde.

1 LIGHT CHICKEN NOODLE SOUP WITH SPRING VEGETABLES

Prep: 6 to 8 minutes   Cook: 11 minutes   Serves: 4

Leftover chicken and almost any vegetables can be used in this soup, with cooking times adjusted accordingly.

1 (46- to 49½-ounce) can chicken broth
2 medium carrots, peeled and cut into small dice
3 cups frozen peas
¾ pound slender asparagus, stalks thinly sliced, tips cut 1 inch long

½ pound skinless, boneless chicken breast, cut into thin strips
1 teaspoon dried tarragon
1 cup thin egg noodles (3 ounces)
¼ teaspoon pepper

1. Skim off and discard any fat from top of chicken broth. In a large saucepan, bring chicken broth, carrots, and 2 cups water to a boil over high heat. Add peas, asparagus, chicken, and tarragon. Reduce heat to medium-low, cover, and cook 5 minutes.

2. Add egg noodles and cook until vegetables and noodles are tender and chicken is white in the center, about 6 minutes. Season with pepper.

2 MEXICAN CHICKEN SOUP

Prep: 5 minutes   Cook: 13 to 15 minutes   Serves: 4

This soup was inspired by one served at Las Mananitas restaurant in Cuernavaca, Mexico. If you have leftover cooked turkey or chicken on hand, total preparation and cooking time can be reduced to about 10 minutes.

1 (46- to 49½-ounce) can chicken broth
2 skinless, boneless chicken breast halves
1 (15-ounce) can black beans, rinsed and drained
1 (11-ounce) can Mexicorn

¾ cup quick-cooking rice
2 scallions, thinly sliced
1½ tablespoons minced cilantro
1 tablespoon green or red salsa
¼ teaspoon ground cumin
4 lime wedges

1. Place chicken broth, chicken, and 2 cups of water in a large saucepan. Cover and bring to a boil over high heat. Reduce heat to medium-low and poach chicken uncovered until barely cooked through, 8 to 10 minutes. Remove and shred chicken.

2. Return chicken to broth. Stir in beans, corn, rice, scallions, cilantro, salsa, and cumin. Cook 5 minutes over medium-high heat.

3. Ladle soup into bowls and serve with lime wedges.

3   GREEK CHICKEN SOUP
Prep: 2 minutes   Cook: 15 minutes   Serves: 4

Lemon and egg combine to give this Greek version of chicken soup a tart flavor and creamy consistency. Heat the soup gently after the eggs have been added, or it may curdle.

1 (46- to 49½-ounce) can chicken broth	Juice of 1 lemon (3 to 4 tablespoons)
2 skinless, boneless chicken breast halves	½ teaspoon dried oregano
1 cup quick-cooking rice	¼ teaspoon salt
1 tablespoon cornstarch	⅛ teaspoon freshly ground pepper
4 eggs	1 tablespoon minced parsley

1. Place chicken broth and chicken in a large saucepan. Cover and bring to a boil over medium-high heat. Reduce heat to medium-low and poach chicken uncovered until barely cooked through, 8 to 10 minutes. Remove chicken and shred it. Return chicken to broth and stir in rice. Cover and remove saucepan from heat.

2. In a small bowl, dissolve cornstarch in ¼ cup water. Whisk in eggs, lemon juice, and oregano.

3. With a ladle, remove about 1 cup hot broth from saucepan. Gradually whisk broth into egg mixture. Return mixture to the saucepan and stir well.

4. Heat gently, stirring constantly, until soup is thickened and creamy. Season with salt and pepper. Serve garnished with parsley.

4   HOT-AND-SOUR CHICKEN AND RICE SOUP
Prep: 7 minutes   Cook: 8 minutes   Serves: 6

3 (14¾-ounce) cans chicken broth	1 tablespoon hot chile oil
1½ cups quick-cooking rice	1 tablespoon rice wine vinegar
1 pound skinless, boneless chicken breasts, cut into ½-inch dice	1 bunch of scallions, thinly sliced
1½ teaspoons minced fresh ginger	

1. In a large saucepan, bring chicken broth, rice, and 3 cups water to a boil over high heat. Add chicken to soup. Reduce heat to medium-low, cover, and cook until rice is tender and chicken is white in center, about 6 minutes.

2. Add ginger, chile oil, vinegar, and scallions and cook 2 minutes to blend flavors.

5 ORIENTAL CHICKEN NOODLE SOUP
Prep: 7 minutes   Cook: 12 to 13 minutes   Serves: 6

Using slender, quick-cooking noodles and thinly sliced vegetables that are prepared while the chicken is poaching speeds up the cooking time for this soup.

1 (46- to 49½-ounce) can chicken broth
4 skinless, boneless chicken breast halves
2 (5-ounce) packages Japanese curly noodles (chucka soba)
1 (6-ounce) package snow peas, thawed

3 medium carrots, peeled and cut into thin strips
3 scallions, thinly sliced
3 tablespoons minced cilantro plus 6 sprigs
1½ tablespoons minced fresh ginger
1½ to 2 teaspoons Chinese chile paste with garlic

1. Place chicken broth, chicken, and 4 cups water in a large saucepan. Cover and bring to a boil over high heat. Reduce heat to medium-low and cook uncovered 8 minutes, skimming off and discarding any foam that rises to the top.

2. Remove chicken and shred or dice it. Return chicken to boiling broth. Add noodles, snow peas, carrots, scallions, minced cilantro, ginger, and chili paste.

3. Cook until noodles and vegetables are tender and chicken white throughout, 4 to 5 minutes. Ladle soup into bowls and garnish with cilantro sprigs.

6 ALPHABET BEEF AND VEGETABLE SOUP
Prep: 5 minutes   Cook: 11 to 13 minutes   Serves: 3 to 4

1 tablespoon vegetable oil
1 pound lean ground beef
½ teaspoon pepper
2 garlic cloves, minced
2 (15-ounce) cans Italian-style stewed tomatoes
1 (14¾-ounce) can beef broth

1½ teaspoons Italian seasoning
1 (1-pound) package frozen mixed vegetables
⅓ cup alphabet noodles or other small pasta
¼ cup chopped parsley
¼ cup grated Parmesan cheese

1. In a large saucepan, heat oil. Season meat with pepper and add to pan. Cook over high heat, stirring, until browned, about 5 minutes. Add garlic and cook 1 minute.

2. Add tomatoes, beef broth, Italian seasoning, frozen vegetables, pasta, and 2 cups water. Bring to a boil over high heat, reduce heat to medium, and cook uncovered until pasta and vegetables are tender, 5 to 7 minutes.

3. Stir in parsley and cheese and serve.

7 ACORN SQUASH BUTTERMILK SOUP
Prep: 5 minutes   Cook: 12 to 15 minutes   Serves: 2 to 3

2 tablespoons butter
2 medium leeks (white and pale green parts only), well rinsed and finely chopped
1 (14¾-ounce) can chicken broth
2½ cups frozen mashed potatoes

1 (12-ounce) package frozen mashed winter squash, such as acorn or Hubbard, thawed
1 cup buttermilk
½ teaspoon ground ginger
½ teaspoon dried leaf sage, crumbled
¼ teaspoon salt
⅛ teaspoon pepper

1. Melt butter in a large saucepan. Add leeks, cover, and cook over medium heat 3 minutes. Uncover, raise heat to medium-high, and cook, stirring frequently, until softened, 2 to 3 minutes longer.

2. Add chicken broth, potatoes, thawed squash, and ¾ cup water. Bring to a boil over high heat. Reduce heat to medium, cover, and cook until potatoes are smooth, 6 to 8 minutes.

3. Add buttermilk, ginger, sage, salt, and pepper and heat through, but do not boil or buttermilk may curdle, about 1 minute.

8 BAKED BEAN AND MOLASSES SOUP
Prep: 3 minutes   Cook: 12 minutes   Serves: 5 to 6

3 tablespoons olive oil
2 medium onions, chopped
5 teaspoons chili powder
1½ teaspoons powdered mustard
2 (15-ounce) cans stewed tomatoes

2 (15-ounce) cans white beans, drained
¼ cup molasses
½ teaspoon salt
¼ teaspoon black pepper

1. In a large saucepan, heat oil. Add onions and cook over medium-high heat, stirring, until softened, about 3 minutes. Add chili powder and mustard and cook, stirring, 1 minute.

2. Add tomatoes and their juice, beans, molasses, and 4 cups water. Bring to a boil over high heat, reduce heat to medium, and cook uncovered 8 minutes.

3. Break up large chunks of tomatoes and mash about one-third of beans with the back of a spoon to thicken soup. Season with salt and pepper.

9   QUICK CUBAN BLACK BEAN SOUP
Prep: 5 minutes   Cook: 11 to 13 minutes   Serves: 6

Adding sherry to this soup is traditional, but not essential.

2 tablespoons canola oil
1 cup chopped smoked ham
   (about ¼ pound)
1 cup chopped onion
3 (15-ounce) cans black beans
2 (14½-ounce) cans vegetable
   broth

¾ teaspoon ground cumin
¾ teaspoon hot pepper sauce
½ teaspoon dried oregano
2 tablespoons dry sherry
¼ teaspoon salt
⅛ teaspoon pepper
½ cup sour cream

1. In a large saucepan, heat oil over medium-high heat. Add ham and ⅔ cup onion. Cook, stirring occasionally, until onion is softened, about 3 minutes.

2. Puree 2 cans of beans with their liquid. Add puree, remaining can of whole beans with liquid, vegetable broth, cumin, hot sauce, and oregano to saucepan. Cook over medium heat, stirring occasionally, until thoroughly heated, 8 to 10 minutes.

3. Add sherry and season with salt and pepper. Serve soup, garnished with remaining chopped onion and a dollop of sour cream.

10   CALIFORNIA AVOCADO SOUP
Prep: 5 minutes   Cook: none   Serves: 4

This lovely, pale green soup requires no cooking. It is perfect as a first course on a warm summer day.

3 ripe avocados
2 tablespoons lime juice
2 tablespoons lemon juice
2 (14¾-ounce) cans chicken
   broth
2 cups half-and-half

¼ teaspoon ground cumin
¼ teaspoon salt
¼ teaspoon pepper
¼ cup good-quality chunky
   salsa

1. Cut avocados in half and remove pits. With an avocado peeler or large spoon, scoop out avocado from skin and place in a food processor. Add lime juice and lemon juice and puree until smooth. With machine on, pour chicken broth and half-and-half through feed tube, processing until smooth. Season with cumin, salt, and pepper.

2. Divide among bowls and top each serving with about 1 tablespoon salsa.

11   QUICK BORSCHT
Prep: 5 to 7 minutes   Cook: 7 to 9 minutes   Serves: 3 to 4

Packages of shredded cabbage sold in the produce section of many supermarkets are a good time-saver.

2 tablespoons vegetable oil	⅛ teaspoon pepper
1 cup shredded cabbage	1 (16-ounce) jar pickled beets,
½ cup chopped onion	liquid reserved
¼ teaspoon caraway seeds	⅓ cup sour cream
¼ teaspoon salt	Fresh dill or parsley sprigs

1. In a large saucepan, heat oil over medium-high heat. Add cabbage, onion, caraway seeds, salt, and pepper. Cook, stirring occasionally, until vegetables are barely tender, 4 to 6 minutes.

2. In a food processor, puree cabbage-onion mixture and pickled beets, with their liquid.

3. Return to saucepan and cook over high heat, stirring occasionally, until heated through, about 3 minutes.

4. Ladle borscht into serving bowls and top each with a dollop of sour cream and a small sprig of dill.

12   WHITE BEAN AND SAUSAGE SOUP
Prep: 4 minutes   Cook: 16 minutes   Serves: 4

A handful of mild cheese tops off this savory bean and sausage soup.

1 tablespoon olive oil	1 (15-ounce) can stewed
12 ounces smoked sausage,	tomatoes
such as kielbasa, cut into	½ cup dry white wine
¼-inch slices	1½ teaspoons dried rosemary
3 medium carrots, thinly	½ teaspoon cayenne
sliced	¼ teaspoon black pepper
1 medium celery rib, thinly	1½ cups shredded Muenster or
sliced	other mild cheese
1 (15-ounce) can white beans,	
drained	

1. In a large saucepan, heat olive oil. Add sausage, carrots, and celery and cook over medium-high heat, stirring frequently, until sausage is browned and vegetables are softened, about 6 minutes.

2. Add beans, tomatoes, wine, rosemary, and 4 cups water. Bring to a boil over high heat, reduce heat to medium-low, and cook uncovered until soup is somewhat reduced and thickened, about 10 minutes. Season with cayenne and black pepper.

3. Ladle soup into bowls and top with cheese.

13   CHEDDAR AND CORN SOUP
Prep: 5 minutes   Cook: 15 minutes   Serves: 4

2 tablespoons butter
1 large onion, chopped
1 pound all-purpose potatoes, peeled and cut into rough ½-inch dice
4 cups frozen corn kernels
1 (14¾-ounce) can chicken broth

2½ teaspoons dried thyme leaves
3 cups half-and-half
4 cups grated medium-sharp Cheddar cheese
¼ teaspoon pepper

1. In a large saucepan, heat butter. Add onion and cook over medium-high heat, stirring, until softened and lightly browned, about 4 minutes.

2. Add potatoes, corn, chicken broth, thyme, and 2 cups water. Bring to a boil over high heat, reduce heat to medium, cover, and cook until potatoes are just tender, about 8 minutes.

3. Add half-and-half and cheese and cook over medium heat, stirring, until cheese is melted, about 3 minutes. Season with pepper and serve at once.

14   SOUTHWESTERN CORN CHOWDER
Prep: 5 minutes   Cook: 6 to 10 minutes   Serves: 6

This distinctive pueblo-style chowder combines corn with potatoes and chiles, two other ingredients that are also native to the Americas.

2 slices of bacon, coarsely chopped
1 small onion, chopped
2 tablespoons flour
½ teaspoon ground cumin
½ teaspoon chili powder
1 (16-ounce) can whole potatoes, drained, rinsed, and diced
1 (16½-ounce) can cream-style corn

2 (14½-ounce) cans reduced-sodium chicken broth
1 (11-ounce) can Mexicorn
1 (4-ounce) can chopped mild green chiles
¼ teaspoon salt
¼ cup sour cream
2 tablespoons minced cilantro

1. In a large skillet, cook bacon with onion over medium heat until fat is rendered, 2 to 3 minutes. Add flour, cumin, and chili powder. Cook, stirring, 1 to 2 minutes.

2. Stir in potatoes, cream-style corn, chicken broth, Mexicorn, chiles, and salt. Bring to a boil over high heat, 3 to 5 minutes.

3. Ladle chowder into bowls and top with sour cream and cilantro.

15   CORN AND RED PEPPER SOUP

Prep: 5 minutes   Cook: 12 minutes   Serves: 3 to 4

2 tablespoons vegetable oil
1 medium onion, chopped
1 garlic clove, minced
5 cups frozen corn kernels
2 (14¾-ounce) cans chicken
  broth

1 (7-ounce) jar roasted red
  peppers, drained and
  chopped
⅛ teaspoon grated nutmeg
¼ teaspoon Tabasco sauce
¾ cup plain yogurt

1. In a large saucepan, heat oil. Add onion and cook over medium-high heat, stirring, until it begins to soften, about 3 minutes. Add garlic and cook 30 seconds. Add corn kernels and 2 cups water. Bring to a boil over high heat. Reduce heat to medium-low, cover, and cook until corn is very tender, about 7 minutes.

2. Process corn mixture in a food processor or blender to make a coarse puree. Return to saucepan and add chicken broth and peppers. Bring to a boil over high heat and cook 1 minute. Season with nutmeg and Tabasco.

3. Ladle into bowls and top with yogurt.

16   GAZPACHO

Prep: 5 minutes   Cook: none   Serves: 2 to 3

In Spain, gazpacho tends to be thicker and pink rather than the thin, tomato juice–like version often served in the United States.

1 medium cucumber, peeled,
  halved lengthwise, and
  seeded
1 small onion, quartered
1 (14½-ounce) can Mexican-
  style stewed tomatoes
  Inside of 2 French rolls,
  crust removed

2 tablespoons balsamic or red
  wine vinegar
2 tablespoons extra-virgin
  olive oil
  Salt
1 cup packaged croutons

1. Finely dice one half of cucumber. Set aside for garnish. Cut remaining cucumber half into 4 pieces.

2. In a food processor, combine coarsely cut-up cucumber, onion, tomatoes, bread, vinegar, oil, and 1 cup cold water. Puree until smooth.

3. Season with salt to taste. Ladle gazpacho into bowls and serve topped with diced cucumber and croutons. If made ahead, refrigerate until serving time.

17   GREEN PEA SOUP WITH SMOKED HAM

Prep: 5 minutes   Cook: 12 minutes   Serves: 4 to 6

2 tablespoons butter
1 large onion, chopped
2 (14¾-ounce) cans chicken
   broth
1 (14-ounce) package frozen
   mashed potatoes

2 cups frozen peas
1 teaspoon dried tarragon
1½ cups milk or light cream
¼ teaspoon pepper
6 ounces smoked ham, finely
   diced

1. In a large saucepan, melt butter. Add onion and cook over medium-high heat, stirring, until softened, about 4 minutes. Add chicken broth, potatoes, peas, tarragon, and 1½ cups water. Bring to a boil over high heat, reduce heat to medium-low, cover, and cook until potatoes are smooth and dissolved, about 8 minutes.

2. Pulse soup in a food processor or blender to make a coarse puree.

3. Return puree to saucepan. Stir in milk and season with pepper. Reheat soup over medium heat. Ladle into bowls and top each serving with smoked ham.

18   LEEK AND POTATO SOUP

Prep: 6 minutes   Cook: 15 to 16 minutes   Serves: 5 to 6

The new frozen mashed potatoes add both body and flavor to this soothing brew.

2 tablespoons butter
4 medium leeks (white and
   pale green parts only),
   well rinsed, finely
   chopped
2 (14¾-ounce) cans chicken
   broth

1 (14-ounce) package frozen
   mashed potatoes
2 cups light cream or half-and-
   half
⅛ teaspoon grated nutmeg
¼ teaspoon pepper

1. In a large saucepan, melt butter. Add leeks, cover, and cook over medium heat 3 minutes. Uncover, raise heat to medium-high, and cook, stirring frequently, until leeks are softened, about 3 minutes longer.

2. Add chicken broth, frozen mashed potatoes, and 1½ cups water. Cover and bring to a boil over high heat; reduce heat to medium and cook uncovered until potatoes are smooth, about 8 minutes.

3. Stir in cream, nutmeg, and pepper. Cook over medium-high heat until hot, 1 to 2 minutes.

19   PASTINA EN BRODO
Prep: 3 minutes   Cook: 10 minutes   Serves: 4

This soothing soup is made with pastina, the very small star-shaped egg pasta. Any small egg noodles can be substituted, with cooking times adjusted if necessary.

1 (46-ounce) can chicken broth
2 medium carrots, peeled and cut into small dice
¾ cup pastina
¾ teaspoon dried oregano

⅔ cup grated Parmesan cheese
2 tablespoons minced fresh parsley
⅛ teaspoon pepper

1. In a large saucepan, bring chicken broth, carrots, and 2 cups water to a boil over high heat. Reduce heat to low, cover, and cook 5 minutes. Add pastina and oregano and cook until carrots and pasta are tender, about 5 minutes longer.

2. Stir in cheese and parsley. Season with pepper.

20   WILD MUSHROOM BISQUE
Prep: 3 minutes   Cook: 10 minutes   Serves: 3 to 4

2 tablespoons butter or vegetable oil
3 ounces shiitake mushrooms, chopped
2 tablespoons minced shallots
1 (10¾-ounce) can condensed cream of mushroom soup, preferably reduced-salt

1 (14¾-ounce) can beef broth, preferably reduced-salt
1 cup half-and-half
2 tablespoons sherry
⅛ teaspoon freshly ground pepper

1. In a large saucepan, melt butter. Add mushrooms and shallots and cook over medium heat, stirring frequently, until softened, about 5 minutes.

2. Raise heat to high and whisk in condensed mushroom soup, beef broth, and half-and-half. Bring to a boil, reduce heat to medium-low, and simmer uncovered 5 minutes.

3. Just before serving, stir in sherry and season with pepper.

21   TORTILLA SOUP
Prep: 4 minutes   Cook: 15 minutes   Serves: 4

To make this soup heartier, you can add leftover cooked chicken or turkey.

1 tablespoon vegetable oil
1 onion, chopped
2 garlic cloves, minced
1 teaspoon ground cumin
2 (14¾-ounce) cans chicken broth
2 (15-ounce) cans Mexican-style stewed tomatoes

1 tablespoon minced jalapeño peppers, fresh or pickled
¼ teaspoon pepper
2 cups shredded Monterey Jack cheese
1 (9-ounce) bag tortilla chips, coarsely crushed

1. In a large saucepan, heat oil. Add onion and cook over medium-high heat, stirring, until softened, about 3 minutes. Add garlic and cumin. Cook, stirring, 1 minute.

2. Add chicken broth, tomatoes, jalapeño peppers, and 2 cups water. Bring to a boil over high heat, reduce heat to medium-low, and cook uncovered 10 minutes. Season with pepper.

3. Ladle soup into bowls. Sprinkle cheese and tortilla chips over each serving.

22   CHESAPEAKE CRAB SOUP
Prep: 5 minutes   Cook: 11 to 14 minutes   Serves: 4

Old Bay Seasoning is a widely available, good-quality ground spice mixture for seafood. Other brands of spice mixes—usually called Chesapeake Bay seasoning—can be substituted.

2 tablespoons olive oil
1 large potato, peeled and cut into ½-inch dice
1 medium carrot, chopped
2 (15-ounce) cans stewed tomatoes
2 cups clam juice
1 cup dry white wine

2 teaspoons Worcestershire sauce
1½ teaspoons Old Bay or other seafood seasoning mix
1 cup frozen peas
12 ounces crabmeat, picked over
½ teaspoon Tabasco sauce

1. In a large saucepan, heat oil. Add potato and carrot; cook over medium-high heat, stirring, 1 minute. Add tomatoes, clam juice, wine, Worcestershire, seafood seasoning, and 1½ cups water. Bring to a boil over high heat, reduce heat to medium, cover, and cook until potatoes are tender, 7 to 10 minutes.

2. Add peas and cook for 2 minutes. Add crabmeat and Tabasco. Simmer 1 minute to heat through.

23   ITALIAN VEGETABLE-RICE SOUP
Prep: 7 minutes   Cook: 8 to 10 minutes   Serves: 4

1 (46- to 49½-ounce) can
    chicken broth
2 medium carrots, peeled and
    diced
1 medium zucchini, scrubbed
    and diced

1 (15.8-ounce) can Great
    Northern white beans,
    undrained
1 cup quick-cooking rice
¼ cup grated Parmesan cheese
2 tablespoons slivered fresh
    basil

1. In a large covered saucepan, bring broth to a boil over high heat, 3 to 5 minutes. Stir in carrots, zucchini, beans with their liquid, and rice. Cook until vegetables are crisp-tender, about 5 minutes.

2. Ladle soup into bowls and sprinkle with Parmesan and basil.

24   NEW ENGLAND CLAM CHOWDER
Prep: 5 minutes   Cook: 12 to 15 minutes   Serves: 4

Chopped frozen hash brown potatoes are a good-quality time-saving product that works well in both soups and stews.

3 slices of bacon, coarsely
    chopped
1 medium onion, chopped
1 teaspoon dried thyme leaves
1 pound frozen hash brown
    potatoes

2 (6½-ounce) cans chopped
    clams with juice
1 cup heavy cream
¼ teaspoon pepper

1. In a large saucepan, cook bacon over medium heat, stirring frequently, until fat is rendered, 4 to 5 minutes. Remove bacon with a slotted spoon and drain on paper towels, leaving 2 tablespoons drippings in pan.

2. Add onion and thyme to drippings and cook over medium-high heat, stirring, until onion is softened, 2 to 3 minutes. Add potatoes and 3 cups water. Bring to a boil over high heat, reduce heat to medium, cover, and cook until potatoes are softened, 5 to 6 minutes.

3. Add clams and their juice, cream, and pepper. Cook just until heated through, about 1 minute.

4. Ladle chowder into bowls and top with reserved cooked bacon.

25   CAPE COD FISH CHOWDER
Prep: 5 minutes   Cook: 13 to 15 minutes   Serves: 4

Almost any kind of firm white fish works beautifully in this rich chowder.

3   slices of bacon, coarsely
    chopped
1   medium onion, chopped
1   teaspoon dried thyme leaves
1   pound frozen hash brown
    potatoes
1   cup clam juice

2   cups half-and-half
1   pound boneless firm white
    fish, such as cod or
    haddock, cut into 1-inch
    pieces
¼   teaspoon pepper

1. In a large saucepan, cook bacon over medium heat, stirring frequently, until lightly browned and fat is rendered, 4 to 5 minutes. Remove bacon with a slotted spoon and drain on paper towels, leaving drippings in saucepan.

2. Add onion and thyme to bacon drippings and cook over medium-high heat, stirring, until onion is softened, 2 to 3 minutes. Add frozen potatoes, clam juice, and 2 cups water. Bring to a boil over high heat, reduce heat to medium, cover, and cook until potatoes are almost softened, about 4 minutes.

3. Add half-and-half and bring to a simmer over high heat. Reduce heat to medium, add fish, and cook uncovered over medium-high heat until potatoes are tender and fish is opaque, about 2 to 3 minutes. Season with pepper.

4. Ladle chowder into bowls. Sprinkle reserved cooked bacon on top and serve hot.

26   TORTELLINI EN BRODO FLORENTINE
Prep: 10 minutes   Cook: 7 minutes   Serves: 4

1   (46- to 49½-ounce) can
    chicken broth
1   (9-ounce) package fresh
    cheese tortellini
1½   cups fresh spinach leaves,
    well rinsed, shredded

1   small bunch of fresh basil,
    chopped
3   to 4 tablespoons grated
    Parmesan cheese

1. In a large saucepan, bring chicken broth to a boil over high heat. Add tortellini and cook 5 minutes.

2. Stir in spinach and basil. Cook until spinach is wilted and pasta is just tender, about 2 minutes.

3. Ladle soup into bowls and sprinkle with Parmesan cheese.

27 OYSTER STEW
Prep: 2 minutes   Cook: 5 to 6 minutes   Serves: 2

Oyster stew makes a quick but elegant last-minute lunch or dinner for two. The recipe below is inspired by one served at the famous Oyster Bar in New York City's Grand Central Station.

2 pints fresh oysters in their liquor	¼ teaspoon paprika
5 tablespoons unsalted butter	2 teaspoons Worcestershire sauce
¼ teaspoon celery salt	2 cups light cream

1. Drain the oysters, reserving liquor. Feel oysters and remove and discard any fragments of shell.

2. Place 4 tablespoons of butter in a saucepan over medium heat. Sprinkle with celery salt and paprika. When butter sizzles, stir in Worcestershire.

3. Add drained oysters and cook until oysters are plump and their edges curl, 1 to 2 minutes. Add oyster liquor and bring to a boil, about 1 minute. Stir in cream and cook until very hot but do not allow to boil, 2 to 3 minutes.

4. Divide remaining butter between 2 serving bowls. Ladle stew into bowls and serve at once.

28 CHARLESTON SHE-CRAB SOUP
Prep: 4 minutes   Cook: 16 minutes
Serves: 6 as first course, 3 as main course

A specialty of the coastal towns of South Carolina, this delicate, rich soup derives its name—and its distinctive flavor—from crab roe, which was cooked, sieved, and sprinkled on top. Sieved hard-boiled egg yolks can be substituted if you have the time.

2 tablespoons butter	½ teaspoon Worcestershire sauce
1 small onion, finely chopped	½ teaspoon salt
2 tablespoons flour	⅛ teaspoon grated nutmeg
3 cups milk	⅛ teaspoon black pepper
1 cup heavy cream	⅛ teaspoon cayenne
2 cups lump crabmeat, picked over	2 tablespoons sherry
1 teaspoon grated lemon zest	

1. In a medium to large saucepan, melt butter. Add onion and cook over medium-high heat, stirring frequently, until softened, 3 minutes. Add flour and cook, stirring, 1 minute. Raise heat to high, whisk in milk and cream, bring to a boil, and cook, stirring, 2 minutes.

2. Reduce heat to medium-low. Add crabmeat, lemon zest, Worcestershire, salt, nutmeg, black pepper, and cayenne. Cook uncovered, stirring occasionally, 10 minutes.

3. Stir in sherry. Ladle into bowls and serve.

29   QUICK LOUISIANA SEAFOOD GUMBO
Prep: 6 minutes   Cook: 14 minutes   Serves: 6

This thick, chunky southern Louisiana soup is usually served in a shallow bowl over a spoonful of cooked white rice.

3 tablespoons vegetable oil	2 teaspoons dried thyme
3 tablespoons flour	leaves
1 medium onion, chopped	1 pound shelled and deveined
1 medium green bell pepper,	medium shrimp
chopped	½ pound crabmeat, picked
1 (28-ounce) can Italian peeled	over
tomatoes with juice	½ teaspoon Tabasco sauce
2 cups clam juice	
1 (10-ounce) package frozen	
sliced okra, thawed	

1. In a large, heavy saucepan, heat oil. Stir in flour and cook over medium heat, stirring constantly with a wooden spoon, until roux turns a rich brown, about 3 minutes. Immediately add onion and bell pepper and cook, stirring, for 2 minutes.

2. Add tomatoes, clam juice, okra, thyme, and 5 cups water. Bring to a boil over high heat, crushing tomatoes with back of a spoon. Reduce heat to medium and boil uncovered until okra is very soft, about 6 minutes.

3. Add shrimp and crabmeat and cook over medium heat until shrimp turn pink, about 2 minutes. Season with Tabasco and pass bottle at table.

30   SPICY TURKEY AND CORN CHILI
Prep: 5 minutes   Cook: 13 to 15 minutes   Serves: 6 to 8

2 tablespoons vegetable oil	2 (15-ounce) cans Mexican-
1½ pounds ground turkey	style stewed tomatoes
2 medium onions, chopped	2 (16-ounce) cans pinto or
1 medium green bell pepper,	kidney beans, drained
chopped	1 (14¾-ounce) can reduced-
3 tablespoons chili powder	sodium chicken broth
2 teaspoons dried oregano	½ teaspoon salt
1 (1-pound) package frozen	¼ teaspoon pepper
corn kernels	

1. In a large flameproof casserole, heat oil. Add turkey, onions, and green pepper and cook over medium-high heat, stirring often, until meat loses its pink color, about 4 minutes. Add chili powder and oregano and cook, stirring, 1 minute.

2. Add corn, tomatoes, beans, chicken broth, salt, pepper, and 1½ cups water. Bring to a boil over high heat, reduce heat to medium, and cook uncovered, stirring occasionally, until chili thickens slightly, 8 to 10 minutes.

31   QUICK PORK CHILI VERDE

Prep: 5 minutes   Cook: 13 to 15 minutes   Serves: 4

This stew is quite incendiary with jalapeño peppers. Serve with rice or plenty of warm flour tortillas.

1¼ pounds lean ground pork
1 large onion, chopped
2 garlic cloves, minced
¾ teaspoon dried oregano
1½ tablespoons flour
1 (14¾-ounce) can chicken broth

1 (4-ounce) can chopped green chiles
1 tablespoon minced jalapeño peppers, fresh or pickled
¼ cup chopped parsley
¼ teaspoon salt

1. In a medium saucepan or large skillet, cook pork and onion over high heat, stirring, until meat loses its pink color and begins to brown, about 5 minutes. Add garlic and oregano and cook, stirring, 1 minute. Add flour and cook, stirring, 1 minute longer. Gradually stir in chicken broth and bring to a boil, stirring.

2. Add green chiles, jalapeños, parsley, and salt. Cook uncovered over medium heat until chili is slightly reduced and thickened, 6 to 8 minutes.

32   NEW WAVE CHILI

Prep: 5 minutes   Cook: 15 minutes   Serves: 4

Chili recipes vary tremendously from one region and from one cook to another. In recent years, ingredients newly fashionable in the United States, such as sun-dried tomatoes and balsamic vinegar, have found their way into chili pots, with intriguing results.

2 ounces sun-dried tomatoes packed in oil plus 2 tablespoons oil
1¼ pounds lean ground beef or turkey
1 small onion, chopped
2 tablespoons chili powder
1½ teaspoons ground cumin
1 teaspoon salt
½ teaspoon dried oregano

⅛ teaspoon cinnamon
1 (15-ounce) can Mexican-style stewed tomatoes
1 (15-ounce) can black beans, undrained
2 tablespoons chopped cilantro
1½ tablespoons raisins
1 tablespoon balsamic vinegar

1. Heat sun-dried tomatoes and their reserved oil in a large skillet over medium-high heat. Add beef, onion, chili powder, cumin, salt, oregano, and cinnamon. Cook, stirring often, until beef is lightly browned and onion is translucent, about 5 minutes.

2. Stir in tomatoes, beans with their liquid, cilantro, raisins, and vinegar. Cook over medium heat 10 minutes, stirring occasionally. If chili seems too thick, stir in up to ½ cup water.

33 PINTO BEAN SKILLET CHILI
Prep: 5 minutes   Cook: 14 minutes   Serves: 2 to 3

This vegetarian chili is great on a cold night, served right out of the skillet.

2 tablespoons vegetable oil
1 medium onion, chopped
1 small green bell pepper,
    chopped
1 tablespoon chili powder
1 (15-ounce) can Mexican-
    style stewed tomatoes

1 (15-ounce) can pinto beans,
    drained
1½ cups grated Monterey Jack
    cheese with jalapeño
    peppers

1. Preheat the broiler. In a medium (about 8-inch) skillet with ovenproof handle, heat oil. Add onion and bell pepper and cook over medium-high heat, stirring, until softened and lightly browned, about 4 minutes. Add chili powder and cook, stirring, 1 minute.

2. Add stewed tomatoes, beans, and ½ cup water. Bring to a boil over high heat, reduce heat to medium, and cook until chili has thickened to a stew-like consistency, about 8 minutes.

3. Sprinkle cheese evenly over top of chili. Place under broiler about 4 inches from heat and cook for 30 seconds to 1 minute to melt cheese.

34 INCENDIARY EL PASO CHILI
Prep: 5 minutes   Cook: 13 to 15 minutes   Serves: 6 to 8

Serve this traditional chili with cornbread or tortillas. You can cut down on the Tabasco if you'd like less heat.

1 tablespoon vegetable oil
1½ pounds ground chuck or
    meatloaf mixture
2 medium onions, chopped
¼ cup chili powder
1 teaspoon ground cumin
1 teaspoon dried oregano
½ teaspoon cayenne
1 (28-ounce) can crushed
    tomatoes in puree

3 (15-ounce) cans pinto or
    kidney beans, drained
¾ teaspoon salt
1 teaspoon black pepper
1 teaspoon sugar
¾ teaspoon Tabasco sauce, or
    to taste

1. In a large flameproof casserole, heat oil. Add ground meat, onions, chili powder, cumin, oregano, and cayenne. Cook over medium-high heat, stirring frequently, until onions begin to soften, about 3 minutes.

2. Add tomatoes, beans, salt, black pepper, sugar, and 2 cups water. Bring to a boil, reduce heat to medium, and cook uncovered until chili has reduced and thickened slightly, 10 to 12 minutes. Stir in Tabasco and serve.

Chapter 2

Substantial Salads

Most of the recipes in this chapter provide a meal in a bowl. As our preferences move toward eating lighter, main-course salads become an ever more popular choice for the evening supper as well as for midday lunch. Particularly in the warmer months, and in climates that are temperate year-round, substantial salads have a great deal of appeal for busy, active, health-conscious people of all ages. As a further plus to the cook on a time budget, a well-balanced substantial salad can easily become an entire meal in itself, requiring only the addition of some good bread to round out the meal nicely.

Supermarkets are responding to this trend by selling more and more ingredients and products for creating an almost-instant salad meal. Both produce departments and deli-bars now offer handy cut vegetables and fruits, washed and bagged salad greens and spinach, and better-quality prepared salads, such as coleslaw and potato salad. In addition, excellent bottled dressings and canned and jarred vegetables, such as roasted red peppers, artichoke hearts, and olives, can be used in combination with fresh ingredients to make for some lively and colorful presentations.

Whether your preference is for a substantial salad, such as Tuscan Bread Salad or Tabbouleh Ham Salad, a salad with a pasta base, such as Dilled Seashell Pasta and Salmon Salad or Greek Orzo Salad, or for something lighter, as in Tuna Salad Provençal or in Santa Fe Chicken Salad, this chapter provides a myriad of options from which to choose.

35 TUSCAN TUNA SALAD
Prep: 20 minutes   Cook: none   Serves: 4 to 6

Except for the lettuce and fresh basil, all of the ingredients in this salad can be purchased ahead and kept on hand in your cupboard.

2 (6½-ounce) jars marinated artichoke hearts
1 small head of romaine lettuce
3 tablespoons balsamic vinegar
2 teaspoons pesto sauce
2 (15-ounce) cans Great Northern beans, drained and rinsed

4 ounces oil-marinated sun-dried tomatoes, diced
⅓ cup oil-cured black olives
2 (6½-ounce) cans solid white tuna in water
4 to 6 fresh basil or parsley sprigs

1. Remove artichokes from jar; reserve marinade. Cut artichokes in half. Line a small platter with lettuce leaves.

2. In a salad bowl, whisk together artichoke marinade, vinegar, and pesto. Add artichokes, beans, sun-dried tomatoes, and olives and toss gently.

3. Spoon mixture onto platter with lettuce. Top with tuna and drizzle with any remaining dressing from bowl. Garnish with basil sprigs and serve at room temperature.

36 TUNA SALAD PROVENÇAL
Prep: 15 minutes   Cook: 3 to 4 minutes   Serves: 2

1½ tablespoons balsamic vinegar
3 to 4 fresh basil leaves, slivered
1 teaspoon Dijon mustard
1 garlic clove, minced
½ teaspoon sugar
¼ teaspoon salt
⅛ teaspoon freshly ground pepper
¼ cup extra-virgin olive oil
¼ pound fresh green beans, cut into 2-inch pieces

1 small fennel bulb, thinly sliced
1 medium red bell pepper, diced
2 scallions, thinly sliced
1 small bunch of arugula
1 (6½-ounce) can solid white tuna in water, drained
6 to 8 Mediterranean black olives

1. In a mixing bowl, combine vinegar, basil, mustard, garlic, sugar, salt, and pepper. Gradually whisk in olive oil.

2. In a steamer or microwave oven, cook beans until just tender, 3 to 4 minutes. Rinse under cold water and drain well.

3. Add beans, fennel, red pepper, and scallions to bowl and toss gently.

4. Arrange arugula leaves on luncheon plates. Spoon salad over greens and top with crumbled tuna. Drizzle with any dressing remaining in bowl. Garnish salads with olives.

---

37 QUICK SALAD NIÇOISE
Prep: 10 minutes   Cook: 10 minutes   Serves: 2 to 3

Using canned potatoes in this classic bistro salad works well and saves time. To remove any tinny taste be sure to rinse them well under cold running water.

2 **eggs**	⅛ **teaspoon ground pepper**
½ **pound fresh green beans**	⅓ **cup extra-virgin olive oil**
2 **tablespoons white wine vinegar**	1 **(16-ounce) can sliced white potatoes, rinsed and drained**
2 **teaspoons grainy mustard**	
1 **garlic clove, crushed through a press**	1 **small head of romaine lettuce**
½ **teaspoon sugar**	1 **(6½-ounce) can solid white tuna in water**
¼ **teaspoon herbes de Provence**	4 **anchovy fillets**
⅛ **teaspoon salt**	8 **to 10 Niçoise olives**

1. Place eggs in a saucepan with lightly salted water to cover. Bring to a boil over high heat, reduce heat to moderately low, and cook for 10 minutes. Place eggs in bowl of cold water until ready to peel.

2. Meanwhile, bring water to a boil in the bottom of a steamer. Place green beans in top of steamer. Steam until barely tender, about 3 minutes. Rinse under cold water; drain well.

3. In a mixing bowl, whisk together vinegar, mustard, garlic, sugar, herbes de Provence, salt, and pepper. Gradually whisk in olive oil. Add beans and potatoes and toss well.

4. Shell and quarter eggs. Line luncheon plates with romaine lettuce. Mound potatoes and beans on lettuce. Toss tuna with any dressing remaining in the bowl. Spoon tuna over potatoes and garnish each salad with crossed anchovy fillets, egg wedges, and Niçoise olives.

38   CUBAN GRILLED CHICKEN SALAD

Prep: 12 minutes   Cook: 4 to 6 minutes   Serves: 4 to 6

4 skinless, boneless chicken breast halves (about 5 ounces each)
2 tablespoons lime juice
¼ cup cilantro plus 4 to 6 sprigs for garnish
1½ teaspoons sugar
½ teaspoon minced garlic
½ teaspoon chili powder
½ teaspoon salt
¼ teaspoon pepper
⅓ cup extra-virgin olive oil
1 (15-ounce) can black beans, rinsed and drained
1 (11-ounce) can Mexicorn
1 small red bell pepper, slivered
⅓ cup thinly sliced scallions (2 to 3)
1 head of romaine lettuce

1. Prepare a medium-hot fire in a charcoal or gas grill or preheat broiler. Pound chicken between sheets of plastic wrap to about ¼-inch thickness.

2. Grill or broil 5 to 6 inches from heat source 2 to 3 minutes per side, turning once, until cooked through. Remove to a plate.

3. In a food processor or blender, combine lime juice, ¼ cup cilantro, sugar, garlic, chili powder, salt, and pepper. Pulse on and off until garlic and cilantro are chopped. With machine on, gradually add olive oil and any juices from grilled chicken.

4. In a salad bowl, combine beans, corn, red pepper, and scallions. Toss to mix. Arrange lettuce on plates, spoon corn and beans over lettuce, and place chicken on top. Drizzle with dressing and garnish with cilantro sprigs.

39   CURRIED CHICKEN SALAD BOMBAY

Prep: 10 minutes   Cook: 5 to 7 minutes   Serves: 4 to 5

1 cup slivered almonds or pecan halves
½ cup heavy cream
1 ripe banana
3 tablespoons lemon juice
½ cup mayonnaise
2 teaspoons curry powder
¼ teaspoon salt
¼ teaspoon freshly ground pepper
4 cups diced cooked chicken (about 1 pound)
2 cups seedless grapes
1 head of Boston or leaf lettuce

1. Preheat oven to 350°F. Spread out almonds on a baking sheet and toast, stirring to turn 2 or 3 times, until golden, 5 to 7 minutes.

2. While almonds are toasting, in a chilled bowl, using an electric mixer or whisk, whip cream until it holds soft peaks.

3. In a large mixing bowl, mash banana with lemon juice. Stir in mayonnaise, curry powder, salt, and pepper. Fold in whipped cream.

4. Add chicken, grapes, and toasted almonds. Toss gently with dressing. Serve salad on luncheon plates lined with lettuce.

40   SANTA FE CHICKEN SALAD

Prep: 12 minutes   Cook: 5 to 6 minutes   Serves: 6 to 8

Jicama is a tropical vegetable that is becoming increasingly available in supermarkets in the United States. It looks like a large brown turnip, but the crisp white flesh under its rough skin has a flavor and texture somewhere between an apple and a cucumber.

1¼ pounds chicken breast
    tenders
6 tablespoons extra-virgin
    olive oil
    Salt and freshly ground
    pepper
½ cup fresh lime juice
1 small red onion, halved
¼ cup cilantro or fresh basil
    leaves, tightly packed

½ jalapeño pepper, seeded
1 ripe papaya, peeled, seeded,
    and cut into 1-inch
    chunks
1 large ripe avocado, cut into
    1-inch chunks
1 cup diced (½-inch) peeled
    jicama or green apple
1 head of romaine lettuce

1. Prepare a medium-hot fire in a charcoal or gas grill or preheat broiler. Toss chicken with 2 tablespoons oil land season lightly with salt and pepper. Grill or broil 5 to 6 inches from heat 2 to 3 minutes per side, until lightly browned on the outside and white but still moist within. Cut into 1-inch chunks and reserve.

2. In a food processor, combine lime juice, red onion, cilantro, and jalapeño. Process until finely chopped. With machine on, gradually add remaining ¼ cup oil. Season with ¼ teaspoon salt and ⅛ teaspoon pepper.

3. In a salad bowl, toss chicken and any juices, papaya, avocado, and jicama with dressing. Serve on a bed of romaine lettuce.

41   CHICKEN SALAD AFRIQUE

Prep: 12 minutes   Cook: none   Serves: 4

1 (11-ounce) can mandarin
    oranges
½ cup mayonnaise
2 teaspoons curry powder
3 tablespoons mango
    chutney, chopped
1 tablespoon cider vinegar

2 scallions, thinly sliced
3 cups diced cooked chicken
1 head of Boston or 2 heads of
    Bibb lettuce
½ cup roasted peanuts,
    chopped

1. Drain mandarin oranges, reserving ¼ cup of the juice. In a medium bowl, combine reserved mandarin orange juice, mayonnaise, curry, chutney, vinegar, and scallions. Whisk to blend well.

2. Add chicken to dressing and toss to coat. Gently fold in orange sections.

3. Mound salad onto a platter lined with lettuce. Sprinkle peanuts on top.

42 TWO-RICE RASPBERRY CHICKEN SALAD

Prep: 15 minutes   Cook: 5 minutes   Serves: 6 to 8

1 (6¼-ounce) package quick-cooking long-grain and wild rice
¼ cup raspberry or balsamic vinegar
2 tablespoons orange juice
1 tablespoon Dijon mustard
¼ cup light olive oil
¼ cup minced chives
2 tablespoons minced fresh tarragon, or 1 teaspoon dried

¼ teaspoon salt
⅛ teaspoon freshly ground pepper
3 cups diced cooked white meat chicken
1 cup chopped fennel or celery
1½ cups fresh raspberries
2 heads of Bibb lettuce

1. Prepare quick-cooking long-grain and wild rice following package directions but omitting seasoning packet and butter. Set aside.

2. In a salad bowl, combine vinegar, orange juice, and mustard. Whisk to blend well. Gradually whisk in oil. Stir in chives and tarragon and season with salt and pepper.

3. Add rice, chicken, and fennel to dressing. Toss well. Add raspberries and toss gently. Serve on a bed of Bibb lettuce.

43 CALIFORNIA CHICKEN PLATTER

Prep: 12 minutes   Cook: 4 to 5 minutes   Serves: 4 to 6

2 slices of bacon
2 ripe avocados, sliced
3 tablespoons lemon juice
3 cups diced cooked chicken
½ cup chopped celery
½ cup creamy blue cheese salad dressing

1 tablespoon minced chives
1 small head of romaine lettuce
2 ripe medium tomatoes, cut into wedges
8 pitted black olives

1. In a large skillet, cook bacon over medium heat, turning until crisp, 4 to 5 minutes. Drain on paper towels, crumble, and set aside.

2. Meanwhile, toss avocado slices gently with 2 tablespoons lemon juice to prevent discoloration.

3. In a medium bowl, gently toss chicken with celery, crumbled bacon, blue cheese dressing, chives, and remaining lemon juice.

4. Mound salad on luncheon plates lined with lettuce. Arrange tomato and avocado slices in a sunburst around chicken salad. Garnish with olives.

44 COBB SALAD
Prep: 8 minutes   Cook: 10 minutes   Serves: 4

2 eggs
4 strips of bacon
1 (10-ounce) package recipe-
  ready fresh spinach
1 small head of leaf lettuce
¼ cup crumbled blue cheese
1½ cups shredded cooked
  chicken or turkey white
  meat

1 medium avocado, sliced and
  tossed with lemon juice
1 tablespoon lemon juice
⅛ teaspoon salt
⅛ teaspoon freshly ground
  pepper
¼ cup extra-virgin olive oil

1. Place eggs in a small saucepan with lightly salted water to cover. Bring to boil over high heat, reduce heat to medium-low, and cook for 10 minutes. Remove eggs to a bowl of cold water until ready to use.

2. Meanwhile, cook bacon between sheets of paper towel in a microwave on High until crisp, 2 to 3 minutes. Crumble bacon.

3. Line 4 luncheon plates with spinach leaves. Tear leaf lettuce into bite-size pieces and place on top of spinach. Arrange blue cheese, chicken, avocado, and bacon on top of lettuce in strips. Peel and quarter eggs. Place 2 wedges on each plate.

4. In a small bowl, combine lemon juice, salt, and pepper. Gradually whisk in oil. Drizzle dressing over salad and serve.

45 TROPICAL TURKEY SALAD
Prep: 15 minutes   Cook: none   Serves: 6

1 ripe papaya, peeled, seeded,
  and sliced
2 bananas, halved crosswise
  and sliced lengthwise
1 ripe avocado, sliced
¼ cup lemon juice
1 pound roasted turkey
  breast, sliced
1 (10-ounce) package recipe-
  ready spinach

¾ cup plain yogurt
¼ cup mayonnaise
1 tablespoon honey
½ teaspoon ground ginger
½ teaspoon ground coriander
⅛ teaspoon salt
⅛ teaspoon freshly ground
  pepper
⅓ cup toasted cashew nuts,
  chopped

1. In a medium bowl, combine papaya, bananas, and avocado. Sprinkle with 2 tablespoons lemon juice and toss gently. Arrange fruit slices and turkey attractively on a serving platter lined with spinach leaves.

2. In a small bowl, whisk together yogurt, mayonnaise, remaining 2 tablespoons lemon juice, honey, ginger, coriander, salt, and pepper.

3. Spoon dressing over salad. Sprinkle chopped cashews on top.

46   CALIFORNIA TURKEY SALAD
Prep: 10 minutes   Cook: 4 to 6 minutes   Serves: 4

This easy but unusual salad is a great way to use leftover turkey.

4 slices of bacon
3 cups diced cooked turkey
 breast
½ cup Catalina French
 dressing
1½ tablespoons minced chives
1 tablespoon lemon juice

1 teaspoon prepared white
 horseradish
½ cup mayonnaise
⅛ teaspoon freshly ground
 pepper
1 small head of iceberg
 lettuce, cut into bite-size
 pieces

1. In a large skillet, cook bacon over medium heat, turning until crisp, 4 to 6 minutes. Drain on paper towels, crumble, and set aside.

2. While bacon is cooking, toss turkey with dressing, chives, lemon juice, and horseradish. Marinate at room temperature 10 minutes.

3. Add mayonnaise and pepper and toss until turkey is well coated. Add lettuce and toss gently. Sprinkle bacon on top and serve.

47   ITALIAN TURKEY SALAD
Prep: 7 minutes   Cook: 2 to 3 minutes   Serves: 4 to 6

2 cups fresh broccoli florets
3 cups diced cooked turkey
1 medium red bell pepper,
 coarsely chopped
¼ cup black olive rings
1 cup sour cream
3 tablespoons mayonnaise

1 tablespoon white wine
 vinegar
1 tablespoon slivered fresh
 basil
1 garlic clove, minced
¼ teaspoon salt
⅛ teaspoon freshly ground
 pepper

1. In a large saucepan of boiling salted water, cook broccoli until bright green and crisp-tender, 2 to 3 minutes. Drain and rinse under cold running water; drain well.

2. Place turkey, broccoli, bell pepper, and olive rings in a salad bowl.

3. In a small bowl, whisk together sour cream, mayonnaise, vinegar, basil, garlic, salt, and pepper. Pour dressing over chicken and vegetables and toss gently to coat evenly.

48   TURKEY SALAD "RITZ"
Prep: 12 minutes   Cook: 5 to 7 minutes   Serves: 6

½ cup coarsely chopped
    pecans or walnuts
½ cup mayonnaise
⅓ cup sour cream
¼ cup minced chives
1 tablespoon lemon juice
1 teaspoon curry powder
¼ teaspoon salt
⅛ teaspoon freshly ground
    pepper

5 cups diced (¾-inch) cooked
    turkey or chicken (about
    1 pound)
1 large red Delicious apple,
    diced
1 large celery rib, diced
3 cups shredded red cabbage
1½ tablespoons minced parsley

1. Preheat oven to 350°F. Spread out nuts in a small baking dish and toast in oven 5 to 7 minutes, until lightly browned and fragrant.

2. In a large bowl, combine mayonnaise, sour cream, chives, lemon juice, curry powder, salt, and pepper. Blend well. Add turkey, apple, celery, and nuts and toss gently.

3. Divide the shredded cabbage among 6 individual luncheon plates. Serve salad mounded on a bed of cabbage. Garnish with parsley.

49   SESAME BEEF AND BROCCOLI SALAD
Prep: 8 minutes   Cook: 6 to 7 minutes   Serves: 4 to 6

Use leftover roast beef or roast beef from the deli for this delicious salad. Time-saving cut broccoli florets are now available in many supermarket produce departments or salad bars.

5 cups broccoli florets (about
    1 pound)
¼ cup sesame seeds
1 pound thinly sliced rare
    roast beef, cut into
    ½-inch-wide strips
1 large red bell pepper, cut
    into thin strips

⅓ cup vegetable oil
¼ cup Asian sesame oil
¼ cup red wine vinegar
2 tablespoons soy sauce
2 garlic cloves, minced
¼ teaspoon crushed hot red
    pepper
12 romaine lettuce leaves

1. In a large pot of salted boiling water, cook broccoli over high heat until crisp-tender, 3 to 4 minutes. Pour into a colander, rinse under cold running water, and drain well.

2. In a small skillet, toast sesame seeds over medium heat, stirring frequently, until golden and fragrant, about 3 minutes.

3. In a large bowl, combine broccoli, beef, red pepper, and sesame seeds.

4. In a small bowl, whisk together vegetable oil, sesame oil, vinegar, soy sauce, garlic, and crushed red pepper. Pour dressing over salad and toss gently. Line a platter with lettuce leaves and spoon salad over the leaves.

50   CHEF'S SALAD
Prep: 10 minutes   Cook: 10 minutes   Serves: 4

Peeled tomatoes are a nice touch, but it takes extra work to blanch and peel them. A shortcut is to firmly scrape the entire outside of a tomato with a sharp knife, being careful not to cut skin. The skin can then be carefully pulled off. This will work only with ripe tomatoes.

4 **eggs**
2 **tablespoons cider vinegar**
1 **teaspoon Dijon mustard**
¾ **teaspoon salt**
½ **teaspoon freshly ground pepper**
½ **cup vegetable oil**
3 **tablespoons heavy cream**
1 **medium head of iceberg lettuce**

12 **radishes, sliced**
¼ **pound thickly sliced honey-baked ham, cut into strips**
¼ **pound thickly sliced cooked chicken or turkey, cut into strips**
¾ **cup Swiss cheese, cut into matchsticks**
4 **medium tomatoes, cut into 6 wedges each**

1. Place eggs in saucepan and cover with water. Bring to boil over high heat, reduce heat to medium-low, and cook for 10 minutes. Plunge eggs into cold water, then peel and quarter them.

2. Meanwhile, in a small bowl, whisk together vinegar, mustard, ½ teaspoon salt, and ¼ teaspoon pepper. Slowly whisk in oil, then stir in cream. Set dressing aside.

3. Line a salad bowl with several outside lettuce leaves. Tear remaining lettuce into bite-size pieces. Toss with radishes and half of dressing. Place in lined bowl.

4. Arrange ham, chicken, and cheese on top of salad. Place tomatoes and eggs around outer edge. Season with remaining ¼ teaspoon each salt and pepper. Spoon remaining dressing over salad.

51   NEAPOLITAN SALAD
Prep: 8 minutes   Cook: none   Serves: 4

This fresh summer salad works well as as an appetizer.

2 **large ripe tomatoes, sliced ¼ inch thick**
8 **to 12 fresh basil leaves**
½ **pound fresh mozzarella cheese, sliced**

¼ **teaspoon coarse (kosher) salt**
2 **tablespoons extra-virgin olive oil**

1. On a serving platter, arrange alternating slices of tomatoes, basil leaves, and mozzarella cheese, overlapping slightly.

2. Sprinkle with salt. Drizzle olive oil over salad. Serve at room temperature.

52 SHRIMP LOUIS
Prep: 5 minutes   Cook: 10 minutes   Serves: 2

1 egg
½ cup mayonnaise
1 tablespoon heavy cream
1 tablespoon chili sauce
¼ teaspoon Worcestershire
   sauce
⅛ teaspoon Tabasco sauce

1 tablespoon minced onion
4 teaspoons lemon juice
¾ cup shredded lettuce
½ pound shelled and deveined
   medium cooked shrimp
   (about 12)
2 tablespoons chopped chives

1. Place egg in a saucepan and cover with water. Bring to boil over high heat, reduce heat to medium-low, and cook for 10 minutes. Shell and slice egg.

2. Meanwhile, in small bowl, whisk together mayonnaise, cream, chili sauce, Worcestershire, Tabasco, onion, and lemon juice.

3. Place lettuce on 2 salad plates. Arrange half of shrimp on each plate. Spoon sauce over shrimp. Arrange egg slices around shrimp and garnish with chives.

53 LOBSTER SALAD
Prep: 7 minutes   Cook: none   Serves: 2

This salad is delicious and elegant when made with lobster, but less expensive tiny salad shrimp, available at most deli counters, also work very well.

¼ cup mayonnaise
1½ tablespoons lemon juice
1 tablespoon chopped fresh
   tarragon plus sprigs for
   garnish
2 teaspoons Dijon mustard
1 teaspoon anise-flavored
   liqueur

⅛ teaspoon freshly ground
   pepper
½ pound diced cooked lobster
   or whole salad shrimp
½ cup chopped fennel or
   celery
2 scallions, thinly sliced
1 head of Bibb lettuce

1. In a medium bowl, whisk together mayonnaise, lemon juice, tarragon, mustard, anise liqueur, and pepper.

2. Add lobster, fennel, and scallions. Toss gently and serve on a bed of lettuce. Garnish with tarragon sprigs.

54   ANTIPASTO SUPPER SALAD

Prep: 5 minutes   Cook: none   Serves: 6 to 8

The list of ingredients here is merely a guideline. Feel free to add or subtract other cured or smoked meats, cheeses, or pickled vegetables. Serve the antipasto with plenty of sliced peasant bread.

1 **small head of romaine lettuce**
½ **pound thinly sliced baked ham**
¼ **pound thinly sliced salami**
¼ **pound provolone cheese, sliced**
¼ **pound mozzarella cheese, sliced**

2 **(7½-ounce) jars roasted red peppers**
2 **(6-ounce) jars marinated artichoke hearts**
1½ **cups black olives, preferably oil-cured**

1. Trim lettuce, separate into leaves, and arrange in one corner of a large platter. Arrange ham, salami, provolone, mozzarella cheese, and roasted peppers on a platter.

2. Drain artichoke hearts, reserving ¼ cup of marinade. Heap artichokes in center of platter, scatter olives over all, and drizzle reserved marinade over lettuce leaves.

55   ALASKAN CRAB SALAD

Prep: 10 minutes   Cook: none   Serves: 2

This salad can be a lifesaver when last-minute guests arrive. The recipe calls for canned crab, a convenient luxury food to keep on hand for just such occasions.

¼ **cup mayonnaise**
2 **teaspoons prepared white horseradish**
1 **teaspoon chili sauce**
1 **teaspoon grated onion**
¼ **teaspoon fresh chopped dill plus 2 small sprigs**
¼ **teaspoon Worcestershire sauce**

1 **(6- to 8-ounce) can fancy white crabmeat, preferably Alaskan**
4 **to 6 leaves red leaf lettuce**
12 **thin slices of European seedless cucumber**
1 **tablespoon salmon roe caviar**

1. In a medium bowl, whisk together mayonnaise, horseradish, chili sauce, onion, chopped dill, and Worcestershire. Add crab and toss gently.

2. Mound salad on 2 lettuce-lined luncheon plates. Surround with cucumber slices, sprinkle with caviar, and garnish with dill sprigs.

56 FRESH TOMATO SALAD WITH FETA CHEESE

Prep: 15 minutes   Cook: none   Serves: 4 to 6

Sweet onions, such as Vidalia, Walla Walla, and Maui, are ideal for salads. Stronger varieties may be "sweetened" by soaking slices in ice water for at least an hour before serving.

4 ripe tomatoes, sliced
1 small sweet onion (Vidalia, Walla Walla, or Maui), thinly sliced
1 cup crumbled feta cheese
1 (2-ounce) jar green olives with pimiento, sliced
¼ cup extra-virgin olive oil

2 tablespoons red wine vinegar
2 tablespoons minced parsley
4 fresh basil leaves, slivered
¼ teaspoon salt
⅛ teaspoon freshly ground pepper

1. Arrange tomato and onion slices on a small, deep serving platter. Sprinkle with a layer of feta cheese and olives.

2. In a small bowl, whisk together oil, vinegar, parsley, basil, salt, and pepper. Pour dressing over salad and serve.

57 GOAT CHEESE, ARUGULA, AND BACON SALAD

Prep: 7 minutes   Cook: 5 to 6 minutes   Serves: 4

8 slices of bacon, coarsely chopped
1 large or 2 small bunches of arugula, stems removed
¾ pound ripe tomatoes, sliced
4 ounces goat cheese, sliced
1 tablespoon red wine vinegar

1 teaspoon Dijon mustard
3 tablespoons extra-virgin olive oil
⅛ teaspoon freshly ground pepper
½ cup thinly sliced scallions

1. In a large skillet, cook bacon over medium heat, stirring frequently, until lightly browned and fat is rendered, 5 to 6 minutes. Remove bacon with a slotted spoon and drain on paper towels. Pour off all but 1 tablespoon drippings from pan.

2. Meanwhile, spread arugula out on a platter or individual plates. Arrange tomato and goat cheese slices overlapping on arugula.

3. Stir vinegar and mustard into warm bacon drippings. Whisk in oil and season with pepper. Drizzle dressing over salad and sprinkle reserved bacon and scallions on top.

58   GRILLED LAMB AND WHITE BEAN SALAD
Prep: 6 to 8 minutes   Cook: 8 to 10 minutes   Serves: 4

If you don't want to fire up a grill, simply cook the lamb and vegetables in the broiler for this colorful and substantial dinner salad.

3 loin lamb chops, cut about 1 inch thick
Salt and pepper
1 large yellow bell pepper, quartered and seeded
1 large red onion, quartered

⅓ cup bottled olive-oil vinaigrette dressing
1 (15-ounce) can white beans, drained and rinsed
4 cups torn chicory or curly endive leaves

1. Prepare a hot barbecue fire or gas grill, or preheat broiler. Season lamb with salt and pepper. Brush bell pepper and onion with about 1 tablespoon of dressing. Place chops and vegetables on oiled grill or under broiler and cook, turning once or twice, until vegetables are charred on the edges and slightly softened and meat is browned outside and still pink inside, 8 to 10 minutes.

2. Toss beans with 3 tablespoons dressing. On a large platter, make a bed of greens and top with beans.

3. Cut lamb meat off bones and slice into strips. Cut roasted vegetables into strips. Arrange meat and vegetables over beans and drizzle with remaining dressing.

59   TASSO AND BLACK-EYED PEA SALAD
Prep: 12 to 15 minutes   Cook: none   Serves: 4 to 6

Tasso, a highly seasoned Cajun smoked ham from Louisiana, is becoming available in fancy food stores across the country. If tasso is available in your area, it is definitely worth tasting, but other smoked ham is also good in this salad.

2 tablespoons Creole or stone-ground mustard
¼ cup cider vinegar
1 teaspoon sugar
¼ teaspoon cayenne
¼ teaspoon salt
⅛ teaspoon freshly ground pepper
⅔ cup olive oil

½ pound tasso or other flavorful ham, diced
2 (15-ounce) cans black-eyed peas, rinsed and drained
1 large red bell pepper, seeded and diced
1 cup chopped celery
6 to 8 scallions, thinly sliced
4 to 6 cups salad greens

1. In a salad bowl, whisk together mustard, vinegar, sugar, cayenne, salt, and pepper. Gradually whisk in olive oil.

2. Add ham, black-eyed peas, bell pepper, celery, and scallions. Toss to mix well. Serve on a bed of greens.

60   HEARTS OF PALM SALAD WITH GOLF SAUCE
Prep: 6 minutes   Cook: none   Serves: 2

This salad is a popular appetizer throughout South America and particularly in Brazil. The title refers to its popularity at country clubs in the Southern Hemisphere.

1 (14-ounce) can hearts of
    palm, drained, cut into
    1-inch-long pieces
1 head of Bibb lettuce
¼ cup mayonnaise
2½ tablespoons ketchup

1 tablespoon lime or lemon
    juice
2 fresh basil leaves, slivered
2 teaspoons minced chives
2 parsley sprigs

1. Arrange hearts of palm on 2 salad plates lined with lettuce.

2. In a small bowl, combine mayonnaise, ketchup, lime juice, basil, and chives. Blend well.

3. Spoon sauce over hearts of palm and garnish with parsley.

61   SWEET AND SOUR FOUR-BEAN SALAD
Prep: 5 minutes   Cook: 3 to 5 minutes   Marinate: 10 minutes
Serves: 8 to 10

12 ounces fresh green beans,
    cut into 1½-inch lengths
1 (15-ounce) can white beans,
    drained and rinsed
1 (15-ounce) can kidney
    beans, drained and
    rinsed
1 (15-ounce) can chick-peas,
    drained and rinsed
3 medium celery ribs, thinly
    sliced

1 medium red onion,
    chopped
¾ cup vegetable oil
¼ cup cider vinegar
2 tablespoons sugar
1 tablespoon Dijon mustard
1 teaspoon salt
½ teaspoon pepper
⅓ cup chopped parsley

1. In a large pot of boiling salted water, cook green beans uncovered over high heat until crisp-tender, 3 to 5 minutes. Pour into a colander, rinse under cold running water, and drain well.

2. In a large bowl, combine green beans, white beans, kidney beans, chick-peas, celery, and red onion.

3. In a small bowl, whisk together oil, vinegar, sugar, mustard, salt, and pepper until sugar is almost completely dissolved, about 1 minute.

4. Pour dressing over salad and toss gently. Stir in parsley. Let stand 10 minutes at room temperature or store up to 6 hours in refrigerator.

62   PASTA, BEAN, AND PEPPER SALAD BALSAMICO

Prep: 5 minutes   Cook: 10 minutes   Serves: 4 to 6

This colorful meatless pasta salad makes a fine supper and is also a welcome addition to a buffet table.

12 ounces penne or other short,
    medium-thick pasta
2 (15-ounce) cans pink beans,
    drained and rinsed
1 large yellow bell pepper,
    coarsely chopped
1 large green bell pepper,
    coarsely chopped

1 small red onion, chopped
½ cup bottled Italian dressing
1 tablespoon balsamic
    vinegar
¾ teaspoon dried oregano

1. In a large pot of lightly salted boiling water, cook penne until tender but firm, about 10 minutes. Pour into a colander and rinse well under cold running water. Drain well.

2. In a large bowl, toss pasta with beans, peppers, and red onion.

3. In a small bowl, whisk together Italian dressing, balsamic vinegar, and oregano. Pour over salad and toss gently to combine.

63   TRI-COLORED TORTELLINI SALAD

Prep: 6 minutes   Cook: 7 minutes   Serves: 4

1 (9-ounce) package fresh
    multicolored cheese-
    filled tortellini
1 (6-ounce) jar marinated
    artichoke hearts
1 tablespoon balsamic
    vinegar
⅛ teaspoon salt
2 tablespoons slivered fresh
    basil, plus 8 to 10 leaves

1 (8½-ounce) jar sun-dried oil-
    marinated tomatoes,
    drained and chopped
¼ cup Niçoise olives or 1
    (2¼-ounce) can sliced
    olives, drained
1 small head of leaf lettuce

1. In a large saucepan of boiling salted water, cook tortellini 7 minutes, or until just tender. Drain and set aside.

2. Drain artichokes, reserving marinade. In a salad bowl, combine marinade, vinegar, salt, and slivered basil.

3. Add tortellini, chopped sun-dried tomatoes, artichokes, and olives. Toss gently and serve on luncheon plates lined with leaf lettuce. Garnish with basil leaves.

64 GREEK ORZO SALAD

Prep: 12 minutes   Cook: 8 minutes   Serves: 4 to 6

If you can't get orzo, which is the rice-shaped Greek pasta, substitute another small pasta, such as ditalini.

1 cup orzo (½ pound)
1 cup crumbled feta cheese
½ European seedless
   cucumber, thinly sliced
½ yellow bell pepper,
   chopped
10 cherry tomatoes, halved

¾ cup black olives, preferably
   Kalamata, halved and
   pitted
½ cup bottled olive-oil
   vinaigrette dressing
½ cup chopped scallions

1. In a large saucepan of lightly salted boiling water, cook orzo until tender but firm, about 8 minutes. Pour into a colander and rinse under cold running water. Drain well.

2. In a medium bowl, combine orzo with feta cheese, cucumber, bell pepper, tomatoes, and olives. Pour dressing over salad, toss gently to combine, and sprinkle scallions on top.

65 DILLED SEASHELL PASTA AND SALMON SALAD

Prep: 8 minutes   Cook: 10 minutes   Serves: 4

Serve this simply lovely pasta salad on a summer evening with sliced tomatoes, a loaf of crusty bread, and a tall glass of iced tea.

8 ounces small or medium
   pasta shells
1 (7½- to 9½-ounce) can
   salmon, drained and
   broken into chunks
1 medium green bell pepper,
   chopped
⅔ cup thinly sliced celery

½ cup chopped red onion
¾ cup mayonnaise
1 tablespoon white wine
   vinegar
2 tablespoons chopped fresh
   dill, or 1½ teaspoons
   dried

1. In a large pot of lightly salted boiling water, cook pasta until tender but still firm, about 10 minutes. Drain into a colander and rinse under cold running water. Drain well.

2. In a large bowl, combine pasta with salmon, green pepper, celery, and red onion.

3. In a small bowl, whisk together mayonnaise, vinegar, and dill. Pour dressing over salad and toss gently to combine.

66 SHRIMP AND PASTA SALAD
Prep: 10 minutes   Cook: 10 minutes   Serves: 4

The look of this salad can be varied by using different shapes of maca-roni.

½ pound pasta shells
1 cup mayonnaise
½ cup French dressing
1 tablespoon lemon juice
1 small garlic clove, minced
½ teaspoon anchovy paste
½ cup tiny cooked shrimp

1 cup chopped celery
¼ cup thinly sliced scallions
¼ teaspoon salt
⅛ teaspoon freshly ground
  pepper
Parsley sprigs

1. In a large saucepan of boiling salted water, cook pasta until tender but still firm, about 10 minutes. Drain and rinse under cold running water; drain well.

2. In a large bowl, whisk together mayonnaise, dressing, lemon juice, garlic, and anchovy paste.

3. Add pasta, shrimp, celery, scallions, salt, and pepper Toss gently and serve on luncheon plates, garnished with parsley.

67 TABBOULEH HAM SALAD
Prep: 20 minutes   Cook: none   Serves: 4

1 (5¼-ounce) package
  tabbouleh wheat salad
  mix
3 tablespoons balsamic
  vinegar
6 tablespoons olive oil
½ teaspoon salt
⅛ teaspoon pepper
1 medium red bell pepper,
  diced

1 medium yellow bell pepper,
  diced
1 cup diced ham
½ cup diced celery
3 tablespoons raisins
⅓ cup thinly sliced scallions
1 head of leaf lettuce

1. In a medium bowl, combine tabbouleh salad mix including seasoning packet with 1 cup warm water, vinegar, oil, salt, and pepper. Let stand 15 minutes at room temperature.

2. Add bell peppers, ham, celery, raisins, and scallions and toss to mix. Serve salad on a bed of lettuce.

68   TUSCAN BREAD SALAD
Prep: 15 minutes   Cook: none   Serves: 6

Known as *panzanella* in Italy, this salad makes the perfect light supper on a summer evening, when both tomatoes and basil are at their peak.

12 ounces day-old Italian or French bread	1 large yellow bell pepper, coarsely chopped
½ cup extra-virgin olive oil	1 pound mozzarella cheese, preferably fresh, cut into ½-inch dice
⅓ cup balsamic vinegar	
¼ teaspoon salt	
¼ teaspoon freshly ground pepper	3 garlic cloves, minced
	1 tablespoon drained capers
3 large ripe tomatoes, coarsely chopped	1 cup basil leaves, slivered
	12 romaine lettuce leaves

1. Cut bread into rough ¾-inch cubes and place in a large bowl.

2. In a small bowl, whisk together olive oil, vinegar, salt, and pepper. Pour dressing over bread and toss to mix well.

3. Add tomatoes, bell pepper, mozzarella cheese, garlic, capers, and basil. Mix gently but thoroughly. Arrange romaine leaves on a serving platter and spoon salad over leaves.

Chapter 3

Pasta Presto

If I had to choose one food to live on, it would probably be pasta. And I know I am not alone. Pasta is the ultimate comfort food, and it's even good for you. There are a variety of pasta dishes within this chapter, from rich Fettuccine Alfredo to low-fat but luscious Linguine with Quick White Clam Sauce. Some dishes are sophisticated: Angel Hair with Roasted Red Pepper Sauce has an exotic hint of ground cumin to intrigue the palate. Other recipes like Tortellini au Gratin are just plain satisfying! The possibilities for pasta are endless, but I have chosen forty-five of my favorites, and I hope you will enjoy them.

Pasta Tips   Fresh egg pasta cooks faster because it retains some of its moisture content. There are at least two national brands of fresh pasta available in the refrigerated section of most supermarkets along with sauces, such as pesto and marinara. Some fresh pastas, particularly the filled varieties such as tortellini, are also widely available in frozen food sections. These cook almost as quickly as fresh pasta.

Some people prefer dried pasta for its longer shelf life and because it contains no eggs. Thin varieties, such as angel hair or spaghettini, cook very quickly, but even the chunky shapes take no more than 10 to 12 minutes. And you can prepare the sauce while the pasta is in the pot.

Pasta should be cooked in a large pot of rapidly boiling water. I recommend first putting the water on to boil and then getting ingredients together for a sauce. Unsalted water boils more quickly than salted water, so add salt after water comes to the boil. A few drops of olive oil added to the boiling, salted water before you add the pasta will keep it from sticking together.

69   FETTUCCINE ALFREDO
Prep: 3 minutes   Cook: 3 to 5 minutes   Serves: 2 to 3

1 (9-ounce) package fresh
   fettuccine
¾ cup heavy cream
3 tablespoons butter
¼ teaspoon grated nutmeg

½ to ¾ cup grated Parmesan
   cheese
⅛ teaspoon freshly ground
   pepper

1. To a large pot of rapidly boiling, lightly salted water, add fettuccine and cook until barely tender, 3 to 5 minutes. Drain well.

2. In a large skillet over medium-low heat, combine cream, butter, nutmeg, and noodles. Cook, tossing gently, until sauce reduces to a slightly thickened, creamy consistency, 3 to 5 minutes.

3. Add Parmesan cheese and pepper. Toss and serve immediately.

70   FETTUCCINE TOSCANO
Prep: 8 minutes   Cook: 8 to 10 minutes   Serves: 4

This vegetarian recipe contains olive oil and butter, both typically used in Northern Italian cooking. Heating these two together gives good flavor and prevents the butter from burning.

1 (9-ounce) package fresh
   fettuccine
1 pound fresh asparagus
4 to 5 cremini mushrooms,
   sliced
4 to 5 fresh shiitake
   mushrooms, stemmed,
   caps sliced
3 tablespoons butter

3 tablespoons olive oil
8 to 10 fresh basil leaves,
   slivered
1 garlic clove, minced
½ cup vegetable broth
¼ cup grated Parmesan cheese
½ teaspoon salt
¼ teaspoon freshly ground
   pepper

1. In a large pot of rapidly boiling, lightly salted water, cook pasta until barely tender, 3 to 5 minutes. Drain well.

2. Meanwhile, slice asparagus into small pieces on an angle. Trim stems and slice mushrooms crosswise into umbrella shapes.

3. In a large skillet, melt butter in oil over medium-high heat. Add asparagus, mushrooms, basil, and garlic. Cook, tossing, until asparagus is crisp-tender and mushrooms have softened, about 5 minutes.

4. Add vegetable broth and bring to a simmer. Add pasta, Parmesan, salt, and pepper to skillet. Toss gently and serve immediately.

71   FETTUCCINE FLORENTINE
Prep: 8 minutes   Cook: 9 to 10 minutes   Serves: 6 to 8

To quickly shred spinach or other leafy vegetables, stack several leaves and roll them up. With a sharp knife, slice crosswise across the roll to make thin strips.

2 (9-ounce) packages fresh
   fettuccine
2 tablespoons butter
2 tablespoons olive oil
1 garlic clove, minced
1 pound fresh spinach,
   shredded

1 cup heavy cream
1½ cups grated Parmesan
   cheese
¼ teaspoon freshly ground
   pepper

1. In a large pot of rapidly boiling, lightly salted water, cook pasta until barely tender, about 3 minutes. Drain well.

2. In a large skillet, melt butter with oil over medium heat. Add garlic and cook until soft, 2 to 3 minutes. Stir in spinach and cook, tossing, 1 minute.

3. Add pasta and cream to spinach mixture, raise heat to medium-high, and cook just until cream thickens slightly, about 3 minutes. Add cheese and pepper, toss gently, and serve at once.

72   FETTUCCINE PRIMAVERA
Prep: 12 minutes   Cook: 5 to 8 minutes   Serves: 4

This is an opportunity to use the microwave, as it cooks the vegetables quickly and preserves their color and texture.

12 ounces fresh fettuccine
 1 cup thinly sliced celery
 1 cup thinly sliced carrots
 1 cup thinly sliced leeks,
   white part only
 1 cup small fresh broccoli
   florets
 2 tablespoons butter

1 cup shredded Swiss cheese
½ cup grated Parmesan cheese
4 to 6 fresh basil leaves,
   slivered
½ teaspoon grated nutmeg
¼ teaspoon salt
¼ teaspoon freshly ground
   pepper

1. To a large pot of rapidly boiling, lightly salted water, add pasta and cook until barely tender, 3 to 5 minutes.

2. Meanwhile, in a microwave-safe container loosely covered with plastic wrap, microwave vegetables, butter, and 2 tablespoons water on High until barely tender, 2 to 3 minutes.

3. Drain pasta and vegetables. In a warm bowl, toss hot pasta and vegetables with Swiss cheese, Parmesan cheese, basil, nutmeg, salt, and pepper until cheese melts. Serve immediately.

73 SKILLET TUNA AND PASTA CASSEROLE

Prep: 5 minutes   Cook: 10 to 13 minutes   Serves: 3 to 4

1 (9-ounce) package fresh
   fettuccine, preferably
   green (spinach)
1 (6½-ounce) can oil-packed
   tuna, oil reserved
2 garlic cloves, minced
1 cup heavy cream
¾ cup milk

1½ teaspoons dried basil
¼ teaspoon salt
⅛ teaspoon pepper
6 tablespoons grated
   Parmesan cheese
2 tablespoons dry bread
   crumbs

1. Preheat broiler. In a large pot of rapidly boiling, lightly salted water, cook fettuccine until tender but still firm, about 3 minutes. Drain into a colander.

2. Meanwhile, in a 9- to 10-inch skillet with ovenproof handle, heat 1½ tablespoons of oil from tuna. Add garlic and cook over medium heat, stirring, 1 minute. Add cream, raise heat to high, and cook until reduced to about ¾ cup, 4 to 6 minutes. Add milk, basil, salt, and pepper and cook for 1 minute, until sauce is hot.

3. Add cooked pasta and toss to combine. Break tuna into chunks and add to pasta. Toss gently to combine.

4. In a small bowl, combine cheese and bread crumbs. Sprinkle evenly over pasta.

5. Broil about 4 inches from heat until crumbs are browned, 1 to 2 minutes, watching carefully to prevent burning. Serve from skillet, cut into wedges.

74 FETTUCCINE CARBONARA

Prep: 6 minutes   Cook: 5 to 7 minutes   Serves: 2

In this recipe, the hot pasta actually cooks the egg mixture, forming a creamy sauce.

4 slices of bacon, diced
6 ounces fresh fettuccine
2 eggs
⅛ teaspoon freshly ground
   pepper

¼ cup grated Parmesan cheese
¼ cup finely chopped parsley,
   preferably Italian

1. In a large skillet, cook bacon over medium heat until crisp, 4 to 6 minutes. Drain off all but 1 tablespoon fat. Set skillet aside.

2. Meanwhile, in a large pot of rapidly boiling, lightly salted water, cook pasta until barely tender, 3 to 5 minutes.

3. In a mixing bowl, beat eggs with pepper. Stir in bacon, cheese, and parsley.

4. Return skillet with bacon to medium heat. Add hot drained fettuccine and toss until well coated and hot, about 1 minute. Remove from heat. Immediately add eggs and toss until creamy. Serve immediately.

---

75   FETTUCCINE WITH MINT AND BALSAMIC VINEGAR
Prep: 10 minutes   Cook: 3 to 5 minutes   Serves: 4

1 (9-ounce) package fresh
   fettuccine
1 medium zucchini, quartered
   lengthwise and thinly
   sliced
1 (14½-ounce) can pasta-ready
   diced tomatoes, drained
12 paper-thin slices medium
   red onion, divided into
   rings

3 tablespoons minced
   parsley, preferably Italian
1 tablespoon chopped fresh
   mint
1 garlic clove, minced
2 tablespoons olive oil
1 tablespoon balsamic or red
   wine vinegar
   Salt and freshly ground
   pepper

1. In a large pot of rapidly boiling, lightly salted water, cook fettuccine until just tender, 3 to 5 minutes.

2. Meanwhile, in a serving dish, combine zucchini, tomatoes, onion, parsley, mint, garlic, oil, and vinegar. Toss to mix. Season with salt and pepper to taste.

3. Drain pasta and lightly toss with sauce. Serve at once.

---

76   OIL AND GARLIC PASTA
Prep: 5 minutes   Cook: 6 to 8 minutes   Serves: 5

The secret ingredient in this typical Umbrian recipe is fresh ginger. According to food historian Waverly Root, Marco Polo was responsible for this exotic addition to Italian cooking.

8 ounces dry spaghettini
3 tablespoons olive oil
2 teaspoons minced fresh
   ginger

2 garlic cloves, minced
2 tablespoons minced
   parsley, preferably Italian

1. In a large pot of rapidly boiling, lightly salted water, cook pasta 5 minutes. Add 1 tablespoon oil and cook until pasta is barely tender, 1 to 3 minutes longer.

2. Meanwhile, in large skillet, heat remaining oil over medium heat. Stir in ginger, garlic, and parsley and remove from heat.

3. Drain pasta and toss with sauce. Serve immediately.

77   HAY AND STRAW
Prep: 3 minutes   Cook: 2 to 3 minutes   Serves: 4

1 (9-ounce) package fresh
   spinach linguine
1 (9-ounce) package fresh
   linguine
1 stick (4 ounces) butter
2 to 3 garlic cloves, crushed

½ teaspoon freshly ground
   pepper
½ teaspoon salt
⅔ cup freshly grated Parmesan
   cheese

1. In large pot of rapidly boiling, lightly salted water, cook pasta until barely tender, 2 to 3 minutes.

2. While pasta is cooking, melt butter in a small saucepan with garlic. Remove and discard garlic, then add pepper and salt.

3. Drain pasta and toss with butter and Parmesan.

78   ANGEL HAIR WITH ROASTED RED PEPPER SAUCE
Prep: 5 minutes   Cook: 9 to 12 minutes   Serves: 2 to 3

To save time, use canned or jarred roasted red peppers.

1 cup chopped onion
2 large garlic cloves, minced
1 tablespoon olive oil
1 (14½-ounce) can pasta-ready
   tomatoes
1 (7-ounce) jar roasted red
   peppers, drained
½ cup chicken broth
¾ teaspoon dried oregano

½ teaspoon red wine vinegar
½ teaspoon ground cumin
¼ teaspoon salt
¼ teaspoon cayenne
1 (9-ounce) package fresh
   angel hair pasta
¼ cup grated Romano or
   Parmesan cheese

1. In a large skillet, cook onion and garlic in oil over medium heat until softened, about 3 minutes.

2. In a food processor or blender, puree tomatoes, roasted peppers, chicken broth, oregano, vinegar, cumin, salt, and cayenne until smooth. Add puree to onion and garlic, raise heat to medium-high, and cook 5 to 7 minutes, or until slightly thickened.

3. Meanwhile, in a large pot of rapidly boiling, lightly salted water, cook pasta until barely tender, 1 to 2 minutes.

4. Drain pasta, transfer to a warm platter, top with sauce, and serve sprinkled with Romano cheese.

79   ANGEL HAIR WITH SMOKED SALMON
Prep: 8 minutes   Cook: 4 minutes   Serves: 3 to 4

A small amount of smoked salmon goes a long way in this elegant pasta dish.

3 tablespoons olive oil	½ teaspoon salt
3 garlic cloves, minced	¼ teaspoon pepper
1¼ cups heavy cream	1 (9-ounce) package fresh
1 medium zucchini, thinly	angel hair pasta
sliced	6 ounces thinly sliced smoked
1 tablespoon lemon juice	salmon, cut into thin
1 teaspoon grated lemon zest	strips
¾ teaspoon dried tarragon	1 tablespoon drained capers

1. In a large skillet, heat oil. Add garlic and cook over medium heat, stirring, 1 minute. Add cream and zucchini, bring to a boil over high heat, reduce heat to medium-low, and cook uncovered until zucchini is crisp-tender, about 3 minutes. Stir in lemon juice, zest, tarragon, salt, and pepper.

2. Meanwhile, in a large pot of rapidly boiling, lightly salted water, cook pasta until tender but still firm, about 2 minutes. Drain into a colander.

3. Add cooked pasta to skillet and toss thoroughly. Transfer to a serving platter. Arrange salmon over pasta and sprinkle with capers.

80   ANGEL HAIR POMODORO
Prep: 6 minutes   Cook: 1 to 2 minutes   Serves: 6

This is an excellent way to use tomatoes from the garden in the summer.

4 to 6 ripe medium tomatoes,	¼ teaspoon freshly ground
quartered	pepper
½ cup lightly packed fresh	2 tablespoons olive oil
basil leaves	2 (9-ounce) packages fresh
2 garlic cloves, chopped	angel hair pasta
¼ teaspoon salt	6 tablespoons freshly grated
	Romano cheese

1. In a food processor, combine tomatoes, basil, garlic, salt, and pepper. Pulse machine to chop coarsely. Stir in 1 tablespoon oil. Marinate 10 minutes.

2. In a large pot of rapidly boiling, lightly salted water, cook pasta until barely tender, 1 to 2 minutes. Drain well, then toss with remaining 1 tablespoon olive oil.

3. Place pasta on a serving platter and pour on fresh tomato sauce. Sprinkle cheese on top.

81 CAULIFLOWER WITH LINGUINE
Prep: 8 minutes   Cook: 12 minutes   Serves: 4 to 6

2 tablespoons olive oil
1 tablespoon butter
1 medium head of
   cauliflower, cut into small
   florets
1½ cups sliced onions
¼ cup chopped parsley,
   preferably Italian
5 to 6 garlic cloves, chopped
2 (14½-ounce) cans pasta-
   ready tomatoes

¾ teaspoon crushed red
   pepper
½ teaspoon lemon juice
¼ teaspoon salt
⅛ teaspoon freshly ground
   pepper
1 (9-ounce) package fresh
   linguine
¼ cup grated Parmesan or
   Romano cheese

1. In a large nonstick skillet over medium-high heat, heat 1 tablespoon oil with butter. When butter begins to bubble, add cauliflower and onions. Cook, stirring occasionally, until florets turn golden, about 5 minutes. Stir in parsley and garlic and cook for 1 minute.

2. Add tomatoes, red pepper, lemon juice, salt, and pepper. Reduce heat to medium-low and simmer 5 minutes, to blend flavors.

3. Meanwhile, in a large pot of rapidly boiling, lightly salted water, cook linguine until just tender, 2 to 4 minutes. Drain well. Transfer to a serving dish and toss with remaining tablespoon olive oil. Spoon sauce over pasta and serve sprinkled with Parmesan cheese.

82 SPAGHETTINI WITH QUICK TOMATO SAUCE
Prep: 5 minutes   Cook: 12 to 15 minutes   Serves: 2 to 3

A pinch of sugar added to this quick-cooking tomato sauce cuts acidity and gives a rounded flavor normally associated with longer-cooking sauces.

6 to 8 ripe medium plum
   tomatoes, quartered
1 small shallot, peeled and
   quartered
¼ cup fresh basil leaves
¼ teaspoon dried thyme leaves
¼ teaspoon salt

¼ teaspoon pepper
¼ teaspoon sugar
6 ounces spaghettini
1 tablespoon olive oil
2 to 3 tablespoons grated
   Parmesan cheese

1. In a food processor, puree tomatoes, shallot, and basil until smooth. Transfer puree to a large nonreactive skillet. Add thyme, salt, pepper, and sugar. Bring to a boil and cook over medium heat, stirring occasionally, 12 to 15 minutes to blend flavors.

2. Meanwhile, in a large pot of rapidly boiling, lightly salted water, cook pasta until tender but still firm, 8 to 10 minutes. Drain well and toss with olive oil.

3. Pour sauce over pasta. Sprinkle cheese on top and serve.

---

83   SPAGHETTINI WITH ARUGULA, GOAT CHEESE, AND SUN-DRIED TOMATOES
Prep: 8 minutes   Cook: 7 to 9 minutes   Serves: 4

Goat cheese adds tanginess and a creamy richness to this sophisticated sauce.

1 **pound spaghettini**	1 **cup dry white wine**
¾ **cup thinly sliced oil-packed**	1½ **teaspoons dried basil**
sun-dried tomatoes, plus	¼ **teaspoon salt**
¼ **cup oil from tomatoes**	¼ **teaspoon pepper**
4 **garlic cloves, minced**	4 **ounces mild chèvre,**
6 **cups thinly sliced arugula**	**crumbled**
leaves and stems	

1. In a large pot of rapidly boiling, lightly salted water, cook pasta until tender but still firm, 7 to 9 minutes. Ladle out ½ cup of cooking water and set aside. Drain pasta into a colander.

2. Meanwhile, in a large skillet, heat oil from tomatoes. Add garlic and cook over medium heat, stirring, 1 minute. Add arugula and toss until wilted. Add wine and basil, raise heat to high, and boil until slightly reduced, about 2 minutes. Season with salt and pepper.

3. Add pasta and reserved cooking water to sauce and toss to combine. Add crumbled goat cheese and sun-dried tomatoes and toss gently so that cheese begins to melt. Serve immediately.

84   SPAGHETTINI WITH QUICK BOLOGNESE SAUCE

Prep: 3 minutes   Cook: 10 minutes   Serves: 4 to 6

If mixed ground meat (often referred to as "meatloaf mixture") isn't available, substitute one pound of ground beef.

1 pound spaghettini	1 (16-ounce) can tomato sauce
1 pound mixed ground meat (beef, pork, and veal)	1 tablespoon Italian seasoning
1 medium onion, chopped	¾ teaspoon salt
2 garlic cloves, minced	½ teaspoon pepper
1 (28-ounce) can crushed tomatoes in puree	¼ cup chopped parsley, preferably Italian

1. In a large pot of rapidly boiling, lightly salted water, cook the spaghettini until tender but still firm, 7 to 9 minutes. Drain into a colander.

2. Meanwhile, in a large skillet, combine mixed ground meat, onion, and garlic. Cook over medium-high heat, stirring frequently, until meat loses its pink color, about 5 minutes. Pour off any excess fat.

3. Add tomatoes, tomato sauce, Italian seasoning, salt, and pepper. Bring to a boil over high heat, reduce heat to medium, and cook uncovered until somewhat thickened, about 5 minutes. Stir in parsley. Spoon sauce over cooked pasta.

85   SPAGHETTINI TRAPANESE

Prep: 5 minutes   Cook: 8 to 12 minutes   Serves: 4

To toast almonds, spread on cookie sheet and bake at 350°F. for 6 to 8 minutes, stirring occasionally, until lightly browned.

2 garlic cloves, chopped	¼ teaspoon salt
2 tablespoons olive oil	¼ teaspoon pepper
1 (28-ounce) can chopped peeled tomatoes, liquid reserved	¼ teaspoon dried oregano
	8 ounces spaghettini
2 tablespoons sun-dried tomato paste	¼ cup sliced almonds, preferably lightly toasted
4 fresh basil leaves, slivered	½ cup grated Romano cheese

1. In a large skillet, over medium heat, cook garlic in oil until soft, about 1 minute. Add tomatoes, with their liquid, tomato paste, basil, salt, pepper, and oregano. Cook, stirring occasionally, until slightly thickened, 8 to 12 minutes.

2. Meanwhile, in a large pot of rapidly boiling, lightly salted water, cook pasta until barely tender, 8 to 10 minutes; drain.

3. Place pasta on a deep platter and cover with sauce. Sprinkle almonds and cheese on top and serve immediately.

86 LINGUINE WITH QUICK WHITE CLAM SAUCE

Prep: 4 to 5 minutes   Cook: 5 to 7 minutes   Serves: 3 to 4

Though traditionally seafood pastas are served without cheese, I like the addition of Parmesan in this dish.

1 (9-ounce) package fresh linguine	¼ cup chopped parsley, preferably Italian
4 garlic cloves, minced	2 tablespoons dry white vermouth
2 tablespoons butter	
1 (6½-ounce) can minced clams, including juice	⅛ teaspoon white pepper
	⅓ to ½ cup grated Parmesan cheese
1¼ cups clam juice	

1. In a large pot of rapidly boiling, lightly salted water, cook linguine until barely tender, 3 to 5 minutes.

2. Meanwhile, in a large skillet, cook garlic in butter over medium heat until soft, about 2 minutes. Add clams and juice. Cook over medium heat until heated through, 2 to 3 minutes. Add parsley, vermouth, and pepper just before serving.

3. Drain pasta, place on heated platter, pour sauce over pasta, and sprinkle with cheese.

87 LINGUINE WITH SUN-DRIED TOMATO SAUCE

Prep: 5 minutes   Cook: 9 minutes   Serves: 3 to 4

¾ cup thinly sliced oil-packed sun-dried tomatoes, plus 3 tablespoons oil from tomatoes	⅓ cup heavy cream
	1 (9-ounce) package fresh linguine
3 garlic cloves, minced	¼ teaspoon pepper
1 (28-ounce) can crushed tomatoes in puree	1 tablespoon balsamic vinegar
	¼ cup grated Parmesan cheese

1. In a large skillet, heat oil from tomatoes. Add garlic and cook over medium heat 1 minute. Add canned tomatoes and sun-dried tomatoes and bring to a boil over high heat. Reduce heat to medium and cook uncovered until slightly reduced, about 5 minutes. Add cream and cook for 3 minutes to blend flavors.

2. Meanwhile, in a large pot of rapidly boiling, lightly salted water, cook linguine until tender but firm, about 3 minutes. Drain into a colander.

3. Season sauce with pepper and stir in vinegar. Spoon over pasta and sprinkle with cheese.

88   LINGUINE WITH CREAMY SPINACH AND HAM SAUCE

Prep: 5 minutes   Cook: 5 minutes   Serves: 3 to 4

2 (9-ounce) packages frozen creamed spinach in microwave pouch
1½ tablespoons olive oil
1 cup diced smoked ham
2 garlic cloves, minced

1 cup ricotta cheese
½ teaspoon salt
¼ teaspoon pepper
¼ teaspoon grated nutmeg
1 (9-ounce) package fresh linguine

1. Thaw spinach in microwave.

2. In a large skillet, heat oil. Add ham and cook over medium-high heat, stirring frequently, until lightly browned, about 4 minutes. Add garlic and cook 30 seconds. Add creamed spinach and whisk in ricotta. Cook, stirring, until sauce is heated through, about 2 minutes. Season with salt, pepper, and nutmeg.

3. Meanwhile, in a large pot of rapidly boiling, lightly salted water, cook pasta until tender but still firm, about 3 minutes. Drain into a colander and transfer to a serving dish. Pour sauce over linguine and serve.

89   SPICY GARLIC EGGPLANT LINGUINE

Prep: 5 minutes   Cook: 13 to 17 minutes   Serves: 3 to 4

Use small Italian eggplants—sometimes called "baby" eggplants—or the long, thin Japanese eggplants for this sauce. They are less bitter than the larger variety and cook to a melting tenderness very quickly.

3 tablespoons olive oil
12 ounces small Italian or Japanese eggplant, cut into ½-inch dice
2 garlic cloves, minced
2 (14½-ounce) cans Italian-style stewed tomatoes
½ cup dry white wine

1½ teaspoons Italian seasoning
½ teaspoon salt
¼ teaspoon crushed hot red pepper
1 (9-ounce) package fresh linguine
½ cup grated Parmesan cheese

1. In a large skillet, heat oil. Add eggplant and cook over medium-high heat, stirring frequently, until softened and lightly browned, 6 to 8 minutes.

2. Add garlic and cook 30 seconds. Add tomatoes, wine, Italian seasoning, salt, and hot pepper. Boil uncovered until sauce is reduced and thickened slightly, 3 to 5 minutes.

3. Meanwhile, in a large pot of rapidly boiling, lightly salted water, cook pasta until tender but still firm, about 3 minutes. Drain into a colander.

4. Transfer pasta to a serving dish. Pour sauce over pasta, toss, and sprinkle cheese on top.

90 CALAMARI LINGUINE

Prep: 8 minutes   Cook: 4 to 6 minutes   Serves: 3 to 4

Calamari, or small squid, are now widely available both fresh and frozen. If you use the tentacles, cut them into small pieces.

3 tablespoons olive oil
4 garlic cloves, minced
2 (14½-ounce) cans Italian-style stewed tomatoes
1½ teaspoons dried oregano
½ teaspoon crushed hot red pepper

¼ teaspoon salt
1 pound cleaned calamari, cut into thin rings
½ cup chopped parsley, preferably Italian
1 (9-ounce) package fresh linguine

1. In a large skillet, heat oil. Add garlic and cook over medium heat, stirring, until softened and fragrant, about 1 minute. Add tomatoes, oregano, hot pepper, and salt. Break up tomatoes with side of a spoon. Bring to a boil over high heat, add calamari, and reduce heat to medium-low. Cook uncovered until calamari is opaque and sauce is slightly reduced, 3 to 5 minutes. Stir in parsley.

2. Meanwhile, in a large pot of rapidly boiling, lightly salted water, cook linguine until tender but still firm, about 3 minutes. Drain into a colander, then transfer to a serving dish.

3. Pour sauce over pasta, toss, and serve.

91 GARLIC SHRIMP LINGUINE

Prep: 10 minutes   Cook: 9 minutes   Serves: 3 to 4

This is really a special-occasion dish, perfect for a quick company supper.

1 (9-ounce) package fresh linguine
3 tablespoons olive oil
2 tablespoons butter
4 garlic cloves, minced
3 tablespoons minced shallots
1 cup bottled clam juice

⅓ cup dry white wine
1 pound medium shrimp, shelled and deveined
½ cup chopped parsley, preferably Italian
½ teaspoon freshly ground pepper

1. In a large pot of rapidly boiling, lightly salted water, cook linguine until tender but still firm, about 3 minutes. Drain into a colander.

2. In a large skillet, heat oil and butter. Add garlic, shallots, clam juice, and wine. Raise heat to medium-high and boil uncovered until sauce is slightly reduced, about 3 minutes.

3. Add shrimp, reduce heat to medium, and cook until they turn pink and are opaque but still moist in the center, about 3 minutes. Stir in parsley and pepper. Spoon sauce over pasta and serve.

92   BUTTER AND CHEESE RAVIOLI

Prep: 3 minutes   Cook: 6 to 7 minutes   Serves: 4

1 (9-ounce) package fresh
   spinach ravioli
4 tablespoons butter, melted
¼ cup chopped parsley,
   preferably Italian

¼ teaspoon freshly ground
   pepper
⅓ cup grated Parmesan cheese

1. In a large pot of rapidly boiling, lightly salted water, cook ravioli until just tender, 6 to 7 minutes. Drain well.

2. In a warm bowl, toss hot ravioli with melted butter, parsley, pepper, and Parmesan cheese. Serve immediately.

93   RAVIOLI WITH SPINACH-PECAN PESTO

Prep: 8 minutes   Cook: 5 to 7 minutes   Serves: 4

The addition of spinach to this variation on traditional pesto makes the sauce lighter and less rich. Pecans work well and are less expensive and easier to find than the shelled pignoli nuts often called for in pesto recipes. Like most nuts, pecans are more flavorful if toasted in a 350°F. oven for about 5 minutes before using in a recipe.

1 (12-ounce) package fresh
   cheese-filled ravioli
1 cup firmly packed spinach
   leaves, well rinsed and
   dried
½ cup firmly packed fresh
   basil leaves
6 tablespoons extra-virgin
   olive oil

⅔ cup grated Parmesan cheese
½ cup pecan pieces, preferably
   lightly toasted
2 garlic cloves
¼ teaspoon salt
   Freshly ground pepper and
   grated nutmeg

1. In a large pot of rapidly boiling, lightly salted water, cook ravioli until just tender, 5 to 7 minutes.

2. Meanwhile, in a food processor, combine spinach, basil, olive oil, ⅓ cup Parmesan cheese, ¼ cup pecans, garlic, and salt. Pulse on and off until pureed.

3. Drain pasta, reserving ⅓ cup of the cooking water. Place pasta in a warm bowl with pesto and reserved water. Season lightly with pepper and nutmeg. Toss gently but thoroughly to coat pasta with sauce. Serve with remaining cheese and pecans sprinkled on top.

94 RAVIOLI PARMA

Prep: 5 minutes   Cook: 7 to 9 minutes   Serves: 3

1 (9-ounce) package fresh
   spinach ravioli
1 (10-ounce) package frozen
   peas
2 tablespoons unsalted butter

¼ pound thinly sliced
   prosciutto, cut into ¼-
   inch-wide strips
⅛ teaspoon freshly grated
   pepper
¼ cup grated Parmesan cheese

1. In a large pot of rapidly boiling, lightly salted water, cook ravioli until barely tender, 6 to 7 minutes. Drain and set aside.

2. Meanwhile, place peas in microwave dish with 1 tablespoon water. Microwave on High 2 to 3 minutes to thaw.

3. In a large skillet, melt butter over medium heat. Add ravioli, peas, prosciutto, and pepper. Cook 1 to 2 minutes to heat through. Transfer to a serving dish and toss gently with Parmesan cheese.

95 TORTELLINI AU GRATIN

Prep: 5 minutes   Cook: 8 to 11 minutes   Serves: 6 to 8

2 cups heavy cream
2 tablespoons butter
2 (9-ounce) packages meat-
   filled tortellini

¼ teaspoon freshly ground
   pepper
¼ teaspoon grated nutmeg
½ cup grated Parmesan cheese

1. Preheat broiler. In a large saucepan, combine cream and butter. Cook over medium heat, stirring frequently, until cream is reduced by about half, 6 to 8 minutes.

2. Meanwhile, in large pot of rapidly boiling, lightly salted water, cook tortellini until barely tender, 5 to 7 minutes; drain.

3. Add drained tortellini, pepper, and nutmeg to cream sauce. Toss gently. Transfer to a 9 x 13-inch gratin dish or 6 individual gratin dishes. Sprinkle Parmesan on top.

4. Broil about 4 inches from heat 2 to 3 minutes, until lightly browned.

96 TORTELLINI WITH TOMATO CREAM SAUCE

Prep: 5 minutes   Cook: 5 to 7 minutes   Serves: 4

A tube of sun-dried tomato paste is worth its weight in gold. A small amount gives distinction to many dishes, and there is no waste.

1 (9-ounce) package meat-filled tortellini	4 teaspoons sun-dried tomato paste
1 cup heavy cream	¼ cup chopped parsley

1. In a large pot of rapidly boiling, lightly salted water, cook tortellini until tender, 5 to 7 minutes.

2. Meanwhile, in a large, heavy saucepan over medium heat, boil cream, stirring frequently, until reduced by about half, 5 to 6 minutes. Add tomato paste and whisk until well blended.

3. Drain tortellini and add to cream sauce. Toss gently and serve sprinkled with parsley.

97 PENNE WITH CAPONATA AND TUNA

Prep: 5 minutes   Cook: 10 minutes   Serves: 2

A good-quality caponata, which is a savory combination of eggplant, tomatoes, olives, and capers, is sold in cans nationwide. It makes a terrific topping for pasta in combination with tuna and some other seasonings.

8 ounces penne	2 teaspoons lemon juice
1 (6½-ounce) can oil-packed tuna, oil reserved	½ cup chopped parsley, preferably Italian
2 garlic cloves, minced	¼ teaspoon crushed hot red pepper
1 (7½-ounce) can caponata	

1. In a large pot of rapidly boiling, lightly salted water, cook penne until tender but still firm, about 10 minutes. Drain into a colander.

2. Meanwhile, in a large skillet, heat 1½ tablespoons oil from tuna. Add garlic and cook over medium heat, stirring, until softened and fragrant, about 1 minute. Add caponata, lemon juice, parsley, and hot pepper. Break tuna into chunks and stir in gently. Cook until heated through, about 2 minutes.

3. Add cooked pasta to sauce and toss to combine. Serve at once.

98   VERMICELLI WITH SCALLOPS AND LEMON

Prep: 5 minutes   Cook: 7 minutes   Serves: 4

1 pound vermicelli	2 teaspoons dried tarragon
¼ cup olive oil	1 pound small bay scallops
2 tablespoons butter	¾ cup thinly sliced scallions
1 cup bottled clam juice	¼ teaspoon freshly ground
¼ cup fresh lemon juice	pepper
2 teaspoons grated lemon zest	

1. In a large pot of rapidly boiling, lightly salted water, cook vermicelli until tender but still firm, about 7 minutes. Drain into a colander. Transfer to a serving dish.

2. Meanwhile, in a large skillet or saucepan, combine olive oil, butter, clam juice, lemon juice, lemon zest, and tarragon. Bring to a boil over high heat and boil until slightly reduced, about 2 minutes.

3. Add scallops, reduce heat to medium-low, and cook uncovered until opaque but still tender, 1 to 2 minutes. Stir in scallions and pepper. Spoon sauce over pasta and serve.

99   SALMON AND PEAS WITH BOW-TIE PASTA

Prep: 8 minutes   Cook: 9 minutes   Serves: 4 to 6

1 pound bow-tie pasta	2 teaspoons Dijon mustard
1½ cups heavy cream	12 ounces salmon fillets, cut
½ cup dry white wine	into thin strips
1½ cups frozen baby peas	½ teaspoon salt
½ cup thinly sliced scallions	¼ teaspoon freshly ground
¼ cup chopped fresh dill	pepper

1. In a large pot of rapidly boiling, lightly salted water, cook pasta until tender but still firm, about 9 minutes. Drain into a colander.

2. Meanwhile, in a large skillet or saucepan, combine cream and wine. Bring to a boil over high heat, add peas, and return to a boil. Reduce heat to medium and cook uncovered until sauce is slightly reduced and peas are tender, 2 to 3 minutes.

3. Add scallions and dill to sauce and whisk in mustard. Add salmon and cook until fish is opaque, about 1 minute. Season with salt and pepper. Spoon sauce over bow-ties and toss to combine.

100 FUSILLI WITH PESTO SHRIMP
Prep: 3 minutes   Cook: 10 minutes   Serves: 4

Fusilli is long, corkscrew pasta. If you can't find it, any strand pasta will do just fine.

1 **pound fusilli**
1 **cup bottled clam juice**
½ **cup dry white wine**
1 **pound shelled and deveined medium shrimp**

1¼ **cups pesto sauce**
½ **cup chopped parsley**
½ **teaspoon pepper**

1. In a large pot of rapidly boiling, lightly salted water, cook fusilli until tender but still firm, about 10 minutes. Drain into a colander.

2. Meanwhile, in a large skillet or saucepan, combine clam juice and wine. Bring to a boil over high heat and cook until liquid is slightly reduced, about 2 minutes. Add shrimp, reduce heat to medium-low, and cook until shrimp turn pink but are still moist in the center, about 3 minutes.

3. Stir in pesto and parsley and season with pepper. Spoon over pasta to serve.

101 ROTELLE WITH SOUTHWESTERN SALSA CRUDA
Prep: 10 minutes   Cook: 10 minutes   Serves: 4

Rotelle pasta is shaped like little wheels. Almost any other medium pasta shape, such as rotini or cavatelli, can be substituted.

1 **pound rotelle**
2½ **pounds tomatoes, seeded and chopped**
3 **cups diced Monterey Jack cheese with jalapeño peppers (12 ounces)**
6 **tablespoons olive oil**

1½ **tablespoons red wine vinegar**
3 **garlic cloves, minced**
1 **teaspoon salt**
½ **teaspoon freshly ground pepper**
⅔ **cup chopped cilantro**

1. In a large pot of rapidly boiling, lightly salted water, cook rotelle until tender but still firm, about 10 minutes. Drain into a colander.

2. Meanwhile, in a large bowl, combine tomatoes, cheese, oil, vinegar, garlic, salt, and pepper. Let stand 5 minutes. Stir in cilantro.

3. Toss hot pasta with room temperature sauce until cheese begins to melt. Serve immediately.

102   FUSILLI WITH TUNA SAUCE

Prep: 5 minutes   Cook: 10 minutes   Serves: 4

Canned pasta-ready tomatoes are diced and seasoned with garlic and herbs.

1 pound fusilli	¼ cup chopped parsley
3 tablespoons olive oil	1 tablespoon lemon juice
2 (14½-ounce) cans diced	2 teaspoons drained capers
pasta-ready tomatoes,	½ teaspoon pepper
liquid reserved	2 (6½-ounce) cans oil-packed
½ cup sliced black olives	tuna, oil reserved

1. In a large pot of rapidly boiling, lightly salted water, cook fusilli until tender but still firm, about 10 minutes. Drain into a colander.

2. Meanwhile, in a large skillet, heat oil. Add tomatoes with their liquid, olives, parsley, and lemon juice. Bring to a boil and cook, stirring, until heated through, 1 to 2 minutes. Stir in capers and season with pepper.

3. Add cooked pasta to pan and toss to combine. Add tuna with oil and toss gently to break tuna into chunks.

103   ZITI WITH BROCCOLI AND WHITE BEANS

Prep: 3 minutes   Cook: 10 to 12 minutes   Serves: 8

Cut broccoli florets, available in the produce department of most supermarkets, keep preparation time to a minimum in this hearty crowd-pleasing recipe.

1 pound ziti	2 (14- to 16-ounce) cans white
8 cups broccoli florets	cannellini beans, drained
(about 1½ pounds)	and rinsed
3 tablespoons olive oil	½ cup grated Parmesan cheese
4 garlic cloves, minced	½ teaspoon salt
2 cups dry white wine	¼ teaspoon pepper

1. In a large pot of boiling salted water, cook ziti until tender but still firm, 10 to 12 minutes. During the last 2 to 3 minutes of cooking, add broccoli so that florets are crisp-tender when pasta is done. Drain into a colander.

2. Meanwhile, heat oil in a large skillet. Add garlic and cook over medium heat, stirring, 1 minute. Add wine and white beans. Bring to a boil, reduce heat to medium, and cook until liquid is slightly reduced, about 5 minutes. Add reserved cooked broccoli.

3. Toss pasta with sauce, add cheese, and toss again. Season with salt and pepper.

104   FAMILY-STYLE MACARONI AND CHEESE WITH SMOKED HAM

Prep: 3 minutes   Cook: 7 to 10 minutes   Serves: 2 to 3

A box of macaroni and cheese mix is handy to have on the pantry shelf for a good, quick meal. Here, it's livened up with smoked ham, scallions, and dry mustard.

1 (7½-ounce) package macaroni and cheese	¾ teaspoon dry mustard
4 tablespoons butter	2 tablespoons chopped scallions
1 cup diced smoked ham	⅛ teaspoon pepper
½ cup milk	

1. In a large pot of rapidly boiling, lightly salted water, cook macaroni from package until tender but firm, 7 to 10 minutes. Drain into a colander.

2. Meanwhile, in a skillet or saucepan, heat butter. Add ham and cook over medium to medium-high heat, stirring frequently, until ham is lightly tinged with brown, about 4 minutes. Add milk and whisk in dry mustard and packet of cheese sauce mix. Bring to a boil over high heat, whisking constantly, until sauce mix is smooth.

3. Remove from heat and stir in cooked macaroni, scallions, and pepper.

105   PASTA PUTTANESCA

Prep: 5 minutes   Cook: 10 minutes   Serves: 6

Use a rather small spoonful of this deliciously potent sauce on each portion of spaghetti. It goes a long way.

1¼ pounds spaghetti	6 anchovy fillets
3 tablespoons olive oil	2 tablespoons drained capers
4 garlic cloves, minced	1 teaspoon dried oregano
1 (28-ounce) can Italian peeled tomatoes, drained, juices reserved	½ teaspoon crushed hot red pepper
1 cup sliced black olives	⅔ cup chopped parsley
	⅔ cup grated Parmesan cheese

1. In a large pot of rapidly boiling, lightly salted water, cook spaghetti until tender but still firm, about 10 minutes. Drain into a colander.

2. Meanwhile, in a large skillet, heat oil. Add garlic and cook over medium heat, stirring, until softened and fragrant, about 1 minute. Add tomatoes to skillet along with olives, anchovies, capers, oregano, and red pepper. Bring to a boil over high heat, breaking up tomatoes into smaller pieces with side of a spoon. Reduce heat to medium and cook uncovered until sauce is quite thick, about 6 minutes.

3. Stir in parsley. If sauce needs more liquid, add up to ½ cup reserved tomato juice. Spoon over pasta and sprinkle cheese on top.

106 SPICY JALAPEÑO MACARONI AND CHEESE
Prep: 3 minutes   Cook: 7 to 10 minutes   Serves: 2

Spiced up with jalapeño peppers and chili powder, this is a Southwestern twist on packaged macaroni and cheese.

1 (7½-ounce) package
  macaroni and cheese
4 tablespoons butter
2 tablespoons chopped onion
¾ teaspoon chili powder

½ cup milk
2 to 3 teaspoons minced
  jalapeño peppers,
  pickled or fresh

1. In a large pot of rapidly boiling, lightly salted water, cook macaroni from package until tender but firm, 7 to 10 minutes. Drain into a colander.

2. Meanwhile, in a skillet or saucepan, heat butter. Add onion and cook over medium heat, stirring, until slightly softened, about 3 minutes. Stir in chili powder and cook, stirring, for 1 minute. Whisk in milk and packet of cheese sauce mix. Bring to a boil over high heat, whisking constantly, until sauce mix is smooth.

3. Remove from heat and stir in cooked macaroni and jalapeños.

107 SPAGHETTI WITH DIABLO CLAM SAUCE
Prep: 5 minutes   Cook: 10 minutes   Serves: 4 to 5

1 pound spaghetti
2 tablespoons olive oil
4 garlic cloves, chopped
1 tablespoon chili powder
1 (28-ounce) can crushed
  tomatoes in puree
2 teaspoons brown sugar

½ teaspoon black pepper
½ teaspoon cayenne
½ teaspoon paprika
2 (10-ounce) cans baby clams,
  drained, juice reserved
½ teaspoon grated lemon zest

1. In a large pot of rapidly boiling, lightly salted water, cook spaghetti until tender but still firm, about 10 minutes. Drain into a colander.

2. Meanwhile, in a large skillet, heat oil. Add garlic and chili powder and cook over medium-high heat, stirring, 1 minute. Add tomatoes, brown sugar, black pepper, cayenne, paprika, and reserved clam juice. Bring to a boil over high heat, reduce heat to medium, and cook uncovered until sauce has reduced and thickened somewhat, about 8 minutes. Add clams and cook 1 minute. Stir in lemon zest. Spoon sauce over cooked spaghetti to serve.

108 ORECCHIETTE WITH BROCCOLI RABE AND BACON

Prep: 4 minutes   Cook: 13 to 16 minutes   Serves: 4

The pleasing pungency of broccoli rabe adds spark and interest to this pasta dish made with orecchiette, or "little ears." All of the broccoli rabe, including stems, leaves, and buds, gets used.

1 large bunch of broccoli rabe (about 1½ pounds)	2 tablespoons olive oil
12 ounces orecchiette	4 garlic cloves, minced
6 slices of bacon, coarsely chopped	1 cup dry white wine
	½ teaspoon pepper
	½ cup grated Parmesan cheese

1. In a large pot of rapidly boiling, lightly salted water, cook broccoli rabe until crisp-tender, 3 to 4 minutes. Lift out with tongs, drain in a colander, rinse under cold water to cool, and drain well. Chop into pieces about ½ inch long. Boil orecchiette in same water until tender but still firm, 10 to 12 minutes. Measure out and reserve ½ cup cooking water and drain pasta into a colander.

2. Meanwhile, in a large skillet, cook bacon over medium heat, stirring frequently, until browned and crisp and fat is rendered, 5 to 6 minutes. Remove with a slotted spoon, drain on paper towels, and discard all but 1 tablespoon fat. Add olive oil and garlic and cook over medium heat, stirring, 1 minute. Add wine, raise heat to high, and boil until slightly reduced, about 2 minutes. Stir in cooked broccoli rabe and season with pepper.

3. Toss cooked pasta and sauce together, along with reserved ½ cup cooking water. Add Parmesan and toss again. Sprinkle with reserved bacon before serving.

109 COUSCOUS WITH BROCCOLI, GARLIC, AND PINE NUTS

Prep: 4 minutes   Cook: 6 to 8 minutes   Stand: 5 minutes Serves: 4

1 large bunch of broccoli (about 1½ pounds)	2 cups vegetable broth or water
3 tablespoons olive oil	1¼ cups instant couscous
¼ cup pine nuts	¼ teaspoon pepper
3 garlic cloves, minced	Salt

1. Trim broccoli to make florets; thinly slice about 3 inches of stems. In a large pot of rapidly boiling, lightly salted water, cook broccoli until tender, 3 to 4 minutes. Drain into a colander.

2. In a large skillet, heat oil. Add pine nuts and cook over medium heat, stirring, until lightly browned, 2 to 3 minutes. Add garlic and cook, stirring, 1 minute. Add broth, couscous, and cooked broccoli.

3. Bring to a boil over high heat, cover, and remove from heat. Let stand until liquid is absorbed and couscous is softened, about 5 minutes. Fluff with a fork. Season with pepper and salt to taste before serving.

110 SPAGHETTINI WITH HOT AND SPICY TOMATO SAUCE

Prep: 5 minutes   Cook: 10 minutes   Serves: 4

Good-quality imported plum tomatoes make all the difference in this sauce.

8 to 10 ounces spaghettini
3 tablespoons olive oil
2 to 3 dried whole hot red chiles, or ¼ teaspoon crushed hot red pepper
1 medium onion, chopped
2 garlic cloves, minced
1 (28-ounce) can Italian peeled tomatoes, with their juices

½ cup dry white wine
½ teaspoon salt
¼ teaspoon pepper
Pinch of sugar
2 tablespoons chopped parsley
¼ cup grated Parmesan cheese

1. In a large pot of rapidly boiling, lightly salted water, cook pasta until tender but still firm, 7 to 9 minutes. Drain into a colander. Transfer to a serving dish.

2. Meanwhile, in a large skillet, heat oil. Add chiles and cook over medium heat 1 minute. Remove and discard chiles. Stir in onion and cook over medium-high heat until it begins to soften, about 3 minutes. Add garlic and cook, stirring, 30 seconds.

3. Add tomatoes with juices, breaking up tomatoes with side of spoon. Add wine, salt, pepper, and sugar. Bring to a boil over high heat, reduce heat to medium, and cook uncovered until most of liquid is evaporated, about 5 minutes.

4. Stir in parsley. Spoon sauce over pasta and sprinkle cheese on top.

111   HAM AND THREE-CHEESE NOODLES

Prep: 5 minutes   Cook: 6 to 8 minutes   Serves: 4

8 ounces dry home-style egg
   noodles
1 (10¾-ounce) can condensed
   cream of mushroom soup
½ cup milk
½ cup sour cream
¼ cup dry sherry

2 teaspoons Dijon mustard
⅛ teaspoon pepper
2 cups diced ham
¼ cup grated Parmesan cheese
¼ cup grated Romano cheese
¼ cup grated Gruyère cheese

1. In a large pot of rapidly boiling, lightly salted water, cook noodles until just tender, 6 to 8 minutes.

2. Meanwhile, in a medium saucepan, combine mushroom soup, milk, sour cream, sherry, mustard, and pepper. Whisk to blend. Add ham and cook over medium heat, stirring until hot, about 3 minutes. Do not boil.

3. Drain noodles, transfer to a bowl, add cheeses, and toss lightly. Place noodles on a platter, top with ham sauce, and serve.

112   NOODLES À LA RUSSE

Prep: 3 minutes   Cook: 6 to 8 minutes   Serves: 3 to 4

9 ounces dry egg noodles
1 cup heavy cream
½ cup sour cream
¼ teaspoon salt
⅛ teaspoon freshly ground
   pepper

1½ teaspoons minced fresh dill
   plus 3 or 4 sprigs
4 ounces thinly sliced smoked
   salmon
1 tablespoon salmon caviar

1. In a large pot of rapidly boiling, lightly salted water, cook noodles until just tender, 6 to 8 minutes.

2. Meanwhile, in heavy skillet over medium heat, boil cream until reduced by half, about 5 minutes. Whisk in sour cream, salt, pepper, and minced dill. Gently stir in salmon.

3. Drain noodles, place on a warm serving plate, and cover with sauce. Top with caviar and sprigs of dill.

113   QUICK MOROCCAN CHICKEN COUSCOUS
Prep: 6 minutes   Cook: 10 to 12 minutes   Serves: 6 to 7

This quick rendition of the classic couscous tastes deliciously authentic. North Africans often serve their couscous with harissa, a condiment made from a combination of hot spices. Harissa can be found in some specialty stores. Tabasco sauce, though not the same flavor, will provide the same kind of heat.

1⅔ cups instant couscous
2¼ cups boiling water
1½ teaspoons salt
3 tablespoons olive oil
½ cup flour
¼ teaspoon cayenne
1½ pounds skinless, boneless chicken thighs, cut into 2-inch cubes
3 garlic cloves, minced
1 teaspoon curry powder

½ teaspoon ground cumin
3 cups chicken broth
1 (1-pound) package frozen baby carrots
2 cups frozen pearl onions
2 medium zucchini, cut into 1-inch lengths
1 tablespoon ketchup
2 cinnamon sticks, broken in half

1. In a large bowl, combine couscous, boiling water, and 1 teaspoon salt. Cover with plastic wrap and let stand until liquid is absorbed and couscous is softened, about 5 minutes. Fluff with a fork. Mound couscous on a large rimmed heatproof platter. Cover loosely with foil and place in a warm oven.

2. Meanwhile, in a large skillet, heat oil. Combine flour, ½ teaspoon salt, and cayenne in a paper or plastic bag and shake chicken pieces in seasoned flour to coat. Add chicken to skillet and cook over medium-high heat until browned on one side, about 2 minutes. Turn chicken with tongs, add garlic, curry powder, and cumin and cook, stirring, 30 seconds.

3. Add broth, carrots, onions, zucchini, ketchup, and cinnamon sticks and bring to a boil over high heat. Cover, reduce heat to medium-low, and cook until chicken is no longer pink in the center and vegetables are tender, 8 to 10 minutes. Spoon stew around mounded couscous and serve.

114   SPICY COUSCOUS WITH CHICK-PEAS AND DRIED FRUITS

Prep: 4 minutes   Cook: 9 minutes   Stand: 5 minutes   Serves: 4 to 5

Marketed nationwide, packaged mixed dried fruits usually consist of apples, pears, apricots, and prunes.

3 tablespoons olive oil
2 medium onions, chopped
1 cup chopped mixed dried fruits
¾ teaspoon ground cumin
½ teaspoon crushed hot red pepper

2 cups vegetable broth or water
1¼ cups instant couscous
1 (15-ounce) can chick-peas, drained and rinsed
   Salt
¼ cup chopped scallions

1. In a large skillet, heat oil. Add onions and cook over medium heat, stirring frequently, until lightly browned and softened, about 5 minutes. Add dried fruits and cook 3 minutes. Add cumin and crushed pepper and cook, stirring, 1 minute longer.

2. Add broth, couscous, and chick-peas. Bring to a boil over high heat, cover, and turn off heat. Let stand until liquid is absorbed and couscous and fruits are softened, about 5 minutes.

3. Fluff with a fork and season with salt to taste. Sprinkle chopped scallions on top before serving.

Chapter 4

Fast Eggs, Frittatas, and Omelets

Eggs are one of the most useful staples you can keep in the refrigerator. They are full of protein and form a complete food in themselves. They can be used with any number of other ingredients to create a myriad of tasty dishes. And best of all for the 20-minute cook, they take only a few minutes to prepare. There are hundreds, if not thousands, of ways to prepare eggs. They can be used to create dishes for almost any meal, but these days I like to use my weekly egg quota for supper or more substantial brunch dishes instead of breakfast. The 25 international recipes in this chapter give a sampling of their almost limitless possibilities.

When cooking eggs, the pan is especially important. Tradition holds that an egg or omelet pan should be made of heavy iron or steel and should be reserved just for cooking eggs. Few households support that sort of specialization and even if they did, these pans require special care. My personal preference is a heavy-duty nonstick skillet with sloping sides and an ovenproof handle.

The principle involved in cooking eggs is the same as for meat. If eggs are exposed to high heat, the albumin (proteins) will shrivel up; hence, most egg dishes are cooked over gentle heat. The eggs used in this book are large unless otherwise specified. When selecting eggs, choose only grade AA or A. Do not use eggs that are cracked, as those openings allow bacteria to enter the egg. Keep eggs and egg dishes refrigerated and wash hands and utensils thoroughly in soapy water when raw eggs are used in a recipe.

115 EGGS SCRAMBLED WITH CHIVES AND CHEDDAR CHEESE

Prep: 3 minutes   Cook: 5 to 7 minutes   Serves: 5 to 6

12 eggs
⅓ cup milk
2 teaspoons grainy Dijon
    mustard
2 tablespoons butter
2 cups grated sharp Cheddar
    cheese

3 tablespoons minced chives
    or minced scallion tops
¼ teaspoon freshly ground
    pepper

1. In a large bowl, whisk eggs with milk and mustard until blended.

2. In a large nonstick skillet, heat butter. Add eggs and cook over low heat, stirring almost constantly, until eggs have formed a creamy mass and are just barely set but still moist, 5 to 7 minutes.

3. Sprinkle cheese, chives, and pepper over scrambled eggs and serve at once.

116 SCRAMBLED EGGS PARMA

Prep: 5 minutes   Cook: 6 to 8 minutes   Serves: 4

Scrambling eggs in a double-boiler produces a delicate custardy texture. Just make sure the pan is not aluminum, which could cause an off color or flavor.

8 eggs
2 slices of ham, diced
2 tablespoons heavy cream
2 tablespoons freshly grated
    Parmesan cheese
1½ tablespoons minced fresh or
    frozen chives

¼ teaspoon salt
⅛ teaspoon pepper
2 tablespoons butter
4 English muffins, split and
    lightly toasted

1. In top of a double-boiler, whisk together eggs, ham, cream, Parmesan cheese, chives, salt, and pepper. Cook over boiling water, stirring constantly, until eggs begin to thicken and small curds form, 6 to 8 minutes.

2. Stir in butter and remove from heat. Immediately spoon over toasted English muffins and serve.

117 PIPERADE
Prep: 7 minutes   Cook: 11 to 12 minutes   Serves: 3 to 4

In a classic piperade, or Basque-style omelet, the eggs and vegetables are scrambled together. Here the filling is spooned over the eggs to provide a contrast of color and texture.

2 tablespoons olive oil	1 garlic clove, minced
1 cup diced smoked or baked ham	¼ teaspoon crushed hot red pepper
1 small onion, sliced	7 eggs
2 large plum tomatoes, chopped	½ teaspoon dried marjoram
1 medium green bell pepper, chopped	¼ teaspoon salt

1. In a large nonstick skillet, heat 1 tablespoon olive oil. Add ham and onion and cook over medium-high heat, stirring, until lightly browned, about 3 minutes. Add tomatoes and bell pepper and cook, stirring often, until tomatoes have released their juice and pepper is somewhat softened, about 4 minutes. Add garlic and hot pepper and cook 1 minute. Remove vegetable mixture with a slotted spoon and set aside. Do not wash pan.

2. In a large bowl, beat eggs lightly with marjoram, salt, and 2 tablespoons water. Heat remaining 1 tablespoon olive oil in skillet. Add eggs and cook over low heat, stirring constantly with spatula, until softly set, 2 to 3 minutes.

3. With a spatula, flatten eggs to make a smooth top. Spoon reserved vegetable and ham topping over eggs, cover, and cook until vegetables are heated through, about 1 minute. Serve from pan, cut into wedges.

118 FRENCH-STYLE SCRAMBLED EGGS
Prep: 2 minutes   Cook: 6 to 8 minutes   Serves: 4 to 5

These custardy, soft scrambled eggs serve well as a light luncheon or brunch dish. For everyday, spoon them over toasted English muffin halves; for an elegant touch, present them in prebaked puff pastry shells.

10 eggs	¼ teaspoon freshly ground pepper
1½ teaspoons minced fresh tarragon, or ½ teaspoon dried	3 tablespoons butter
½ teaspoon salt	Fresh tarragon sprigs

1. In top of a double-boiler, beat eggs with tarragon, salt, and pepper. Place over boiling water and stir with a wooden spatula until mixture begins to thicken, 4 to 5 minutes.

2. Add butter 1 tablespoon at a time, stirring and scraping sides and bottom of pan until soft curds form, 2 to 3 minutes longer. Serve immediately, garnished with tarragon sprigs.

119 MEXICAN SCRAMBLED EGGS WITH TORTILLAS

Prep: 3 minutes   Cook: 4 to 6 minutes   Serves: 4

Thrifty Mexican cooks call this dish *migas*, and they prepare it as a tasty way to use day-old tortillas. I like the dish so much that I seldom wait for the tortillas to age! For an even quicker version, use crumbled corn tortilla chips.

1½ **tablespoons butter or canola oil**	½ **cup shredded Monterey Jack cheese**
4 **corn tortillas, cut into ½-inch strips**	⅓ **cup medium-hot salsa**
10 **eggs**	½ **teaspoon salt**

1. In a large nonstick skillet, melt butter over medium-high heat. Add tortilla strips and cook until crisp, 3 to 4 minutes.

2. In a mixing bowl, beat eggs until blended. Add cheese, salsa, and salt and whisk to blend.

3. Add eggs to skillet and reduce heat to low. Stir constantly with a wooden spatula until eggs form soft curds, 1 to 2 minutes.

120 HUEVOS RANCHEROS

Prep: 5 minutes   Cook: 6 to 8 minutes   Serves: 2 to 4

This is a quick and easy recipe that can be served at any time of the day. For a spicier dish, add chopped jalapeño peppers.

2 **to 3 tablespoons olive or canola oil**	¼ **cup shredded Monterey Jack cheese**
4 **corn tortillas**	½ **cup salsa**
1 **cup refried beans**	**Fresh cilantro or parsley sprigs**
4 **eggs**	

1. Preheat oven to 325°F. In a large nonstick skillet, heat oil to sizzling. Lightly fry tortillas one at a time, turning once, about 30 seconds per side. Place on a baking sheet. Spread ¼ cup of refried beans over each tortilla and place in oven to keep warm.

2. Reduce heat to medium-low and break eggs into skillet. Fry eggs until whites are set and yolks are still shiny, 1½ to 2 minutes.

3. Sprinkle 1 tablespoon cheese over each fried egg. Top each tortilla with a fried egg. Spoon salsa over each serving and garnish with cilantro sprigs.

121   BREAKFAST BURRITOS

Prep: 6 minutes   Cook: 7 to 10 minutes   Serves: 2

This is a versatile recipe that can be altered to suit many tastes. Brown-and-serve bacon or sausage or cooked vegetables can be used in place of leftover meat. Choose a red or green (hot or mild) salsa depending on the desired degree of heat. Grate the potato on the large holes of a hand grater or, to save time, in a food processor using the shredding disk.

2 **large (10-inch) flour tortillas**
2 **tablespoons vegetable or
    canola oil**
1 **medium red potato, peeled
    and shredded**
¾ **cup diced leftover chicken,
    beef, pork, or shrimp**

3 **eggs**
¼ **teaspoon salt**
⅛ **teaspoon pepper**
¼ **cup salsa**
2 **tablespoons Monterey Jack
    cheese**

1. Warm tortillas on a griddle or in a large skillet or microwave oven.

2. Meanwhile, heat oil in a large nonstick skillet. Add potato and meat to pan and cook over medium heat, stirring often, until potato is soft and just beginning to brown and meat is heated through, 6 to 8 minutes.

3. In a small bowl, beat eggs with salt and pepper. Stir eggs into skillet. Cook, stirring, until eggs are set to desired consistency, 1 to 2 minutes.

4. Spoon half of egg filling across middle of each warm tortilla. Fold in right and left sides to overlap filling slightly. Bring up bottom and roll into a cylinder that is closed at both ends. Top each burrito with 2 tablespoons salsa and 1 tablespoon cheese. Serve at once.

122   CAMPFIRE EGGS

Prep: 5 minutes   Cook: 5 minutes   Serves: 4

This recipe is a favorite with children. Use star- or heart-shaped cookie cutters to cut out different-shaped holes for a holiday breakfast treat.

2 **tablespoons butter, softened**
4 **slices of whole wheat bread**

4 **slices of ham**
4 **eggs**

1. Heat a griddle or large nonstick skillet over medium-high heat. Butter one side of bread. Top unbuttered side with a slice of ham. Using a 3½-inch round cookie cutter, press out a circle or other shape in the bread and ham. Set buttered side down on hot griddle.

2. One at a time, break eggs into a shallow bowl and gently slide one into each hole. Cook until white is set, 2 to 3 minutes.

3. Using a long spatula, flip bread over to warm ham and cook yolk to desired consistency. Serve immediately.

123   MOROCCAN EGGS
Prep: 5 minutes   Cook: 10 to 13 minutes   Serves: 6

Moroccan cooking is famous for its sophisticated blend of sweet and savory flavors. This typical recipe should be served right from the skillet.

1 tablespoon olive oil	⅛ teaspoon cayenne
1 small onion, chopped	2 tablespoons chopped
1 (14½-ounce) can pasta-ready	cilantro
tomatoes	6 eggs
½ teaspoon cumin	⅛ teaspoon salt
½ teaspoon cinnamon	
½ teaspoon freshly ground	
pepper	

1. Heat oil in large nonstick skillet over medium heat. Add onion and cook until softened, 2 to 3 minutes.

2. Add tomatoes, cumin, cinnamon, pepper, cayenne, and 1 tablespoon of chopped cilantro. Raise heat to high and add ½ cup water. Bring to a boil. Carefully crack eggs and slip into skillet, being sure not to overlap eggs. Cook until whites are set, about 5 minutes. Season yolks with salt.

3. Reduce heat to medium-low and cover skillet. Cook until yolks are cooked to taste, 3 to 5 minutes. Garnish with remaining cilantro and serve immediately.

124   MUSTARDY FRIED EGGS AND HOT PASTRAMI
Prep: 3 minutes   Cook: 7 to 8 minutes   Serves: 2

2 tablespoons butter	⅛ teaspoon pepper
¼ pound thinly sliced	1 garlic clove, minced
pastrami, cut into 1-inch	1 tablespoon grainy Dijon
strips	mustard
4 eggs	

1. In a large nonstick skillet, heat 1 tablespoon butter. Add pastrami strips and cook over medium-high heat until golden and slightly crispy, about 3 minutes. Remove with tongs to paper towels.

2. Add remaining butter to skillet and reduce heat to medium-low. Carefully break eggs into skillet and cook uncovered until whites are almost set, 2 to 3 minutes. Turn over, sprinkle with pepper, and cook until set, about 1 minute. Transfer fried eggs to plates and top with pastrami.

3. Stir garlic into skillet drippings and cook, stirring, 1 minute. Whisk in mustard. Spoon mustard over eggs and serve at once.

125   CREAMED EGGS ON TOAST
Prep: 7 minutes   Cook: 4 to 5 minutes   Serves: 2 to 4

2 tablespoons butter
3 small shallots, minced
2 tablespoons flour
1¼ cups milk
¼ cup heavy cream
4 hard-boiled eggs, peeled and chopped
2 tablespoons chopped parsley

1 tablespoon slivered fresh basil
¼ teaspoon salt
½ teaspoon white pepper
2 English muffins, split and toasted

1. In a large nonstick skillet, melt butter over medium heat. Add shallots and cook until just soft, about 2 minutes.

2. Add flour to skillet and cook, stirring, 1 minute. Add milk and cream and bring to a boil, whisking until sauce begins to thicken, 1 to 2 minutes.

3. Gently stir in eggs, parsley, basil, salt, and white pepper. Spoon over toasted English muffins and serve while hot.

126   EGG AND SPINACH GRATIN
Prep: 5 minutes   Cook: 12 to 15 minutes   Serves: 4

1 (10-ounce) package frozen chopped spinach, thawed
1 tablespoon butter
½ cup heavy cream or half-and-half

¼ teaspoon salt
⅛ teaspoon pepper
¼ teaspoon grated nutmeg
8 eggs
1 cup grated Swiss cheese

1. Preheat oven to 325°F. Place spinach in a sieve and press to squeeze out as much water as possible.

2. Use butter to grease 4 shallow 1-cup ramekins or individual French gratin dishes. Spread spinach in bottoms of dishes, drizzle 1 tablespoon of cream over each portion, and season with salt, pepper, and nutmeg. Carefully break 2 eggs, side by side, into each dish. Drizzle with remaining cream and sprinkle ¼ cup grated cheese over each.

3. Bake in preheated oven 12 to 15 minutes, until whites are just set and cheese is melted.

127   BAKED EGGS FLORENTINE
Prep: 3 minutes   Cook: 12 to 15 minutes   Serves: 2

If you use low-fat frozen creamed spinach, low-fat ham, and part-skim mozzarella, this quick and elegant recipe will taste much richer than it is.

2 slices of ham	Salt and freshly ground
1 (10-ounce) package frozen	pepper
creamed spinach, thawed	3 to 4 tablespoons shredded
2 eggs	mozzarella cheese

1. Preheat oven to 375°F. Butter a 6 x 9-inch baking dish, oval gratin dish, or 2 individual gratin dishes.

2. Place ham slices in baking dish. Spread thawed creamed spinach over ham. Make 2 indentations in spinach with back of a large spoon.

3. Break eggs into indentations. Season lightly with salt and pepper. Sprinkle mozzarella on top and bake on middle rack of oven 12 to 15 minutes, until eggs are set.

128   GARLIC, GREENS, AND BACON FRITTATA
Prep: 3 minutes   Cook: 15 to 17 minutes   Serves: 3 to 4

1 (10-ounce) package frozen	3 garlic cloves, minced
chopped greens—turnip,	7 eggs
collard, or mustard—	½ teaspoon pepper
thawed	¼ teaspoon salt
4 slices of bacon, coarsely	2 tablespoons grated
chopped	Parmesan cheese
1 tablespoon olive oil	

1. Squeeze out as much moisture from greens as possible; set aside. In a large skillet with ovenproof handle, cook bacon over medium-high heat, stirring frequently, until almost crisp and fat is rendered, about 5 minutes. Remove bacon with a slotted spoon and drain on paper towels. Pour off all but 1 tablespoon drippings.

2. Add oil to drippings in pan. Reduce heat to medium, add garlic, and cook, stirring, 1 minute. Stir in greens. In a bowl, whisk eggs with pepper, salt, and 1 tablespoon water until blended. Pour eggs over greens, stir gently to combine, reduce heat to low, and cook, covered, until eggs are almost set, 8 to 10 minutes. Meanwhile, preheat broiler.

3. Sprinkle reserved bacon and Parmesan cheese over frittata and broil 5 inches from heat about 1 minute, until top is just set and bacon is crisp. Cut into wedges to serve.

129   CANADIAN BAKED EGGS
Prep: 3 minutes   Cook: 12 to 15 minutes   Serves: 4

1 tablespoon butter
4 slices of Canadian bacon
8 eggs
1½ cups grated medium-sharp
   Cheddar cheese

2 teaspoons finely chopped
   parsley
⅛ teaspoon pepper

1. Preheat oven to 325°F. Use butter to generously grease 4 shallow 1-cup ramekins or individual French gratin dishes. Line bottoms of dishes with Canadian bacon, cutting to fit if necessary.

2. Carefully break 2 eggs, side by side, into each dish. Sprinkle cheese evenly over eggs and bake 12 to 15 minutes, until whites are just set and cheese is melted.

3. Sprinkle with parsley and pepper and serve at once.

130   ASPARAGUS AND SCALLION FRITTATA
Prep: 6 minutes   Cook: 10 to 13 minutes   Serves: 3 to 4

Make this omelet in the spring, when asparagus is at its peak.

½ pound slender asparagus,
   cut into ½-inch pieces
2 tablespoons butter
½ cup thinly sliced scallions
7 eggs
1 teaspoon Dijon mustard

¼ teaspoon salt
⅛ teaspoon pepper
1½ cups shredded Swiss cheese
2 tablespoons grated
   Parmesan cheese

1. Cook asparagus in a large pot of lightly salted boiling water until crisp-tender, 2 to 3 minutes. Drain into a colander and rinse under cold water; drain well.

2. Preheat broiler. In a large skillet with ovenproof handle, heat butter. Add scallions and cook over medium heat until slightly softened, about 1 minute.

3. In a bowl, whisk eggs with mustard, salt, and pepper. Stir in Swiss cheese. Reduce heat to medium-low, pour egg mixture into skillet, and stir gently to combine. Scatter cooked asparagus over eggs. Cover and cook until eggs are almost set on top, 6 to 8 minutes.

4. Sprinkle Parmesan cheese on top and broil about 5 inches from heat about 1 minute, until top is set and lightly flecked with brown. Cut into wedges to serve.

131 NEAPOLITAN FRITTATA
Prep: 5 minutes   Cook: 12 to 15 minutes   Serves: 4

This frittata tastes quite a lot like a pepperoni pizza, with the eggs here acting as the "crust."

2 tablespoons olive oil
1 medium onion, thinly sliced
7 eggs
1 teaspoon dried oregano
⅛ teaspoon pepper
1 cup shredded mozzarella
   cheese

1½ cups thinly sliced plum
   tomatoes (6 ounces)
1 cup thinly sliced pepperoni
   (¼ pound)
2 tablespoons grated
   Parmesan cheese

1. Preheat broiler. In a large skillet with ovenproof handle, heat oil. Add onion and cook over medium heat, stirring frequently, until softened, about 3 minutes.

2. In a bowl, whisk eggs with oregano and pepper. Stir in mozzarella. Reduce heat to low, pour egg mixture over onion, and stir gently to combine. Scatter tomatoes and pepperoni over eggs, cover skillet, and cook until eggs are almost set, 8 to 10 minutes.

3. Sprinkle frittata with Parmesan cheese and broil about 5 inches from heat 1 to 2 minutes, until top is just set and lightly flecked with brown. Cut into wedges to serve.

132 PASTA AND VEGETABLE FRITTATA
Prep: 8 minutes   Cook: 12 minutes   Serves: 4 to 6

A frittata is typically made with leftovers. This one calls for cooked pasta, and the shape could be anything, from ziti to spaghetti. Garnish a plate with fresh parsley for an attractive presentation.

2 tablespoons olive oil
1 small zucchini, chopped
1 medium green bell pepper,
   chopped
1 garlic clove, minced
1 cup leftover cooked pasta

1 teaspoon Italian seasoning
8 eggs
½ cup shredded mozzarella
   cheese
½ teaspoon salt
¼ teaspoon pepper

1. Preheat oven to 400°F. Heat olive oil in a large skillet with an ovenproof handle. Add zucchini, bell pepper, and garlic and cook over medium heat, stirring occasionally, until vegetables are just softened, about 3 minutes. Add pasta and Italian seasoning.

2. Beat eggs with cheese, salt, and pepper and stir into skillet. Cook until eggs are set on bottom and cheese begins to melt, about 2 minutes.

3. Transfer skillet to oven and bake about 7 minutes, until eggs are cooked and a knife comes out clean when inserted in middle. With a spatula, loosen edges and invert frittata onto platter or serve directly from pan.

133   SPANISH ONION OMELET
Prep: 3 minutes   Cook: 10 to 12 minutes   Serves: 3 to 4

Called a *tortilla* in Spain, this onion and potato omelet is more akin to an Italian frittata than a French omelet.

3 tablespoons olive oil
1 (16-ounce) can sliced white
  potatoes, rinsed and
  drained

1 large onion, thinly sliced
6 eggs
½ teaspoon salt
¼ teaspoon pepper

1. Preheat broiler. In a large skillet with ovenproof handle, heat oil. Add potatoes and onion, cover, and cook over medium-low heat, stirring occasionally, until onions are tender, about 5 minutes.

2. In a bowl, whisk eggs with salt, pepper, and 1 tablespoon water. Pour eggs over potato-onion mixture. Raise heat to medium and cook, uncovered, lifting up edges of omelet with a spatula so uncooked egg can run underneath, until bottom is pale golden and top is almost set, about 4 minutes.

3. Place pan under broiler about 5 inches from heat and cook 1 to 2 minutes, until top is just set. Cut into wedges and serve crust side up.

134   BACON AND WILD MUSHROOM OMELET
Prep: 7 minutes   Cook: 4 to 6 minutes   Serves: 2

Cultivated fresh "wild" mushrooms such as shiitake and cremini are becoming increasingly available in supermarkets across the country. Buy a few and try them in this easy, elegant omelet. Unless you are an expert, never gather your own mushrooms.

1 tablespoon butter
⅓ cup finely chopped wild
  mushrooms
2 slices of bacon, finely
  chopped

2 shallots, finely chopped
½ teaspoon dried thyme
4 eggs
¼ teaspoon salt
⅛ teaspoon pepper

1. In an 8- to 10-inch nonstick skillet, melt butter over medium-high heat. Add mushrooms, bacon, shallots, and thyme. Cook, stirring occasionally, until mushrooms are softened and bacon is golden, 3 to 4 minutes.

2. In a bowl, whisk eggs with 1 tablespoon water, salt, and pepper. Add eggs to skillet and stir with a wooden spoon to combine with mushroom mixture. Cook 1 to 2 minutes, fold omelet in half, turn out onto a large plate, and serve at once.

135   CHILI OMELET

Prep: 3 minutes   Cook: 4 to 6 minutes   Serves: 2 to 3

To produce a light, fluffy omelet, add a small amount of water to the eggs when beating them. The steam produced by the water helps the omelet to puff up.

1 (15-ounce) can chili with beans
6 eggs
⅛ teaspoon salt
⅛ teaspoon pepper

2 teaspoons butter or canola oil
½ cup shredded Monterey Jack cheese

1. In a saucepan, heat chili over medium heat, stirring occasionally. Meanwhile, in a medium bowl, whisk eggs with 1½ tablespoons water, salt, and pepper until well combined.

2. In a large nonstick skillet, melt butter over medium heat, swirling to cover pan with an even film. Stir in eggs. Using a wooden spatula, gather in cooked edges toward center of omelet.

3. When omelet is set but still moist, 1 to 2 minutes, spoon half of chili and all but 2 tablespoons cheese down center. Fold in sides of omelet to enclose filling.

4. Turn omelet out onto a serving plate and divide into 2 to 3 portions. Top with remaining chili and cheese and serve at once.

136   GOAT CHEESE AND SUN-DRIED TOMATO OMELETS

Prep: 5 minutes   Cook: 4 minutes   Serves: 2

4 eggs
1 tablespoon slivered fresh basil, or ¼ teaspoon dried
⅛ teaspoon pepper
2 tablespoons butter

2 tablespoons slivered oil-packed sun-dried tomatoes
2 ounces mild goat cheese, crumbled (about ½ cup)

1. In a bowl, whisk eggs with basil, pepper, and 1 tablespoon water until combined but not frothy.

2. In a 7- to 8-inch omelet pan, heat 1 tablespoon butter over medium-high heat. When butter foams, pour half of egg mixture into pan. Shake pan and when bottom of omelet begins to set, lift edges with a small spatula or fork and tilt pan so uncooked egg runs underneath. Cook until edges are set but center is still moist, about 1 minute. Sprinkle half of tomatoes and goat cheese over omelet. Use a spatula or fork to fold omelet into thirds to enclose filling. Turn omelet out onto a plate, seam side down.

3. Wipe out pan with a paper towel and repeat with remaining ingredients to make 1 more omelet.

137 CREOLE OMELET

Prep: 7 minutes   Cook: 13 minutes   Serves: 2

1 cup thinly sliced andouille
  or kielbasa sausage
  (about 4 ounces)
1 small onion, chopped
½ medium green bell pepper,
  chopped
1 garlic clove, minced
2 medium tomatoes, chopped

¼ teaspoon dried thyme leaves
¼ teaspoon sugar
⅛ teaspoon pepper
4 eggs
¼ to ½ teaspoon Tabasco
  sauce, to taste
2 teaspoons butter

1. In a large skillet, cook sausage over medium-high heat, stirring occasionally, until lightly browned, about 5 minutes. Remove with a slotted spoon, leaving fat in pan.

2. Add onion, bell pepper, and garlic and cook, stirring occasionally, until softened, about 3 minutes. Raise heat to high and add tomatoes, thyme, sugar, and pepper. Cook, stirring often, until most of liquid is evaporated, about 3 minutes. Return sausage to sauce and remove from heat. Cover to keep warm.

3. Beat eggs with Tabasco sauce and 2 teaspoons water until blended. In a 7- to 8-inch nonstick omelet pan, heat 1 teaspoon butter over medium-high heat. When butter foams, pour half the egg mixture into pan. Shake pan and when bottom of omelet begins to set, lift edges with a small spatula or fork and tilt pan so uncooked portion runs underneath. Cook until edges are set but center is still moist, about 1 minute. Use a spatula to fold omelet into thirds and turn out onto a plate, seam side down.

4. Wipe out pan with a paper towel and repeat with remaining butter and egg mixture to make a second omelet. Spoon warm sauce over omelets and serve at once.

138   DENVER OMELET
Prep: 4 minutes   Cook: 8 to 10 minutes   Serves: 2

Also known as a Western, this omelet is a specialty in diners across the country. It's often served with toast to make a sandwich.

1½ tablespoons butter
½ cup chopped onion
½ cup chopped green bell
   pepper

½ cup diced smoked or baked
   ham
3 eggs
⅛ teaspoon cayenne

1. In a large nonstick skillet, heat butter. Add onion, green pepper, and ham and cook over medium heat, stirring occasionally, until vegetables are softened and ham is lightly browned, about 5 minutes.

2. Meanwhile, whisk eggs with cayenne and 2 teaspoons water. Reduce heat to low, pour eggs over vegetables, and stir gently to combine. Cook, uncovered, until bottom is lightly golden, 2 to 3 minutes.

3. With a large spatula, turn eggs over and cook until pale golden on other side, 1 to 2 minutes. Center should remain moist. Divide in half to make 2 servings.

139   SMOKED SALMON AND CAVIAR OMELET
Prep: 5 minutes   Cook: 3 to 4 minutes   Serves: 1 to 2

Serve this elegant omelet for brunch or as a quick after-theater supper.

3 eggs
  Pinch of salt
  Pinch of ground pepper
1 tablespoon butter
2 tablespoons sour cream

1 ounce thinly sliced smoked
  salmon, cut into thin
  strips
1 tablespoon black caviar
  Fresh dill sprigs

1. In a bowl, beat eggs with 1 tablespoon water, salt, and pepper until blended.

2. In a 7- to 8-inch omelet pan, melt butter over medium heat. When butter foams, stir in eggs. Using a wooden spatula, gather in cooked edges toward center of omelet. When eggs are set but still moist, 1 to 2 minutes, use a spatula to fold omelet into thirds; turn out onto a plate.

3. With a sharp knife, slit omelet down center. Spoon sour cream into slit and top with smoked salmon strips. Arrange caviar on top of salmon and garnish with dill.

140   PUFFED OMELET, SOUTHWEST STYLE

Prep: 4 minutes   Cook: 10 to 12 minutes   Serves: 3

This omelet, in which egg whites are beaten separately and folded into the yolks, rises to airy heights much like a soufflé.

6 **eggs, separated**	1½ **cups shredded Monterey**
½ **teaspoon salt**	**Jack cheese with jalapeño**
⅛ **teaspoon pepper**	**peppers**
2 **tablespoons butter**	1¼ **cups bottled salsa**

1. Preheat oven to 375°F. In a medium bowl, whisk egg yolks with salt, pepper, and ¼ cup water until well blended. In a large bowl, beat egg whites to soft peaks. Pour yolks over whites and gently fold together with a rubber spatula.

2. In a large nonstick skillet with ovenproof handle, heat butter. Pour eggs into skillet and cook over medium-low heat until bottom begins to set, about 2 minutes. Place skillet in preheated oven and cook until omelet is puffed and top begins to color, 8 to 10 minutes.

3. Using a heavy potholder, remove skillet from oven. Sprinkle with cheese, make a crease down center with a large spatula, and fold in half, pressing firmly for 15 seconds so omelet stays folded. Spoon salsa on top and cut into thirds to serve.

Chapter 5

Sandwiches, Pizzas, and Other Quick Pick-Ups

Sandwiches and pizzas are both modern and very old. People today like them for the same reasons they always did—these foods are fast, filling, and easy to eat out of hand.

In the 90s, a sandwich is not just a "ham on rye." The choice of spreads, fillings, and condiments found in supermarkets has increased dramatically in the last decade. Dijon mustard has descended from its Rolls-Royce status to join ketchup and yellow mustard at the fast-food franchise. Intriguing ingredients, such as tapenade, an intense olive puree, Boursin cheese, pesto, and sun-dried tomatoes, combine with more expected sandwich fixings like ham, cheese, and turkey in innovative interpretations. A variety of ethnic breads, wrappers, and bases, such as tortillas, flatbreads, and biscuits, are readily available to further expand the horizons of creative sandwich makers.

Over the years sandwiches in one form or another have become part of food culture worldwide. The recipes in this chapter, from Croque Monsieur and New Orleans Oyster Loaf to Smoked Turkey and Avocado Melt and Mexican Pizza, reflect that diversity.

---

141 CROQUE MONSIEUR
Prep: 3 minutes   Cook: 6 to 7 minutes   Serves: 2

This elegant sandwich is perfect for the sandwich maker machines that have become so popular. However, below are instructions for achieving that same effect in a skillet.

1 to 2 tablespoons softened butter	1 teaspoon Dijon mustard
4 slices of white bread	4 slices of baked ham
	4 slices of Swiss cheese

1. Spread butter on 1 side of each slice of bread. Spread mustard on unbuttered side.

2. Place a slice of ham and a slice of Swiss on mustard-coated sides of 2 slices of bread. Top ham and cheese slices with remaining bread.

3. Place sandwiches in a large skillet over medium heat and cook until lightly toasted on 1 side, 3 to 4 minutes. Turn and toast on other side, about 3 minutes. Serve hot.

142   SUPPER-STYLE GRILLED CHEESE AND TOMATO

Prep: 4 minutes   Cook: 6 minutes   Serves: 2

4 slices of cracked wheat
   bread
¾ cup thinly sliced sharp
   Cheddar cheese
1 small tomato, thinly sliced
2 eggs

1 tablespoon milk
½ teaspoon dried oregano
¼ teaspoon salt
¼ teaspoon pepper
2 teaspoons olive oil
2 teaspoons butter

1. Make 2 sandwiches with bread, cheese, and tomato.

2. In a wide, shallow bowl, whisk eggs with milk, oregano, salt, and pepper. Place sandwiches in egg mixture, turn to coat, and let stand until almost all egg is absorbed.

3. In a large skillet, preferably nonstick, heat oil and butter over medium-low heat. Add sandwiches and cook until browned on 1 side, about 3 minutes. Turn, press lightly with spatula, and cook on other side until browned, about 3 minutes. Cut in half diagonally to serve.

143   HAM AND CHEDDAR RAREBIT

Prep: 2 minutes   Cook: 9 to 11 minutes   Serves: 4 to 6

1 (10-ounce) package frozen
   Welsh rarebit
6 slices of white bread

1 tablespoon Dijon mustard
12 thin slices of ham
   Paprika

1. Preheat oven to 375°F. Prepare Welsh rarebit following package directions; this will take 7 to 8 minutes.

2. While rarebit is cooking, toast bread. Halve slices diagonally and spread 1 side of each with mustard.

3. Arrange 2 slices of ham on top of each mustard-covered triangle. Place points up in a small baking dish or pie plate, overlapping triangles slightly on top of each other.

4. Spoon welsh rarebit sauce over all. Bake in oven 2 to 3 minutes to heat through. Sprinkle with paprika.

144 GRILLED EGGPLANT AND MOZZARELLA SANDWICHES

Prep: 7 minutes   Cook: 7 minutes   Serves: 2

¼ cup olive-oil Italian dressing
12 ounces baby eggplant or Japanese eggplant, cut in ½-inch-thick lengthwise slices

2 Portuguese rolls or other large crusty rolls, split
¾ cup sliced mozzarella cheese
1 large tomato, thinly sliced
¼ cup fresh basil leaves

1. Prepare a moderately hot fire in a charcoal or gas grill. On a platter, pour 2 tablespoons dressing over eggplant slices; turn to coat well.

2. Grill eggplant over moderate heat, brushing with 1 tablespoon more dressing, until charred on both sides and soft within, about 5 minutes.

3. Meanwhile, brush cut sides of rolls with remaining 1 tablespoon dressing, place around edge of grill, and toast until pale golden, about 2 minutes.

4. Layer rolls with eggplant, cheese, tomato, and basil leaves and replace tops.

145 TUNA AND BLACK OLIVE MELTS

Prep: 7 minutes   Cook: 3 to 4 minutes   Serves: 3 to 4

6 English muffins, split
2 (6½-ounce) cans tuna, drained
½ cup finely chopped celery
¼ cup sliced black olives
3 tablespoons chopped red onion

½ cup mayonnaise
⅛ teaspoon pepper
2 tablespoons butter
6 ounces medium-sharp Cheddar cheese, sliced

1. Preheat broiler. Lightly toast English muffins. In a bowl, flake tuna into small chunks. Toss with celery, olives, and red onion. Add mayonnaise, stir to blend well, and season with pepper.

2. Place muffin halves cut sides up on a baking sheet and toast lightly under broiler, about 2 minutes. Remove from oven and spread with butter. Divide tuna salad among muffins and top with cheese.

3. Broil about 5 inches from heat 1 to 2 minutes, until cheese is melted and bubbly.

146   SMOKED TURKEY AND AVOCADO MELT

Prep: 4 minutes   Cook: 2 to 3 minutes   Serves: 3

6 slices of cracked wheat
   bread
½ cup bottled Russian or
   Thousand Island
   dressing
2 medium tomatoes, thinly
   sliced

½ pound smoked turkey
   breast, thinly sliced
1 large avocado, peeled and
   thinly sliced
1½ cups shredded Monterey
   Jack cheese with jalapeño
   peppers

1. Preheat broiler. Arrange bread on a baking sheet and toast lightly on 1 side, about 1 minute.

2. Spread dressing over toasted sides of bread. Layer with tomatoes and smoked turkey. Arrange avocado slices in a spoke pattern over turkey. Sprinkle cheese on top.

3. Broil about 5 inches from heat 1 to 2 minutes, until cheese is melted and bubbly.

147   BRUSCHETTA WITH TOMATOES AND FRESH MOZZARELLA CHEESE

Prep: 10 minutes   Cook: 6 to 9 minutes   Serves: 4

Fresh mozzarella is softer and tangier than the aged packaged variety. Either one works well in this sandwich, but use the fresh if you can get it.

12 slices of Italian bread,
   cut ½ inch thick
2 pounds ripe tomatoes,
   halved, seeded, and
   chopped
⅓ cup slivered fresh basil,
   plus sprigs for garnish
2 garlic cloves, minced

⅓ cup extra-virgin olive oil
3 tablespoons balsamic
   vinegar
½ teaspoon salt
¼ teaspoon crushed hot red
   pepper
8 ounces mozzarella cheese,
   preferably fresh, sliced

1. Preheat oven to 400°F. Place bread in a single layer on a baking sheet and toast in oven 3 to 5 minutes, until pale golden on top. Turn and toast 3 to 4 minutes, until second side is pale golden.

2. In a large bowl, combine tomatoes, basil, garlic, oil, vinegar, salt, and hot pepper. Toss to mix well.

3. Place 3 toasts on each plate. Spoon tomatoes and juice over bread and arrange cheese slices on top. Garnish with sprigs of fresh basil. Eat sandwiches with a knife and fork.

148   CLUB SANDWICH
Prep: 8 minutes   Cook: 5 to 7 minutes   Serves: 2

5 slices of bacon, cut in half
⅓ cup mayonnaise
2 tablespoons minced
   scallions
½ teaspoon dried tarragon
4 slices of firm-textured white
   bread, preferably thinly
   sliced

1 large tomato, thinly sliced
2 slices of whole wheat bread,
   preferably thinly sliced
¼ pound roast turkey, thinly
   sliced
2 large leaves of green leaf
   lettuce

1. In a large skillet, cook bacon over medium-high heat, turning frequently, until browned and crisp, 5 to 7 minutes. Drain on paper towels.

2. In a small bowl, mix mayonnaise with scallions and tarragon until well blended. Spread herb mayonnaise over 1 side of each white bread slice.

3. Arrange bacon and tomato over mayonnaise on 2 mayonnaise-coated bread slices. Top with 2 slices of whole wheat bread. Arrange turkey and lettuce over whole wheat bread slices. Top each sandwich with last 2 white bread slices, mayonnaise side down. Cut each sandwich in half diagonally and secure with toothpicks, if desired.

149   HOT FRENCH TURKEY SANDWICH
Prep: 5 minutes   Cook: 6 to 8 minutes   Serves: 3 to 4

Want a turkey sandwich with a twist? Try this tarragon and mushroom special. Use leftover sliced turkey or deli turkey breast.

2 tablespoons butter
2 tablespoons flour
1 (14½-ounce) can chicken
   broth
1 teaspoon minced fresh
   tarragon, or ¼ teaspoon
   dried

1 teaspoon Dijon mustard
   Salt and pepper
1 cup thinly sliced fresh
   mushrooms
8 slices of cooked turkey
4 slices of white or whole
   wheat bread

1. Melt butter in a large skillet over medium heat. Add flour and cook, stirring, 2 to 3 minutes, until golden. Gradually whisk in broth. Bring to a boil, whisking, until gravy is smooth and thickened, 1 to 2 minutes.

2. Whisk in tarragon and mustard. Season with salt and pepper to taste.

3. Add mushroom slices to gravy and simmer 2 minutes. Add turkey and cook 1 minute longer, until hot.

4. Toast bread and cut diagonally to form triangles. Arrange turkey slices on toast and spoon mushrooms and gravy over all.

150   HOT AND TANGY TURKEY SANDWICH
Prep: 5 minutes   Cook: 10 to 13 minutes   Serves: 8

The sauce for this unusual knife-and-fork sandwich can be made ahead and kept in the refrigerator for two to three days. Other possible fillings might include ham and Cheddar cheese or turkey, ham, and Swiss cheese.

½ cup condensed tomato soup
½ cup prepared yellow
    mustard
½ cup sugar
½ cup cider vinegar
1 tablespoon butter

2 eggs, beaten
8 slices of dark or whole
    wheat bread
8 slices of cooked turkey
8 (¼-inch) slices of mozzarella
    cheese

1. In the top of a double boiler, combine soup, mustard, sugar, vinegar, butter, and beaten eggs. Cook over boiling water, stirring constantly, until mixture thickens to a custard, 8 to 10 minutes. Preheat broiler.

2. Toast bread. Spread 1 tablespoon custard over each slice. Top with turkey and cheese.

3. Place under broiler 2 to 3 minutes, until cheese melts. Pass with extra sauce on the side.

151   SWISS TURKEY BURGERS
Prep: 8 minutes   Cook: 10 to 12 minutes   Serves: 4

This burger, made with lean ground turkey or chicken, will appeal to health-conscious eaters.

1 pound ground turkey or
    chicken
1 teaspoon salt
½ teaspoon dried dill
2 tablespoons vegetable oil
1 cup thinly sliced fresh
    mushrooms

1 cup shredded Swiss cheese
4 kaiser rolls, split, lightly
    toasted
2 teaspoons Dijon mustard
3 to 4 tablespoons light sour
    cream

1. In a mixing bowl, combine ground turkey, salt, and dill. Mix well. Shape poultry mixture into 4 patties about ¾ inch thick.

2. Heat oil in a large skillet over medium-high heat. Add burgers and cook, turning, until brown on both sides, 3 to 4 minutes. Reduce heat to medium. Add mushrooms to skillet and continue cooking 4 minutes.

3. Turn burgers and top each with ¼ cup cheese. Cover and continue to cook until cheese is melted and burgers are no longer pink inside, 3 to 4 minutes.

4. Spread rolls with mustard. Place a burger on each bottom half of roll and top with mushrooms and a dollop of sour cream. Place tops on burgers and serve.

152 SLOPPY JOES
Prep: 2 minutes   Cook: 8 to 11 minutes   Serves: 4 to 6

This classic favorite appeals to kids of all ages. Serve with a big basket of potato chips.

1 pound ground beef	Salt and pepper
1 (12-ounce) jar chili sauce	6 hard rolls
2 tablespoons brown sugar	

1. Preheat broiler. Place beef in a large skillet, preferably nonstick, and cook over medium-high heat, stirring occasionally and breaking up large lumps, until meat is browned, 5 to 8 minutes.

2. Add chili sauce and brown sugar to skillet and stir. Cook 2 minutes. Season with salt and pepper to taste.

3. Split rolls and toast lightly under broiler, about 1 minute. Spoon beef mixture over 6 roll bottoms. Top with remaining halves.

153 STEAK SANDWICH
Prep: 5 minutes   Cook: 8 to 9 minutes   Serves: 2 or 3

Steak sandwiches take on a sophisticated and slightly different appeal when seasoned with Dijon mustard and bourbon.

2 tablespoons olive oil	2 teaspoons Dijon mustard
2 medium onions, sliced into rings	1 (12-inch) loaf of Italian bread, split
½ pound beef round sandwich steaks	2 tablespoons Worcestershire sauce
Salt and freshly ground pepper	1 tablespoon bourbon
	8 or 9 cherry tomatoes

1. Preheat broiler. Heat oil in a large skillet. Add onions and cook over medium-high heat, stirring occasionally, until softened, about 3 minutes. Remove to a plate and cover with foil to keep warm.

2. Season steaks with salt and pepper to taste. Spread Dijon mustard over meat. Place steaks in skillet and cook over medium-high heat, turning, until cooked to desired doneness, 3 to 4 minutes. Meanwhile, lightly toast bread under broiler, about 2 minutes.

3. Place steaks on bottom half of loaf. Stir Worcestershire and bourbon into skillet. Top with onions and pan drippings. Put top on sandwich and cut in half or thirds. Serve with cherry tomatoes.

154 ROAST BEEF PHILLY CHEESE STEAKS

Prep: 3 minutes   Cook: 11 to 12 minutes   Serves: 4

An updated version of the traditional Philadelphia cheese steak, this recipe calls for rare roast beef as a substitute for the more classic "chip," or sandwich steaks. To save time, be sure to have your deli slice the roast beef and cheese for you.

4 tablespoons butter
1 large onion, thinly sliced
¼ cup dry red wine
½ teaspoon dried thyme leaves
2 teaspoons Dijon mustard
1 teaspoon prepared white
  horseradish
4 submarine or grinder rolls,
  6 to 7 inches long

1 pound thinly sliced rare
  roast beef, at room
  temperature
½ teaspoon salt
¼ teaspoon pepper
¼ pound Muenster cheese,
  thinly sliced

1. Preheat broiler. In a medium skillet, heat 1 tablespoon butter. Add onion and cook over medium heat, stirring occasionally, until softened and lightly browned, about 8 minutes. Add wine and thyme, raise heat to high, and boil until wine evaporates, 1 to 2 minutes. Remove onion with a slotted spoon and set aside.

2. Melt remaining 3 tablespoons butter in skillet; remove from heat. Whisk in mustard and horseradish. Slice rolls lengthwise and brush with flavored butter. Place on a baking sheet and broil until lightly browned, about 45 seconds.

3. Divide onion equally over bottom halves of rolls. Top each with roast beef and season with salt and pepper. Lay cheese over meat, return to broiler, and broil about 45 seconds, until cheese is melted. Place tops on sandwiches and serve.

155 SANTA FE CHEESEBURGERS

Prep: 7 minutes   Cook: 5 to 7 minutes   Serves: 2

Southwestern influence is strong in American cooking, and nowhere in the Southwest is the food more interesting than in Santa Fe, New Mexico. Serve these tasty burgers with tortilla chips.

½ pound ground beef	2 hard rolls or burger buns
½ teaspoon salt	1 plum tomato, chopped
½ teaspoon chili powder	2 thin slices of mild onion
¼ teaspoon ground cumin	4 pickled jalapeño slices
2 tablespoons vegetable oil	¼ cup shredded lettuce
½ cup shredded Monterey Jack cheese	¼ cup salsa ketchup

1. In a mixing bowl, combine beef, salt, chili powder, and cumin. Mix well. Shape mixture into 2 patties.

2. Heat oil in medium skillet to medium-high. Add burgers and cook, turning once, until just under desired doneness, 3 to 5 minutes.

3. Place cheese on top of burgers. Cover pan and continue cooking until cheese has melted, 2 to 3 minutes.

4. While burgers are cooking, split and lightly toast rolls. Place burgers on rolls and top with tomato, onion, jalapeño, lettuce, and salsa ketchup.

156 BLACKENED CAJUN CHEESEBURGERS

Prep: 2 minutes   Cook: 6 to 8 minutes   Serves: 4

Commercial "blackened" seasoning blends are readily found in the spice section of the market these days. They vary in quality and in degree of spiciness, so find one you prefer.

1 pound lean ground chuck	4 crusty rolls or hamburger buns
1 tablespoon "blackened" spice seasoning blend	4 slices of meaty tomato
4 slices of Monterey Jack cheese (about 2 ounces)	4 leaves of lettuce

1. Prepare a moderately hot fire in a charcoal or gas grill, or preheat broiler. Divide beef into 4 portions and form into patties about ½ inch thick. Sprinkle both sides evenly with seasoning blend.

2. Grill or broil patties, turning once, 6 to 8 minutes, until nicely browned outside and medium-rare inside. Place a slice of cheese on each burger to melt as it finishes cooking.

3. Split rolls and place around edge of grill to toast lightly. Place cheeseburgers on rolls and top with tomato and lettuce. Replace tops and serve.

157 SPICED PORK POCKET SANDWICHES
Prep: 8 minutes   Cook: 3 to 4 minutes   Serves: 4

The mild, citrusy flavor of ground coriander seed, readily found on the spice shelf in most supermarkets, pairs nicely with pork. If you have time, warm the pita breads in the oven or microwave.

1 pound boneless pork loin chops, cut into thin strips	½ teaspoon salt
3 tablespoons olive oil	½ teaspoon pepper
1½ tablespoons grainy Dijon mustard	4 pita breads, 7 to 8 inches in diameter
2 garlic cloves, minced	½ cup plain yogurt
1 teaspoon ground coriander	2 medium tomatoes, chopped
	¾ cup alfalfa or radish sprouts

1. In a bowl, combine pork strips with 1½ tablespoons oil, mustard, garlic, coriander, salt, and pepper. Toss well to coat meat.

2. In a large skillet or wok, heat remaining 1½ tablespoons oil over high heat. Add pork and stir-fry until lightly browned outside and no longer pink inside, 3 to 4 minutes.

3. Split pita breads in half, fill with pork, and top with yogurt, tomatoes, and sprouts.

158 CENTRAL GROCERY MUFFALETTA
Prep: 6 minutes   Cook: none   Serves: 2 to 4

Olive salad, an essential ingredient in this New Orleans specialty, which is prepared in step 1, can also be purchased in jars or in many Italian delicatessens.

¾ cup sliced pimiento-stuffed green olives, drained and rinsed (2½-ounce jar)	¼ teaspoon pepper
1 medium celery rib, thinly sliced	1 (10-inch) round loaf Italian bread
1 medium tomato, seeded and chopped	2 ounces thinly sliced Genoa salami
1 garlic clove, chopped	2 ounces thinly sliced baked ham
3 tablespoons olive oil	2 ounces thinly sliced provolone cheese
2 teaspoons red wine vinegar	2 ounces sliced mozzarella cheese
½ teaspoon dried oregano	

1. In a small bowl, combine sliced olives, celery, tomato, garlic, olive oil, vinegar, oregano, and pepper. Toss to mix well.

2. Split loaf of bread in half around circumference. Layer with salami, ham, provolone, and mozzarella cheese. Top with a layer of olive salad. Replace top of bread and cut into 4 quarters.

159 SAUSAGE AND PEPPER SUBS
Prep: 3 minutes   Cook: 15 to 17 minutes   Serves: 4

1 pound Italian link sausage,
  sweet or hot
½ cup dry white wine
2 cups bottled spaghetti sauce
1 tablespoon olive oil
1 medium onion, thinly sliced

1 medium green bell pepper,
  thinly sliced
4 grinder or submarine rolls,
  split
1 cup shredded mozzarella
  cheese

1. Prick sausages with a fork. In a large skillet, combine sausages, wine, and ½ cup water. Bring to a boil over high heat, reduce heat to medium-low, cover, and cook 5 minutes. Uncover, raise heat to medium, and cook, turning sausages occasionally, until most of liquid is evaporated and sausages are browned and no longer pink in center, 5 to 7 minutes. Remove sausages with tongs and pour any remaining liquid into spaghetti sauce. Do not wash skillet.

2. Add olive oil to skillet. Add onion and green pepper and cook over medium-high heat, stirring occasionally, until softened and lightly browned, about 4 minutes. Cut sausages into ½-inch slices and add to skillet. Stir in spaghetti sauce and cook for 1 minute, or until heated through.

3. Split rolls, spoon sausage and sauce onto bottom halves, sprinkle with cheese, and place tops on sandwiches.

160 HOT CORNED BEEF SANDWICH WITH RUSSIAN DRESSING
Prep: 3 minutes   Cook: 5 minutes   Serves: 4

1 tablespoon butter
1 pound lean corned beef,
  sliced medium-thin
8 slices of seeded rye bread,
  lightly toasted
¾ cup bottled Russian or
  Thousand Island
  dressing

½ pound thinly sliced Swiss
  cheese
1½ cups shredded iceberg
  lettuce

1. In a large skillet, melt butter over medium heat. Add corned beef in batches without crowding and cook until hot and edges begin to curl, about 5 minutes total.

2. Spread toasted bread with Russian dressing. Heap hot corned beef on 4 bread slices. Layer with cheese and lettuce and top with remaining bread. Cut sandwiches in half and serve.

161   BEEF AND BEAN BURRITOS

Prep: 5 minutes   Cook: 6 to 7 minutes   Serves: 3 to 4

Southwestern cooking is not complete without burritos. The jalapeño peppers make this recipe especially interesting and tasty.

1 tablespoon vegetable oil	1 jalapeño pepper, seeded
½ pound ground beef	and chopped
1 teaspoon chili powder	8 (10-inch) flour tortillas
½ teaspoon salt	¾ cup salsa
¼ teaspoon ground cumin	¾ cup shredded Monterey
½ cup refried beans	Jack cheese
1 (4-ounce) can chopped mild	
chiles	

1. Heat oil in a large skillet over medium-high heat. Add beef and cook, stirring, until browned, 4 to 5 minutes.

2. Place beef, chili powder, salt, cumin, refried beans, chiles, and jalapeño pepper in a food processor and process for 3 to 4 seconds.

3. Wrap 2 batches of 4 tortillas each in microwave-safe paper towels and microwave on High about 1 minute per batch, until warm.

4. Place 1 to 2 tablespoons filling in a strip just below middle of each tortilla. Fold ends over filling to enclose it partially, then roll up tortilla into a tight cylinder. Arrange burritos on a platter and top with salsa and cheese.

162   TURKEY TACOS

Prep: 10 minutes   Cook: 7 to 10 minutes   Serves: 3 to 4

8 taco shells	Salt and pepper
1½ tablespoons vegetable oil	½ cup salsa
2 cups shredded cooked	1 cup shredded iceberg lettuce
turkey (about ½ pound)	1 cup shredded Monterey
½ cup chopped white onion	Jack cheese
1 teaspoon chili powder	2 tablespoons chopped
½ teaspoon ground cumin	cilantro

1. Preheat oven to 350°F. Wrap taco shells in aluminum foil and warm in oven for 5 minutes.

2. Meanwhile, in a large skillet, heat oil over medium-high heat. Add turkey, onion, chili powder, and cumin. Cook, stirring often, 2 to 3 minutes, until onion is slightly softened. Season with salt and pepper to taste.

3. Fill each taco shell with ¼ cup turkey mixture. Top with salsa, lettuce, cheese, and cilantro.

163   QUICK QUESADILLAS
Prep: 3 minutes   Cook: 10 to 14 minutes
Serves: 3 to 4 as first course, 2 to 3 as main course

Quesadillas may be the most Mexican of sandwiches. They are quick to make, tasty to eat, and a good way to use up leftovers.

2 tablespoons vegetable oil
½ pound ground beef
½ cup finely chopped onion
   Salt and pepper
2 to 3 tablespoons canned
   chopped mild green
   chiles

6 to 8 (8-inch) flour tortillas
1 cup shredded Colby and
   Monterey Jack cheese
1 cup mild salsa

1. In a medium skillet, heat 1 tablespoon oil. Add ground beef and onion. Cook over medium-high heat, stirring often, until meat is browned and onion softened, 4 to 5 minutes. Season with salt and pepper to taste.

2. Place 1 to 2 tablespoons ground beef and 1 to 2 teaspoons chiles on lower half of each tortilla. Top each with ¼ cup cheese and fold tortilla over top to form a half circle.

3. In a large nonstick skillet, heat remaining 1 tablespoon oil over medium-high heat. Place 2 quesadillas in skillet and brown on both sides, 2 to 3 minutes. Repeat with remaining quesadillas. Serve hot. Pass salsa separately.

164   TOSTADAS GRANDES
Prep: 10 minutes   Cook: 8 to 10 minutes   Serves: 4

Nachos like these made with whole tortillas are the Mexican equivalent of pizza.

1 cup refried beans
   Vegetable oil, for frying
4 corn tortillas
1 cup chopped fresh tomato
1 avocado, peeled, pitted, and
   sliced

1 cup shredded iceberg lettuce
1 cup shredded Monterey
   Jack cheese
1 cup salsa
¼ to ½ cup sour cream

1. In a small saucepan, heat refried beans over medium heat, stirring often, until hot, 3 to 5 minutes. Remove from heat and cover to keep warm.

2. Place enough oil in a medium skillet to make a depth of ½ inch. Heat over medium-high heat until a bread cube placed in oil browns in 10 seconds. Fry tortillas one at a time until golden and crispy, about 15 seconds per side. Remove from skillet and keep warm.

3. Place tortillas on individual plates and spread one-fourth of refried beans over each. Layer on tomato, avocado, lettuce, and cheese. Top with salsa and sour cream.

165   TEXAS PINTO BEAN TOSTADAS
Prep: 8 minutes   Cook: 6 minutes   Serves: 2

Tostadas, sometimes also called *chalupas*, are skyscraperlike concoctions. The word *chalupa* in Mexico means a sort of canoe, or a tortilla with sides that come up to keep in fillings. Some cooks make their own "boats" by pressing a large ladle into the middle of tortillas as they deep-fry. I've found the taco bowls sold in packages to be good and a lot less trouble.

2 packaged taco bowls	1/8 teaspoon cinnamon
2 tablespoons vegetable oil	1/2 cup canned pinto beans,
1/2 pound ground beef	drained and rinsed
1/2 cup finely chopped onion	1/4 cup shredded lettuce
1/2 cup finely chopped tomato	1/2 cup shredded Monterey
2 teaspoons brown sugar	Jack cheese
1 teaspoon chili powder	3 tablespoons sour cream
1/2 teaspoon salt	1/3 cup salsa
1/8 teaspoon ground cumin	

1. Preheat oven to 350°F. Place taco bowls on a baking sheet and heat in oven for about 5 minutes, until hot.

2. Meanwhile, in a large skillet, heat oil over medium-high heat. Add ground beef and 1/4 cup onion. Cook, stirring often, until meat is browned, 4 to 5 minutes. Add 1/4 cup tomato, brown sugar, chili powder, salt, cumin, and cinnamon.

3. Place beans with water clinging to them in a 2-cup glass measure. Cover with saucer or microwave-safe plastic wrap and microwave on High 1 minute, or until hot.

4. Place taco bowls on dinner plates. Spoon half of beans into each bowl. Top with meat, lettuce, and remaining tomato and onion. Sprinkle 1/4 cup cheese over each tostada and top with a dollop of sour cream. Serve salsa on the side.

166   OYSTER LOAF
Prep: 5 minutes   Cook: 6 minutes   Serves: 2 to 4

In New Orleans, this sandwich is made with fresh, crusty French bread. When heaped high with shredded lettuce and sliced tomatoes, an oyster loaf becomes a "po' boy," the overstuffed specialty of that city.

½ cup mayonnaise
2 teaspoons lemon juice
½ teaspoon grated lemon zest
½ teaspoon Tabasco sauce
    Vegetable oil, for frying
⅔ cup yellow cornmeal

½ teaspoon salt
½ teaspoon pepper
1 pint shucked oysters
    (about 2 dozen)
4 (3- to 4-ounce) long French
    or grinder rolls

1. In a small bowl, whisk together mayonnaise with lemon juice, lemon zest, and Tabasco until well blended.

2. In a large heavy skillet, preferably cast-iron, heat about ½ inch of oil over medium heat to 350°F. If a cube of bread browns in 20 seconds, oil is correct temperature.

3. On a plate, combine cornmeal, salt, and pepper. Roll oysters in seasoned cornmeal to coat completely. Add half of coated oysters to hot oil and fry until golden brown, about 3 minutes. Drain on paper towels. Repeat with remaining oysters.

4. Split rolls lengthwise and pull out some soft bread to make a cavity for oysters. Spread lemon mayonnaise inside rolls. Arrange oysters in sandwich, replace tops, and cut each sandwich in half diagonally.

167   DOWN EAST LOBSTER ROLLS
Prep: 5 minutes   Cook: 2 minutes   Serves: 2

New England-style frankfurter rolls, favored by Down Easters (people who live in Maine) for their lobster rolls, are split through the top instead of the side. Sealegs (surimi), or another good-quality compressed seafood product, can substitute for the lobster, if necessary.

1½ cups lobster meat, cut into
    chunks (about ½ pound)
2 teaspoons lemon juice
¼ cup finely chopped celery
¼ cup mayonnaise
¼ teaspoon salt

    Pinch of cayenne
2 teaspoons butter
4 frankfurter rolls, preferably
    New England-style
4 leaves of butter lettuce

1. In a bowl, toss lobster meat with lemon juice. Add celery and mayonnaise and stir gently. Season with salt and cayenne.

2. On a griddle or in a large skillet, melt butter over medium heat. Add rolls, cut sides down, and toast until golden brown, about 2 minutes.

3. Lay a leaf of lettuce into each roll and divide lobster salad among rolls.

168   SMOKY MOUNTAIN SAUSAGE AND BISCUIT SANDWICHES

Prep: 2 minutes   Cook: 12 to 14 minutes   Serves: 3

These little sandwiches are a favorite in the mountains of North Carolina. Served with coleslaw and baked beans, they make a great lunch or supper.

2½ teaspoons cornmeal
1 (12-ounce) tube baking powder biscuit dough (10 biscuits)
1 (12-ounce) package pork sausage meat

½ teaspoon dried leaf sage, crumbled
3 tablespoons honey mustard
1 large tomato, cut into 10 slices
10 leaves of green leaf lettuce

1. Preheat oven to 400°F. Sprinkle baking sheet with 2 teaspoons cornmeal. Arrange biscuits 1 inch apart on baking sheet and sprinkle tops with remaining ½ teaspoon cornmeal. Bake in center of preheated oven 10 to 12 minutes, until risen and golden brown.

2. Meanwhile, cut sausage (if in a cylindrical package) into 10 rounds ½ inch thick or shape loose sausage into 10 (½-inch-thick) patties. Sprinkle sage over one side of each patty. Cook in a large skillet over medium-low heat until browned on both sides and no longer pink in center, 12 to 14 minutes. Drain on paper towels.

3. Split biscuits and spread cut sides with honey mustard. Place sausage patties on biscuit bottoms, top with tomato and lettuce, and replace tops.

169   PEPPERY CORN MUFFINS

Prep: 5 minutes   Cook: 15 minutes   Serves: 4 to 6

A batch of these pepper-spiked corn muffins can make any meal feel special!

1 cup cornmeal
1 cup flour
2 tablespoons sugar
1 tablespoon baking powder
½ teaspoon salt

¼ teaspoon cayenne
1 egg
¼ cup vegetable oil
1 cup milk

1. Preheat oven to 425°F. Lightly grease 12 muffin cups or line with paper liners.

2. In a large bowl, combine cornmeal with flour, sugar, baking powder, salt, and cayenne. Whisk to blend well.

3. In a small bowl, whisk egg with oil and milk until thoroughly mixed. Pour egg mixture into flour mixture and stir gently but thoroughly until just blended. Do not overmix. Spoon batter into muffin cups.

4. Bake in preheated oven about 15 minutes, until golden brown. Serve hot.

170   CHEDDAR CHEESE DROP BISCUITS

Prep: 5 minutes   Cook: 12 to 14 minutes   Serves: 4 to 6

Serve these easy cheese-flavored drop biscuits with a soup or salad supper.

2 cups buttermilk baking
  mix, such as Bisquick
1 cup grated sharp Cheddar
  cheese

⅛ teaspoon cayenne
1 cup milk

1. Preheat oven to 425°F. In a large bowl, stir baking mix with cheese and cayenne to mix well. Add milk and stir until dough comes together. Drop by rounded tablespoons onto a lightly greased baking sheet about 1 inch apart to make 12 biscuits. Flatten tops slightly.

2. Bake 12 to 14 minutes, until biscuits are a rich golden brown. Serve hot.

171   CHICKEN-FONTINA WAFFLES

Prep: 7 minutes   Cook: 5 to 7 minutes   Serves: 4

Combined with chicken and cheese, waffles make an interesting open-faced sandwich. Use leftover roast chicken or buy sliced cooked chicken at your supermarket deli.

8 (4- to 5-inch) frozen waffles
2 tablespoons mayonnaise
8 slices of cooked chicken
  Salt and pepper

2 teaspoons Dijon mustard
1 large tomato, cut into 8 slices
½ cup grated Parmesan cheese
2 cups grated fontina cheese

1. Preheat broiler. Toast waffles until nicely browned, 2 to 3 minutes. Spread mayonnaise over waffles. Arrange chicken slices on waffles and season lightly with salt and pepper to taste.

2. Spread mustard over chicken. Place a tomato slice on each waffle. Sprinkle with Parmesan cheese and top with fontina cheese.

3. Place sandwiches on a baking sheet and broil 4 to 5 inches from heat 3 to 4 minutes, until cheese is melted. Serve hot.

172   WAFFLES WITH SMOKED SALMON AND CHIVE CREAM

Prep: 2 minutes   Cook: 5 to 6 minutes   Serves: 2

This quick recipe makes an elegant light lunch or after-theater supper.

1½ tablespoons butter
1½ tablespoons flour
 1 cup milk
 2 tablespoons grated
     Parmesan cheese
⅛ teaspoon pepper

¼ cup minced chives or
    scallion greens
 4 (4- to 5-inch) frozen waffles
 3 ounces thinly sliced smoked
    salmon, cut into thin
    strips

1. In a small saucepan, melt butter. Add flour and cook over medium heat, whisking constantly, until bubbly, about 1 minute. Whisk in milk, bring to a boil over high heat, and cook, whisking, until sauce is smooth and thickened, about 2 minutes. Off heat, whisk in cheese and pepper; stir in chives.

2. Toast waffles until lightly browned and crisp, 2 to 3 minutes. Arrange on 2 plates, spoon sauce over waffles, and top with strips of smoked salmon.

173   WAFFLES WITH HAM AND RED-EYE GRAVY

Prep: 2 minutes   Cook: 6 to 7 minutes   Serves: 2

Good-quality frozen waffles—particularly the whole-grain variety—make a terrific base for this knife-and-fork supper sandwich. The gravy is a Southern specialty.

 1 tablespoon butter
 4 slices of smoked ham or
     Canadian bacon, cut
     ¼ inch thick (about
     3 ounces)
¼ cup heavy cream

¼ teaspoon instant coffee
    granules
⅛ teaspoon pepper
 4 (4- to 5-inch) frozen waffles,
    preferably whole-grain
 1 teaspoon chopped parsley

1. In a large skillet, heat butter. Add ham and cook over medium heat, turning once, until edges are lightly browned and beginning to curl, about 4 minutes. Remove with tongs to a plate.

2. Add cream, coffee granules, and ¼ cup water to pan drippings. Bring to a boil over high heat and cook, stirring, until coffee granules are dissolved and sauce is somewhat reduced and thickened, 2 to 3 minutes. Season with pepper.

3. Meanwhile, toast waffles until lightly browned and crisp. Arrange on 2 plates, place ham over waffles, and pour gravy over ham. Sprinkle with parsley.

174 GARLIC CHEESE BREAD
Prep: 5 minutes   Cook: 1 to 2 minutes   Serves: 4

3 tablespoons olive oil
2 tablespoons softened butter
2 garlic cloves, minced
1 (1-pound) loaf Italian or
  French bread, split
  lengthwise

3 tablespoons grated
  Parmesan cheese
Paprika

1. Preheat broiler. In a small bowl, combine oil, butter, and garlic, stirring well to blend. Place bread on a baking sheet. Spread garlic butter on cut sides of bread, sprinkle evenly with cheese, and dust with paprika.

2. Broil about 5 inches from heat 1 to 2 minutes, until cheese is bubbly and flecked with brown. Cut into slices and serve hot.

175 PEPPERONI FRENCH BREAD PIZZA
Prep: 5 minutes   Cook: 10 to 12 minutes   Serves: 4

If you don't have pizza dough in the house, use French bread. The taste is great, and it's so easy to prepare.

1 (24-inch) loaf French bread
2 tablespoons olive oil
1 cup marinara sauce

48 thin pepperoni slices
1½ cups shredded mozzarella
   cheese

1. Preheat oven to 425°F. Halve bread lengthwise and brush with olive oil.

2. Spread marinara sauce over cut sides of bread. Arrange pepperoni slices over sauce. Top with mozzarella cheese.

3. Bake 10 to 12 minutes, until cheese has melted and crust is golden.

176 MEXICAN PIZZA
Prep: 3 minutes   Cook: 10 to 12 minutes   Serves: 3 to 4

1 (12-inch) prepared pizza
  shell
2 tablespoons olive oil
1 cup fresh salsa, drained
1 (4-ounce) can chopped mild
  green chiles

2 tablespoons chopped
  cilantro
1½ cups shredded Monterey
   Jack and Colby cheese

1. Preheat oven to 425°F. Arrange pizza dough on a baking sheet and brush with olive oil.

2. Spread salsa over dough. Sprinkle with chiles and cilantro. Top pizza with cheeses.

3. Bake 10 to 12 minutes, until cheese has melted and crust is golden.

177   BACON, CHEDDAR, AND TOMATO PITA PIZZAS

Prep: 5 minutes   Cook: 13 to 14 minutes   Serves: 2 to 3

10 slices of bacon, coarsely
      chopped
6 whole wheat pita breads
      (6 to 7 inches in diameter)
3 tablespoons olive oil
1 teaspoon dried basil

6 thin slices of red onion
2 medium tomatoes, thinly
      sliced
1½ cups shredded Cheddar
      cheese
¼ teaspoon pepper

1. Preheat oven to 450°F. In a large skillet, cook bacon over medium-high heat, stirring frequently, until crisp, 5 to 6 minutes. Remove with a slotted spoon and drain on paper towels.

2. Place unsplit pita breads concave sides up on a baking sheet. Drizzle with oil and sprinkle with basil. Divide onion, tomatoes, and bacon over breads and sprinkle cheese on top.

3. Bake about 8 minutes, until cheese is melted and bubbly. Grind pepper over pizzas and cut in wedges to serve.

178   ONION, HAM, AND SAGE FOCACCIA

Prep: 4 minutes   Cook: 13 to 15 minutes   Serves: 2

Originating in Genoa, focaccia ("flatbread") are similar to pizzas, but usually have fewer and less runny toppings. This one is made with refrigerated pizza dough.

2 teaspoons yellow cornmeal
2 tablespoons olive oil
1 large onion, thinly sliced
1½ teaspoons crumbled dried
      sage leaf
½ teaspoon pepper

1 (10-ounce) tube refrigerated
      pizza dough
¾ cup chopped smoked ham
      (3 ounces)
1 cup shredded mozzarella
      cheese

1. Preheat oven to 450°F. Sprinkle cornmeal on a baking sheet.

2. In a large skillet, heat oil. Add onion and cook over high heat, stirring often, until lightly browned and slightly softened, about 3 minutes. Stir in sage and pepper.

3. Unroll pizza dough, place on baking sheet, and stretch gently to an even thickness. Spread onion over dough. Sprinkle ham and cheese evenly on top.

4. Bake 10 to 12 minutes, until dough is golden brown and crusty and cheese is melted and bubbly. Cut in squares to serve.

179   PIZZA MARGHARITA
Prep: 5 minutes   Cook: 10 to 12 minutes   Serves: 2

Fresh flavorful tomatoes and fresh basil and a good-quality olive oil are the secrets of this traditional summer pizza.

2 to 3 ripe plum tomatoes, halved
3 to 4 sprigs fresh basil
1 garlic clove
   Salt and freshly ground pepper

2 (8-inch) Italian flatbreads
1½ tablespoons olive oil
½ cup shredded fontina cheese
½ cup shredded mozzarella cheese

1. Preheat oven to 425°F. In a food processor, combine tomatoes, basil, and garlic. Puree until coarsely chopped. Season with salt and pepper to taste.

2. Brush flatbreads with oil. Spoon half of tomato sauce over each. Sprinkle each pizza with fontina, then mozzarella.

3. Bake pizzas 10 to 12 minutes, until cheese is melted and crust is nicely browned.

180   PIZZA POSITANO
Prep: 8 minutes   Cook: 12 to 15 minutes   Serves: 2 to 4

This pizza recipe comes from Positano, a once sleepy fishing village south of Naples that has become the St. Tropez of Italy.

½ pound shrimp, shelled and deveined
2 tablespoons olive oil
1 garlic clove, minced
½ teaspoon dried oregano
½ medium green bell pepper, cut into julienne strips

1 cup marinara sauce
1 (12-inch) prepared pizza shell
1 cup shredded mozzarella cheese

1. Preheat oven to 425°F. Split shrimp in half lengthwise and place in a small bowl. Add 1 tablespoon oil, garlic, and oregano and toss to coat.

2. In a medium skillet, heat remaining 1 tablespoon olive oil. Add bell pepper strips and cook over medium-high heat until slightly softened, 2 to 3 minutes.

3. Spread marinara sauce over pizza shell. Arrange shrimp over sauce. Top with bell peppers and mozzarella cheese.

4. Bake 10 to 12 minutes, until cheese is melted.

181 PIZZA CAPRICCIOSA

Prep: 6 minutes   Cook: 10 to 12 minutes   Serves: 2 to 4

The combination of artichoke hearts, olives, ham, and capers gives this pizza a flavorful zip.

2 tablespoons olive oil
1 (12-inch) flatbread, such as Boboli
1 cup marinara sauce
½ cup chopped marinated artichoke hearts
¼ cup chopped Greek olives

2 to 3 thin slices of baked ham, coarsely chopped
2 tablespoons capers
1 cup shredded mozzarella cheese
1 tablespoon grated Parmesan cheese

1. Preheat oven to 425°F. Spread olive oil over bread and coat crust with marinara sauce. Arrange artichokes, olives, ham, and capers on top. Sprinkle mozzarella cheese and Parmesan cheese evenly over pizza.

2. Bake 10 to 12 minutes, until cheese is melted and crust is lightly browned.

182 PIZZA SARDENAIRE

Prep: 5 minutes   Cook: 10 to 12 minutes   Serves: 3 to 4

Fish and Italy go hand-in-hand, so the addition of tuna and anchovies is a natural. Add sun-dried tomatoes and seasonings for a terrific pizza combination.

1 frozen (10-ounce) pizza dough
2 tablespoons olive oil
1 (6⅛-ounce) can white tuna packed in water, drained
1 cup sun-dried tomatoes, packed in oil, drained

1 (2¼-ounce) can sliced ripe olives, drained
1 to 2 tablespoons chopped anchovy fillets
1 teaspoon Italian seasoning
1 cup shredded mozzarella cheese

1. Preheat oven to 425°F. Place dough on baking sheet and brush with olive oil.

2. Top pizza with tuna, sun-dried tomatoes, olives, anchovies, and Italian seasoning. Sprinkle cheese over all.

3. Bake 10 to 12 minutes, until cheese is melted and crust is lightly browned.

183   PIZZA QUATRO FORMAGGI
Prep: 5 minutes   Cook: 10 to 12 minutes   Serves: 3 to 4

This pizza is especially designed for cheese lovers. Peaked by the addition of the Gorgonzola cheese, it is a real treat.

1 (12-inch) Italian flatbread	½ cup crumbled Gorgonzola
1 tablespoon olive oil	cheese
1 cup pizza sauce	½ cup shredded fontina cheese
½ cup shredded mozzarella	1 tablespoon grated Parmesan
cheese	cheese

1. Preheat oven to 425°F. Place flatbread on baking sheet and brush with olive oil.

2. Spread pizza sauce over flatbread. Sprinkle mozzarella, Gorgonzola, and fontina cheeses over sauce. Top with Parmesan.

3. Bake 10 to 12 minutes, until cheese has melted and crust is golden.

184   THREE-PEPPER PIZZA
Prep: 5 minutes   Cook: 12 to 15 minutes   Serves: 2 to 4

1 (7-ounce) jar roasted red	1 (12-inch) prepared pizza
peppers	shell
2 tablespoons olive oil	1 cup shredded mozzarella
½ medium green bell pepper,	cheese
cut in thin strips	
1 fresh jalapeño pepper,	
seeded and minced	

1. Preheat oven to 425°F. Place roasted peppers in a food processor and process 3 to 4 seconds to make a puree.

2. In a small skillet, heat 1 tablespoon of oil. Add bell pepper and jalapeño. Cook over medium-high heat until softened, 2 to 3 minutes.

3. Brush remaining oil over pizza shell. Spread roasted pepper puree over pizza. Top with sáuteed peppers and mozzarella cheese.

4. Bake 10 to 12 minutes, until cheese is melted and crust is lightly browned.

185 THREE-ONION PIZZA

Prep: 7 minutes   Cook: 12 to 15 minutes   Serves: 2 to 4

The combination of sun-dried tomato sauce and three onion flavors makes this a delightful and very interesting pizza.

2 tablespoons olive oil
1 medium Spanish onion, thinly sliced
1 medium leek (white part only), thinly sliced
1 teaspoon minced garlic
3 scallions, thinly sliced

Salt and pepper
⅓ cup sun-dried tomato paste or dried tomato tapenade
1 (12-inch) frozen pizza shell
1 cup grated mozzarella cheese

1. Preheat oven to 425°F. In a large skillet, heat oil over medium-high heat. Add Spanish onion, leek, and garlic. Cook, stirring often, until slightly softened, 2 to 3 minutes. Stir in scallions. Remove from heat and season lightly with salt and pepper.

2. Spread tomato sauce over pizza shell. Arrange onion mixture over pizza and top with mozzarella cheese.

3. Bake 10 to 12 minutes, until cheese is melted and crust is lightly browned.

Chapter 6

Variety with Vegetables, Rice, and Grains

Health experts recommend cutting down on fat and cholesterol in our diet and increasing consumption of complex carbohydrates. That means eating more vegetables, rices, and other grains. This chapter offers many quick dishes that are based on just these foods. Quite a few of these are intended as main courses or starters; some are substantial side dishes. Many recipes use quick-cooking rice (both white and brown) and canned beans. If meat appears in these recipes, it is usually a small amount of a highly flavored (and quickly cooked) meat, such as bacon or smoked ham, as a seasoning.

International dishes are featured in this chapter because most cultures around the world have always relied more on well-seasoned grain, rice, corn, and bean combinations for their mainstay meals. Recipes such as New Orleans Red Beans and Rice, Risotto Primavera, Broiled Cheese Polenta with Tomato-Mushroom Sauce, and Oaxacan Brown Rice with Corn and Tomatoes are both healthful and delicious. When served with a green salad and dessert, they make a complete meal.

186 ROASTED ASPARAGUS WITH LEMON
Prep: 5 minutes   Cook: 8 to 10 minutes   Serves: 4

1½ **pounds medium-thick asparagus**	⅛ **teaspoon pepper**
2 **tablespoons olive oil**	1 **tablespoon lemon juice**
¼ **teaspoon salt**	½ **teaspoon grated lemon zest**
	6 **thin lemon slices**

1. Preheat oven to 475°F. Snap off tough ends of asparagus and spread spears out on a rimmed baking sheet. Pour oil over asparagus and toss to coat spears. Season with salt and pepper.

2. Roast 8 to 10 minutes, turning once, until asparagus is tender and begins to caramelize.

3. Transfer to a serving dish, toss with lemon juice and lemon zest, and garnish with lemon slices.

187   GARLIC-ROASTED BROCCOLI WITH BALSAMIC VINEGAR

Prep: 4 minutes   Cook: 7 to 9 minutes   Serves: 4

Vegetables roasted this way develop a slightly charred, smoky flavor.

3 tablespoons olive oil
1 garlic clove, minced
1 large bunch of broccoli
¼ teaspoon salt

⅛ teaspoon pepper
1 tablespoon balsamic
   vinegar

1. Preheat oven to 475°F. In a small bowl, combine olive oil and garlic.

2. Cut broccoli into florets with 2 to 3 inches of stem and spread on a rimmed baking sheet. Pour garlic oil over broccoli and toss to coat. Season with salt and pepper.

3. Roast 7 to 9 minutes, turning once, until broccoli is tender and charred at edges. Transfer to a serving dish and sprinkle with vinegar.

188   GINGERED CARROT PUREE

Prep: 3 minutes   Cook: 10 minutes   Serves: 2 to 3

If you use fresh carrots, just add a few minutes to the cooking time.

1 (1-pound) package frozen
   sliced carrots
1 tablespoon butter
¼ teaspoon salt
⅛ teaspoon pepper

¼ teaspoon sugar
¼ teaspoon ground ginger
3 tablespoons heavy cream or
   half-and-half

1. In a medium saucepan of boiling salted water, cook carrots until very soft, about 10 minutes; drain.

2. In a food processor, combine carrots, butter, salt, pepper, sugar, and ginger. Process to a coarse puree.

3. With machine on, pour cream through feed tube and process to a smooth puree, stopping machine and scraping down sides once or twice. If not serving immediately, return to saucepan; rewarm over low heat.

189   CARROT AND RAISIN SLAW
Prep: 8 minutes   Cook: none   Stand: 10 minutes   Serves: 4

Grate the carrots on the shredding disk of a food processor or use the large holes of a hand grater.

¾ cup mayonnaise
1 tablespoon grainy Dijon
    mustard
2 tablespoons chopped
    shallots
1 teaspoon lemon juice

3 cups packed coarsely grated
    carrots
½ cup raisins
¼ teaspoon salt
⅛ teaspoon pepper

In a large bowl, whisk mayonnaise with mustard, shallots, and lemon juice. Stir in carrots and raisins and season with salt and pepper. Refrigerate at least 10 minutes to blend flavors.

190   CREAMY SAVOY CABBAGE SLAW
Prep: 10 minutes   Cook: none   Stand: 10 minutes   Serves: 4

Savoy cabbage is a first cousin to green cabbage and is distinguished by its wrinkled leaves. Because of its milder flavor and softer texture, savoy cabbage makes an "instant" coleslaw that requires no standing time.

⅓ cup mayonnaise
1 tablespoon white wine
    vinegar
2 tablespoons finely chopped
    red onion
2 teaspoons sugar
½ teaspoon powdered
    mustard

½ teaspoon salt
¼ teaspoon pepper
4 cups shredded savoy
    cabbage (about ½ pound)
1 medium carrot, coarsely
    grated

1. In a large bowl, whisk mayonnaise with vinegar, red onion, sugar, mustard, salt, and pepper.

2. Stir in cabbage and carrot, tossing well to coat with dressing. Cover and refrigerate 10 minutes to blend flavors.

191 GOAT CHEESE POTATO CAKES WITH SMOKED SALMON

Prep: 10 minutes   Cook: 9 minutes
Serves: 2 as a main course, 4 as a first course

3 cups partially thawed frozen
 mashed potatoes (about
 12 ounces)
1¼ cups milk
⅓ cup crumbled mild goat
 cheese (1 ounce)

⅓ cup chopped smoked
 salmon (1 ounce)
1 tablespoon chopped fresh
 dill or ½ teaspoon dried
¼ teaspoon pepper
2 tablespoons butter

1. In a medium saucepan, combine potatoes and milk. Bring to a boil over medium-high heat and cook, stirring, until smooth, about 3 minutes. Off heat, beat in goat cheese, smoked salmon, dill, and pepper.

2. In a large skillet, melt butter. Shape potato mixture into 6 patties ½ inch thick. Cook over medium-low heat, turning once, until golden brown on both sides, about 6 minutes total. Serve hot.

192 DILLED OYSTER POTATO CAKES

Prep: 5 minutes   Cook: 11 to 15 minutes   Serves: 4

⅔ cup milk
1⅓ cups frozen mashed
 potatoes
1 egg yolk
¼ cup thinly sliced scallions
1 tablespoon minced fresh
 dill or 1 teaspoon dried

1 tablespoon flour
½ teaspoon salt
¼ teaspoon pepper
2 tablespoons canola oil
1 (3¾-ounce) can smoked
 oysters, drained

1. In a medium saucepan, heat milk until steaming, 1 to 2 minutes. Add potatoes and cook over medium heat uncovered, stirring constantly to avoid scorching, until hot and smooth, 5 to 7 minutes. Let stand 1 to 2 minutes.

2. In a medium bowl, combine potatoes, egg yolk, scallion, dill, flour, salt, and pepper. Stir until blended.

3. In a large nonstick skillet, heat oil over medium heat. Place ¼ cup potatoes for each cake in pan. Put 1 oyster in center of each cake and with a spatula, cover with remaining potato mixture. Cook, turning once, until golden on both sides, 5 to 6 minutes.

193 SKILLET SCALLOPED POTATOES
Prep: 7 minutes   Cook: 12 minutes   Serves: 2

1 tablespoon butter	1½ teaspoons flour
¾ pound all-purpose or russet potatoes, peeled and thinly sliced	¼ teaspoon salt
	⅛ teaspoon pepper
	1 cup milk
½ cup thinly sliced red onion	1 tablespoon chopped parsley

1. In a heavy 8- or 9-inch nonstick skillet, melt ½ tablespoon butter. Off heat, spread half of potato slices in skillet and cover with red onion. Sprinkle on half of flour, salt, and pepper. Top with remaining potato slices, flour, salt, and pepper and dot with remaining ½ tablespoon butter.

2. Pour milk over potatoes and bring to a boil over high heat. Reduce heat to medium-low, cover, and cook until potatoes are tender, about 12 minutes.

3. Sprinkle with parsley before serving.

194 POTATOES SAUTÉED WITH LEMON AND PARSLEY
Prep: 4 minutes   Cook: 13 to 16 minutes   Serves: 2 to 3

Leaving the potato skins on adds texture and flavor to these delicious lemon-scented potatoes, but you may peel them if you prefer.

1 pound all-purpose or russet potatoes, thinly sliced	1 tablespoon lemon juice
	½ teaspoon grated lemon zest
2½ tablespoons olive oil	¼ teaspoon salt
1 tablespoon chopped parsley	⅛ teaspoon pepper

1. Cook potatoes in a large saucepan of boiling salted water until barely tender, 6 to 8 minutes. Drain into a colander.

2. In a large skillet, heat oil over medium-high heat. Add potatoes and cook until soft and lightly browned, 7 to 8 minutes.

3. Stir in parsley, lemon juice, and lemon zest and season with salt and pepper.

195   GARLIC-CHIVE MASHED POTATOES

Prep: 3 minutes   Cook: 10 minutes   Serves: 4

The new frozen mashed potatoes are a tremendous improvement over the dehydrated mashed potatoes of yore. They already contain butter and seasonings, but you may wish to add a bit more salt and pepper to taste.

4 **large garlic cloves, coarsely chopped**
1 **(14-ounce) package frozen mashed potatoes**
2 **cups milk**

3 **tablespoons minced chives or scallion tops**
   Salt and freshly ground pepper

1. In a small saucepan, cover garlic with 2 inches water. Bring to a boil over high heat, reduce heat to medium-low, and simmer uncovered until garlic is very tender, about 10 minutes. Drain into a sieve and mash with a fork to a puree.

2. Meanwhile, in a medium-large saucepan, combine potatoes and milk. Bring to a boil over high heat, stirring. Reduce heat to medium and cook, stirring frequently, until smooth, 3 to 6 minutes.

3. Stir in garlic and chives and season potatoes with salt and pepper to taste.

196   BROILED DEVILED TOMATOES

Prep: 10 minutes   Cook: 3 to 4 minutes   Serves: 4

Fresh bread crumbs can be made by pulsing four slices of good-quality white or whole wheat bread in a food processor.

4 **large tomatoes**
¼ **teaspoon salt**
⅛ **teaspoon pepper, plus additional for top**
2 **tablespoons olive oil**

1 **large garlic clove, minced**
1½ **teaspoons Dijon mustard**
2 **cups fresh bread crumbs**
2 **teaspoons chopped parsley**

1. Preheat broiler. Cut tomatoes in half crosswise and squeeze out most of seeds. Sprinkle cavities with salt and pepper and arrange in an oiled baking dish.

2. In a small skillet, heat oil. Add garlic and cook over medium heat, stirring, 1 minute. Remove from heat and whisk in mustard. Scrape into a medium bowl.

3. Add bread crumbs and toss with garlic-mustard mixture until well blended. Divide among tomatoes. Sprinkle parsley on tops. Season with another grinding of pepper.

4. Broil about 5 inches from heat 2 to 3 minutes, until crumbs are a rich, dark brown and tomatoes are warm.

197 ROSEMARY ROASTED WINTER VEGETABLES

Prep: 2 minutes   Cook: 18 minutes   Serves: 4

Packages of frozen "stew vegetables" are marketed nationwide. They usually include potatoes, carrots, onions, and celery.

1 **(1-pound) package frozen stew vegetables**	1 **teaspoon dried rosemary**
4 **unpeeled garlic cloves**	¼ **teaspoon sugar**
2 **tablespoons olive oil**	¼ **teaspoon salt**
	⅛ **teaspoon pepper**

1. Preheat oven to 475°F. Place vegetables in a colander and rinse under hot water to dissolve ice crystals and thaw slightly. If potatoes are more than 1 inch in diameter, cut in half.

2. In a shallow roasting pan, toss vegetables and garlic with oil, rosemary, sugar, salt, and pepper.

3. Roast uncovered, about 18 minutes, stirring once, until vegetables are tender and begin to caramelize.

198 SAUTÉED ZUCCHINI AND TOMATOES PROVENÇAL

Prep: 10 minutes   Cook: 7 to 8 minutes   Serves: 3 to 4

Serve this dish with grilled meats or roast chicken.

2 **tablespoons olive oil**	½ **teaspoon herbes de Provence, or ¼ teaspoon each dried oregano and basil**
1 **pound slender zucchini, sliced ¼ inch thick**	
1 **cup seeded and chopped tomato**	¼ **teaspoon salt**
1 **large garlic clove, minced**	⅛ **teaspoon pepper**

1. In a large skillet, heat oil over medium-high heat. Add zucchini and cook, stirring frequently, until lightly browned and crisp-tender, about 5 minutes.

2. Add tomato, garlic, herbes de Provence, salt, and pepper. Cook, stirring frequently, until tomatoes give off their liquid and zucchini is tender but not mushy, 2 to 3 minutes.

199   SANTA FE VEGETABLE RAGOUT
Prep: 6 minutes   Cook: 10 to 12 minutes   Serves: 2 to 3

3 tablespoons olive oil
1 medium green bell pepper, cut in ½-inch pieces
2 garlic cloves, minced
1 tablespoon chili powder
1 (14½- to 16-ounce) can Mexican-style or recipe-ready stewed tomatoes
1½ cups diced canned or precooked sweet potatoes

1 cup frozen corn kernels
1 (15-ounce) can pinto beans, drained
¼ teaspoon salt
⅛ teaspoon pepper
2 tablespoons chopped cilantro

1. In a large saucepan, heat oil over medium-high heat. Add green pepper and cook, stirring frequently, until slightly softened, about 3 minutes. Add garlic and chili powder and cook, stirring, 1 minute.

2. Add tomatoes with juice, sweet potatoes, corn, beans, salt, pepper, and ½ cup water. Bring to a boil over high heat, reduce heat to medium-low, and cook uncovered until liquid thickens, 6 to 8 minutes. Stir in cilantro.

200   GRILLED SUMMER VEGETABLES VINAIGRETTE
Prep: 10 minutes   Cook: 4 to 6 minutes   Serves: 4

2 small, narrow Asian eggplant
2 medium zucchini
1 red onion
1 red bell pepper

1 yellow bell pepper
About ½ cup bottled olive-oil vinaigrette
1 tablespoon chopped parsley

1. Prepare a medium-hot fire in a charcoal or gas grill. Trim eggplant, zucchini, and onion and slice ½ inch thick. Seed peppers and cut into 2-inch strips. On a platter, pour ¼ cup dressing over vegetables; turn to coat well.

2. Grill vegetables, brushing with 2 tablespoons more dressing, until browned on both sides, 4 to 6 minutes. Eggplant should be soft within; other vegetables should retain some texture.

3. Toss vegetables with remaining dressing and garnish with parsley.

201   RUM-MAPLE BAKED BEANS

Prep: 3 minutes   Cook: 12 to 15 minutes   Serves: 3 to 4 as main course, 5 to 6 as side dish

⅓ cup maple syrup
3 tablespoons dark rum
1 tablespoon ketchup
2 teaspoons Dijon mustard

1 small onion, chopped
2 (1-pound) cans baked beans
4 slices of bacon, halved

1. Preheat broiler. In a large nonreactive saucepan, whisk maple syrup with rum, ketchup, and mustard. Add onion and baked beans. Bring to a boil over high heat, reduce heat to medium, and cook uncovered until onion is softened and sauce is reduced and thickened, 10 to 12 minutes.

2. Meanwhile, in a large skillet, cook bacon over medium heat until shriveled and fat is translucent but not quite crisp, about 5 minutes.

3. Pour beans into a shallow 2-quart baking dish and lay bacon strips over beans. Broil about 5 inches from heat 2 to 3 minutes, until bacon is browned and crisp and beans bubble around the edges.

202   QUICK HOPPIN' JOHN WITH BACON

Prep: 6 minutes   Cook: 9 minutes   Serves: 4 to 6

A traditional New Year's Day dish in the South, Hoppin' John is guaranteed to bring good luck in the coming year!

8 slices of lean bacon, coarsely
   chopped
2 medium onions, chopped
1 large celery rib, chopped
2 garlic cloves, minced
2 (15-ounce) cans black-eyed
   peas, drained

1¾ cups quick-cooking rice
¾ teaspoon salt
¼ teaspoon pepper
   Tabasco sauce

1. In a large heavy saucepan, cook bacon over medium-high heat, stirring frequently, until browned and crisp, about 5 minutes. Remove bacon with a slotted spoon and drain on paper towels.

2. Add onions to bacon drippings and cook over medium-high heat until beginning to soften, about 3 minutes. Stir in celery and garlic and cook 1 minute. Add beans, rice, salt, pepper, and 3 cups water. Bring to a boil over high heat, remove from heat, cover, and let stand until rice is tender, about 5 minutes. Hoppin' John should have a thick souplike consistency. Sprinkle with reserved bacon and pass Tabasco at the table.

203   HAVANA BLACK BEANS AND RICE
Prep: 5 minutes   Cook: 13 to 15 minutes   Serves: 4

3 tablespoons olive oil
1 large onion, coarsely
   chopped
2 garlic cloves, minced
1 jalapeño pepper, minced
1½ teaspoons chili powder
2 (15-ounce) cans black beans,
   drained

1 (14¾-ounce) can chicken
   broth
1 bay leaf
1 tablespoon red wine vinegar
½ teaspoon pepper
1 teaspoon salt
2 cups quick-cooking rice
¾ cup chopped red onion

1. In a large skillet, heat oil over medium-high heat. Add onion and cook, stirring frequently, until softened, about 4 minutes. Add garlic, jalapeño pepper, and chili powder. Cook, stirring, 1 minute. Add beans, chicken broth, and bay leaf. Raise heat to high, bring to a boil, reduce heat to medium-low, and cook uncovered until reduced to a thick souplike consistency, 8 to 10 minutes. Remove bay leaf, stir in vinegar, and season with pepper.

2. Meanwhile, in a medium saucepan, bring 2 cups water and salt to a boil over high heat. Add rice, stir, remove from heat, cover, and let stand until water is absorbed, about 5 minutes. Fluff with a fork.

3. Serve beans alongside or over rice and sprinkle with red onion.

204   RISOTTO WITH FENNEL AND PROSCIUTTO
Prep: 5 minutes   Cook: 12 to 15 minutes   Serves: 4

3 tablespoons olive oil
2 cups thinly sliced fennel
   bulb (1 small bulb)
2 garlic cloves, minced
3 cups quick-cooking rice
½ cup dry white wine

6 cups reduced-sodium
   chicken broth
1 cup finely diced prosciutto
½ cup grated Parmesan cheese
¼ teaspoon freshly ground
   pepper

1. In a large heavy saucepan, heat oil over medium-high heat. Add fennel and cook, stirring frequently, until lightly browned and somewhat softened, about 3 minutes. Add garlic and cook, stirring, until fragrant, about 1 minute.

2. Add rice and stir to coat grains. Add wine and cook, stirring, until liquid is absorbed, about 2 minutes. Add broth about 1 cup at a time and cook, stirring, until most of liquid is absorbed. Continue adding broth, stirring after each addition, until most of liquid is absorbed. Total cooking time is 12 to 15 minutes.

3. After last addition of broth, remove pan from heat, stir in prosciutto and cheese, and season with pepper. Rice should be tender, swimming in a creamy broth. Serve in soup bowls.

205   NEW ORLEANS RED BEANS AND RICE
Prep: 4 minutes   Cook: 14 to 16 minutes   Serves: 6

Red beans and rice are traditionally served on Monday (which was washday) in old New Orleans. Andouille is spicy Cajun sausage. If you can't get it, use any kind of well-seasoned smoked sausage.

1 tablespoon olive oil	3 (15-ounce) cans red beans or
1 pound spicy smoked	kidney beans, drained
sausage, such as	2 bay leaves
andouille or kielbasa, cut	1 teaspoon dried thyme
½ inch thick	¼ teaspoon cayenne
1 large onion, coarsely	2½ cups quick-cooking rice
chopped	1¼ teaspoons salt
1 large green bell pepper,	Tabasco sauce
coarsely chopped	

1. In a large flameproof casserole, heat oil over medium-high heat. Add sausage, onion, and green pepper and cook, stirring, until sausage is browned, about 6 minutes. Add beans, bay leaves, thyme, cayenne, and 3 cups water. Bring to a boil over high heat, reduce heat to medium, and cook uncovered, stirring occasionally, until reduced and thickened, 8 to 10 minutes. Remove and discard bay leaves. Use back of a spoon to mash about one-third of beans to thicken sauce.

2. Meanwhile, in a large saucepan, bring 2½ cups water to a boil over high heat. Add rice and salt and stir. Cover, remove from heat, and let stand until water is absorbed, about 5 minutes.

3. Ladle beans over rice and pass Tabasco at the table.

206   MEXICAN RISOTTO
Prep: 5 minutes   Cook: 6 to 7 minutes   Serves: 4 to 6

This is a quick and easy comfort food for Mexican food enthusiasts. Serve it from the saucepan or spoon into a gratin dish. If you like, sprinkle extra cheese on top and place under broiler until bubbly, 1 to 2 minutes.

¾ cup quick-cooking rice	1 (11-ounce) can Mexicorn,
1 tablespoon olive or canola	with juice
oil	¼ cup green or red salsa
⅓ cup chopped onion	½ cup shredded Monterey
1 (16-ounce) can refried beans	Jack cheese
with green chiles	

1. Cook rice following package instructions; set aside.

2. In a medium saucepan, heat oil over medium heat. Add onion and cook, stirring occasionally, until slightly softened, about 3 minutes.

3. Stir in refried beans, corn with its liquid, salsa, and cheese. Cook, stirring, until heated through, 3 to 4 minutes. Stir in cooked rice and serve.

207   WILD MUSHROOM RISOTTO

Prep: 5 minutes   Cook: 10 to 12 minutes   Serves: 2

Use any kind of wild mushrooms from the produce department in this fragrant, autumnal rice dish.

2 tablespoons butter
2 tablespoons chopped
    shallots
1¾ cups sliced shiitake or other
    wild mushrooms
    (6 ounces)
1½ cups quick-cooking rice
¾ teaspoon dried savory

¼ cup dry white wine
3½ cups reduced-sodium
    chicken broth
¼ cup grated Parmesan cheese
⅛ teaspoon freshly ground
    pepper
2 tablespoons chopped
    parsley

1. In a medium saucepan, melt butter over medium-high heat. Add shallots and mushrooms and cook, stirring, until mushrooms are slightly wilted, about 2 minutes.

2. Add rice and savory, stirring to coat rice grains. Add wine and cook, stirring, until liquid is absorbed, about 2 minutes. Add broth, about ¾ cup at a time, and cook, stirring, until most of liquid is absorbed. Continue adding broth, stirring after each addition until most of liquid is absorbed. Total cooking time is 10 to 12 minutes.

3. After last addition of broth, remove pan from heat, stir in cheese, and season with pepper. Rice should be tender, swimming in a creamy broth. Serve in shallow soup bowls and sprinkle with parsley.

208   HERBED RICE PILAF

Prep: 4 minutes   Cook: 1 minute   Serves: 4 to 6

Serve this simple rice pilaf as a side dish to almost any type of meat, chicken, or fish.

1½ tablespoons butter
½ cup chopped scallions
¼ cup chopped fresh parsley,
    dill, and/or basil
2 cups quick-cooking rice

2 cups vegetable or chicken
    broth
¼ teaspoon pepper
Salt

1. In a medium saucepan, melt butter over medium heat. Add scallions and herbs and cook, stirring, 1 minute. Add rice, stir to coat grains, and add broth. Bring to a boil over high heat, cover, remove from heat, and let stand until liquid is absorbed and rice is tender, about 5 minutes.

2. Season with pepper and salt to taste. Fluff with a fork before serving.

209   RISOTTO PRIMAVERA

Prep: 5 minutes   Cook: 8 to 10 minutes   Serves: 2

True risotto is always made with short-grain Arborio rice, which, when cooked and stirred with broth for approximately 20 minutes, produces a creamy sauce. Since Arborio is sometimes difficult to find and also exceeds our time limit, I tried this version made with quick-cooking rice, and I liked the results. Make this "primavera" in early spring when fresh asparagus comes into season.

1 tablespoon butter	1 teaspoon dried basil
1½ cups quick-cooking rice	¼ cup heavy cream
¼ cup dry white wine	3 tablespoons grated
3 cups reduced-sodium	Parmesan cheese
chicken broth	⅛ teaspoon freshly ground
1 cup sliced asparagus (½ inch	pepper
thick)	¼ cup thinly sliced scallions
¾ cup frozen peas	
⅓ cup chopped red bell	
pepper	

1. In a medium saucepan, melt butter over medium-high heat. Add rice and stir to coat grains. Add wine and cook, stirring, until liquid is absorbed, about 2 minutes. Add broth, about ¾ cup at a time, and cook, stirring, until most of liquid is absorbed. Continue adding broth, stirring after each addition until most of liquid is absorbed.

2. After last addition of broth, add asparagus, peas, red pepper, and basil. Bring to a boil over high heat, reduce heat to low, and cook until vegetables are tender but still firm, about 2 minutes. Total cooking time is 8 to 10 minutes.

3. Off heat, stir in cream and cheese and season with pepper. Rice should be tender, swimming in a creamy broth. Serve in shallow soup bowls and sprinkle with scallions.

210 VEGETABLE FRIED RICE
Prep: 10 minutes   Cook: 6 minutes   Serves: 3

You can save time here by buying cut broccoli florets in the produce section or salad bar of the supermarket.

1½ cups quick-cooking rice
¾ teaspoon salt
3 tablespoons peanut oil
1¼ cups thinly sliced
    mushrooms, either
    shiitake or white button
    mushrooms
1¼ cups small broccoli florets

1 cup thinly sliced red bell
    pepper
1 tablespoon minced fresh
    ginger
1¼ cups thinly sliced scallions,
    including green tops
2 tablespoons soy sauce

1. In a medium saucepan, bring 1½ cups water to a boil over high heat. Add rice and salt and stir. Cover, remove from heat, and let stand until water is absorbed, about 5 minutes.

2. Meanwhile, in a large skillet or wok, heat oil over high heat. Add mushrooms, broccoli, red pepper, and ginger and stir-fry until vegetables are just tender, about 3 minutes. Add scallions and cook 1 minute.

3. Add cooked rice and soy sauce, reduce heat to medium, and cook, stirring, until thoroughly blended and heated through, about 1 minute. Serve with additional soy sauce at the table.

211 OAXACAN BROWN RICE WITH CORN AND TOMATOES
Prep: 3 minutes   Cook: 10 minutes
Serves: 4 as a main course, 6 as a side dish

2 tablespoons olive oil
1 medium onion, coarsely
    chopped
1½ teaspoons chili powder
2 cups quick-cooking brown
    rice
1 (14½-ounce) can diced
    recipe-ready tomatoes

1 (4-ounce) can chopped green
    chiles, drained
1 cup frozen corn kernels
1½ cups vegetable broth or
    water
¼ teaspoon salt or to taste
¼ teaspoon pepper

1. In a large saucepan, heat oil over medium heat. Add onion and cook until softened, about 4 minutes. Add chili powder and cook, stirring, until fragrant, 1 minute.

2. Add rice and stir to coat grains. Add tomatoes with their juice, green chiles, corn, and broth. Bring to a boil over high heat, reduce heat to low, cover, and cook 5 minutes.

3. Remove from heat and let stand until liquid is absorbed and rice is tender, about 5 minutes. Season with salt and pepper and fluff with a fork before serving.

212 SPICED BROWN RICE PILAF WITH ALMONDS AND RAISINS

Prep: 2 minutes   Cook: 9 to 10 minutes
Serves: 4 as a main course, 6 as a side dish

2 tablespoons olive oil
1 medium onion, chopped
3 tablespoons sliced almonds
½ teaspoon curry powder
¼ teaspoon cinnamon
2 cups quick-cooking brown rice

2 cups vegetable broth or broth and water
½ cup raisins
¼ teaspoon salt
⅛ teaspoon cayenne

1. In a medium saucepan, heat oil over medium heat. Add onion and almonds and cook, stirring, until they both begin to brown, 3 to 4 minutes. Add curry powder and cinnamon and cook, stirring, until spices are fragrant, about 1 minute.

2. Add rice and stir to coat grains. Add broth, raisins, salt, and cayenne and bring to a boil over high heat. Reduce heat to low, cover, and cook 5 minutes.

3. Remove from heat and let stand until liquid is absorbed and rice is tender, about 5 minutes. Fluff with a fork before serving.

213 BROILED CHEESE POLENTA WITH TOMATO-MUSHROOM SAUCE

Prep: 3 minutes   Cook: 10 to 12 minutes   Serves: 4

Polenta, like mashed potatoes, is a great comfort food. Serve it with a green salad and a bottle of Chianti for a quick, satisfying dinner.

1¼ cups yellow cornmeal
½ teaspoon salt
¼ teaspoon pepper
6 tablespoons grated Parmesan cheese

1 (26-ounce) jar tomato sauce with mushrooms

1. Preheat broiler. In a large saucepan, bring 2½ cups water to a boil over high heat. In a bowl, whisk cornmeal into 1½ cups cold water. Gradually whisk cornmeal paste into boiling water. Reduce heat to low and cook uncovered, whisking frequently, until very thick, 6 to 8 minutes. Season with salt and pepper and whisk in 4 tablespoons cheese. Spoon into a greased 9-inch baking dish or ovenproof skillet. Sprinkle remaining 2 tablespoons cheese on top.

2. Broil polenta about 5 inches from heat 2 minutes, until cheese melts and bubbles and polenta begins to brown around edges.

3. In a medium saucepan, cook tomato sauce over medium heat until heated through, about 2 minutes. Cut polenta into wedges or squares and serve with sauce spooned over.

214 PEPPER, OLIVE, AND GARLIC RICE
Prep: 6 minutes   Cook: 4 minutes   Serves: 4 to 6

2 tablespoons olive oil
1 medium red bell pepper,
   chopped
3 garlic cloves, minced
2 cups quick-cooking rice

2 cups chicken broth or broth
   and water
¾ cup sliced pimiento-stuffed
   green olives
¼ teaspoon pepper

1. In a medium saucepan, heat oil. Add red pepper and cook over medium heat until beginning to soften, about 3 minutes. Add garlic and cook, stirring, 1 minute.

2. Add rice, stir to coat grains, and add broth. Bring to a boil over high heat, cover, remove from heat, and let stand until liquid is absorbed and rice is tender, about 5 minutes.

3. Stir in olives and season with pepper. Fluff with a fork before serving.

215 BROILED CHEDDAR GRITS AND GREENS
Prep: 3 minutes   Cook: 9 to 11 minutes   Serves: 3 to 4

Frozen cooked greens taste good and are a great time-saver. Use any kind here—turnip, collards, or mustard.

1 (10-ounce) package frozen
   turnip or other greens
⅔ cup quick-cooking grits
¼ teaspoon salt
1¼ cups grated sharp Cheddar
   cheese (5 ounces)

1 tablespoon butter
2 garlic cloves, finely chopped
¼ teaspoon Tabasco sauce

1. Preheat broiler. Thaw greens in a microwave; drain in a colander and press out moisture.

2. In a medium saucepan, bring 2¼ cups water to a boil over high heat. Gradually whisk grits into water and stir in salt. Reduce heat to low, cover, and cook, stirring occasionally, until grits are very thick, 5 to 7 minutes. Whisk in 1 cup cheese.

3. Meanwhile, in a medium skillet, melt butter over medium heat. Add garlic and cook, stirring, 1 minute. Add greens and heat through, about 1 minute. Season with Tabasco.

4. Spread greens into bottom of a buttered 1-quart dish. Spoon grits over greens and sprinkle with remaining cheese. Broil 5 inches from heat 2 minutes, until cheese melts and bubbles and grits begin to brown around edges.

Chapter 7

Fish and Shellfish in a Flash

These days you do not have to live by the sea to enjoy its bounty. Modern fish markets and supermarket seafood departments offer impressive variety, including convenient boneless fish fillets, packages of peeled and deveined raw or cooked shrimp, and cooked lobster and crabmeat. Even small whole fish cook in under 20 minutes, so seafood is a natural choice for hurried cooks. In fact, overcooking ruins good fish, so be sure to follow the cooking instructions in the recipes carefully for delicious results.

Practically everyone loves shrimp, and it takes a mere 2 or 3 minutes for them to turn pink and curl, the signs they are cooked through. To ensure they remain tender and succulent, it's important not to leave them over heat much longer. Because of their speed and versatility, I've included a generous sampling of shrimp recipes. All of these call for shelled and deveined shrimp. If they don't come that way, most fish markets will perform that task for you for an additional charge. If you'd rather spend time than money, then add another 5 to 10 minutes when calculating your preparation time.

Fish lends itself well to many cooking methods, including grilling, sautéing, baking, broiling, and poaching. Often the simplest treatment for fish is the best treatment. Heavy sauces and intensely flavored seasonings can obscure the delicate flavor and texture of good seafood.

For midweek family meals, try Crispy Oven-Fried Fish or Baked Halibut Steaks with Tomato-Wine Sauce. Stir-Fried Scallops and Snow Peas or Poached Salmon Steaks with Vegetables Orientale are perfect for the person who wants a light, low-fat meal. And for those elegant dinners, a dish such as Lobster Thermidor, Seafood Brochettes, or Montego Bay Seafood Stew proclaims much louder than words that this is indeed a special evening.

216   HALIBUT WITH HERBS

Prep: 3 minutes   Cook: 7 to 11 minutes   Serves: 4 to 6

2 tablespoons flour
2 teaspoons dried oregano
¼ teaspoon salt
¼ teaspoon pepper
1½ to 2 pounds halibut steaks,
    cut about ¾ inch thick

2 tablespoons olive oil
2 tablespoons butter
3 garlic cloves, minced
4 teaspoons lemon juice

1. On a plate, combine flour with oregano, salt, and pepper. Coat halibut with seasoned flour; shake off any excess.

2. In a large skillet, heat oil over medium heat. Add halibut and cook, turning, until fish just flakes, 3 to 5 minutes per side. Remove fish to warm serving platter.

3. Add butter to skillet, stir in garlic, and cook 30 seconds. Add lemon juice and pour butter over fish. Serve at once.

217   GRILLED HALIBUT WITH HORSERADISH BUTTER

Prep: 3 minutes   Cook: 7 to 11 minutes   Serves: 4

When making this sauce, just melt the butter. If the butter is too hot, it will cause the sauce to separate.

1½ to 2 pounds halibut steaks,
    cut about ¾ inch thick
1 tablespoon canola oil
¼ teaspoon salt
¼ teaspoon pepper

4 tablespoons butter
2 tablespoons prepared white
    horseradish
2 teaspoons minced fresh dill

1. Prepare a hot fire in a charcoal or gas grill, or preheat broiler. Rub halibut with oil and season with salt and pepper. Grill, 3 to 5 minutes per side, turning, until firm and just opaque throughout.

2. While halibut is grilling, melt butter in small saucepan, but do not boil. Remove butter from heat and stir in horseradish. Spoon horseradish butter over halibut. Sprinkle dill over top and serve.

218   BAKED HALIBUT STEAKS WITH TOMATO-WINE SAUCE

Prep: 5 minutes   Cook: 11 to 14 minutes   Serves: 4

3 tablespoons chopped
   shallots
1 to 1½ pounds halibut steaks,
   1 inch thick, cut into
   4 pieces
1 cup dry white wine

2 medium plum tomatoes,
   chopped
½ teaspoon dried tarragon
¼ teaspoon salt
⅛ teaspoon pepper
2 tablespoons olive oil

1. Preheat oven to 450°F. Sprinkle shallots over bottom of a 1½- to 2-quart baking dish. Place fish in shallow baking pan and pour in wine. Sprinkle chopped tomato, tarragon, salt, and pepper over fish. Drizzle with oil.

2. Bake 10 to 12 minutes, until fish is opaque throughout. Remove fish with a slotted spatula to a serving dish and peel off skin.

3. Set baking pan (if metal) over a stove burner or pour liquid and vegetables into a small saucepan. Boil over high heat until sauce reduces slightly, 1 to 2 minutes. Spoon sauce over fish and serve.

219   POACHED SALMON WITH SORREL SAUCE

Prep: 6 minutes   Cook: 8 minutes   Serves: 4

Sorrel is a tangy, lemony leaf with both a spring and a fall season. To make this sauce, roll sorrel leaves into a cylinder and cut with a large knife into thin ribbons.

4 salmon steaks, cut 1 inch
   thick (about 6 ounces
   each)
2 tablespoons butter
¼ cup chopped shallots
1 bunch of sorrel, cut into
   slivers (4 to 6 ounces)

¾ cup heavy cream
¼ teaspoon salt
⅛ teaspoon white pepper
⅛ teaspoon grated nutmeg

1. In a large skillet, bring 3 cups salted water to a boil over high heat. Place fish in water, adding additional water if necessary to cover. Return to a boil, reduce heat to low, cover, and cook until fish is opaque throughout, about 8 minutes. Remove with a slotted spatula and peel off skin.

2. Meanwhile, in a medium nonreactive saucepan or skillet, heat butter over medium heat. Add shallots and cook, stirring, until softened, about 1 minute. Add sorrel and cream and cook, stirring occasionally, until sorrel softens and cream reduces slightly, 3 to 4 minutes. Season with salt, pepper, and nutmeg. Spoon sauce over fish to serve.

220   POACHED SALMON STEAKS WITH VEGETABLES ORIENTALE

Prep: 8 minutes   Cook: 9 to 11 minutes   Serves: 4

1 cup dry white wine
2 teaspoons grated fresh
  ginger
½ teaspoon salt
1 pound salmon or halibut
  steaks, cut into 4 pieces
1 medium carrot, peeled and
  thinly sliced

2 ounces snow peas, trimmed
1½ teaspoons Asian sesame oil
1 teaspoon soy sauce
5 scallions, trimmed, halved
  lengthwise, and cut into
  1-inch lengths

1. In a large nonreactive skillet, combine wine, ginger, salt, and 1 cup water. Bring to a boil over high heat. Place fish in poaching liquid, adding additional water if necessary to cover. Return to a boil, reduce heat to medium-low, cover, and cook until fish is opaque throughout, 6 to 8 minutes. Remove fish from broth with a slotted spoon or spatula and peel off skin.

2. Add carrot and boil uncovered 2 minutes. Add snow peas and boil until carrots are crisp-tender and snow peas remain bright green, about 1 minute longer.

3. Stir in sesame oil, soy sauce, and scallions. To serve, spoon vegetables and some poaching broth over fish.

221   FILLET OF SOLE AMANDINE

Prep: 4 minutes   Cook: 6 to 8 minutes   Serves: 4

¼ cup flour
¼ teaspoon salt
¼ teaspoon pepper
1 pound fillets of gray sole or
  other thin fish fillets

2 tablespoons butter
2 tablespoons vegetable oil
½ cup sliced almonds
2 tablespoons lemon juice
1 tablespoon chopped parsley

1. On a plate, combine flour, salt, and pepper. Rinse fish under cold water and dip in seasoned flour to coat lightly.

2. In a large skillet, heat 1 tablespoon each of butter and oil over medium-high heat. Add fish and cook, turning once, until lightly browned outside and opaque in center, 4 to 5 minutes total. Remove fish to a serving platter.

3. Reduce heat to medium-low and add remaining butter and oil to pan. Add almonds and cook, stirring often, until nuts are fragrant and begin to color, 2 to 3 minutes. Stir in lemon juice and parsley. Spoon almonds over fish and serve.

222   SWORDFISH SYRACUSE
Prep: 5 minutes   Cook: 7 to 9 minutes   Serves: 4

This sauce has an interesting balance of sweet, salty, and tart flavors. If it is too sharp for your taste, swirl a tablespoon of butter into the sauce before serving.

3 **tablespoons flour**	¼ **cup pimiento-stuffed olives,**
¼ **teaspoon salt**	**sliced**
¼ **teaspoon pepper**	¼ **cup raisins**
2 **pounds swordfish steaks,**	4 **teaspoons capers**
cut ½ inch thick	¼ **cup red wine vinegar**
2 **tablespoons olive oil**	4 **teaspoons chopped mint**

1. On a plate, mix flour with salt and pepper. Dredge fish steaks in flour and pat off excess.

2. In large skillet, heat oil over medium-high heat. Add fish and cook, turning, until firm and just opaque throughout, 3 to 4 minutes per side. Stir in olives, raisins, and capers.

3. Remove fish to a warm serving platter. Add vinegar and mint to skillet and heat, stirring, for 1 minute. Spoon sauce over swordfish and serve.

223   CAJUN BLACKENED SNAPPER
Prep: 2 minutes   Cook: 14 to 16 minutes   Serves: 4

You can use almost any fish, though redfish, pompano, or black drum work particularly well in this Cajun specialty created by Paul Prudhomme. Be sure your stove is equipped with a good vent, because this cooking method can create a lot of smoke.

4 **skinless red snapper fillets,**	4 **teaspoons butter, melted**
6 to 8 ounces each	
4 **teaspoons "blackened"**	
spice seasoning blend	

1. Heat a large cast-iron skillet over medium-high heat until very hot, about 10 minutes. Skillet is correct temperature if a drop of water evaporates almost immediately when dropped on surface.

2. Sprinkle both sides of fish fillets with spice mixture to coat well. Place fish in hot skillet and cook until underside is dark brown, 2 to 3 minutes. Carefully spoon ½ teaspoon melted butter over each fillet. (Try to avoid spilling butter into pan; it may flare up).

3. Use a wide spatula to turn fish and spoon ½ teaspoon butter over blackened side of each fillet. Cook until underside is dark brown and fish is opaque but still moist in center, 2 to 3 minutes longer. Transfer to plates and serve at once.

224   GRILLED SWORDFISH WITH LEMON-CAPER BUTTER

Prep: 3 minutes   Cook: 6 to 10 minutes   Serves: 2 to 3

1 pound swordfish steaks, cut
    about ½ inch thick
2 teaspoons olive oil
⅛ teaspoon salt
⅛ teaspoon pepper

2 tablespoons butter
1 tablespoon lemon juice
1 tablespoon drained capers
2 garlic cloves, minced
⅛ teaspoon salt

1. Prepare a hot fire in a charcoal or gas grill, or preheat broiler. Brush swordfish with oil and season with salt and pepper. Grill or broil 3 to 5 minutes per side, until browned outside and just opaque throughout.

2. While fish is grilling, in a small saucepan, combine butter, lemon juice, capers, garlic, and salt. Heat on grill or stovetop until butter is melted and flavors have combined, 2 to 3 minutes.

3. Serve swordfish with butter sauce spooned on top.

225   GRILLED TUNA WITH TROPICAL SALSA

Prep: 10 minutes   Cook: 8 to 10 minutes   Serves: 4

1 ripe medium papaya,
    peeled, seeded, and
    chopped
½ cup chopped red onion
¼ cup chopped cilantro
2 tablespoons lime juice
1 tablespoon finely chopped
    jalapeño peppers, fresh
    or pickled

Salt
4 tuna steaks, ¾ inch thick
    (about 6 ounces each)
1 tablespoon olive oil
½ teaspoon paprika

1. Prepare a moderately hot fire in a charcoal or gas grill. In a medium bowl, combine papaya, red onion, cilantro, lime juice, and jalapeño peppers. Toss to mix. Season with salt to taste. (If using pickled jalapeños, no salt may be needed.)

2. Brush tuna steaks with oil and season with ½ teaspoon salt and paprika. Grill tuna, turning once, 8 to 10 minutes, until fish is lightly browned outside and just opaque in center. (For medium-rare center, cook a few minutes less.)

3. Transfer tuna to plates and top each fish steak with a spoonful of salsa. Pass remaining salsa on the side.

226 BEER BATTER–FRIED FISH
Prep: 5 minutes   Cook: 4 to 5 minutes   Serves: 4

Baking soda and beer are the secret ingredients to produce a crispy, crackly coating encasing the moist fish within. Any type of non-oily fish, including cod, catfish, scrod, sole, or haddock will work fine. Serve with French fries for a "fish and chips" meal.

1 cup flour	Vegetable oil, for frying
½ teaspoon baking soda	1 pound fish fillets, about
¼ teaspoon salt	½ inch thick
1 cup beer	Malt or cider vinegar

1. In a large bowl, whisk flour with baking soda and salt. Slowly whisk in beer and 2 tablespoons water. Whisk just until smooth; do not overmix.

2. In a large heavy (preferably cast-iron) skillet, heat about ½ inch of oil over medium heat to 375°F. When oil is correct temperature, a cube of bread will brown in 30 seconds.

3. Cut fish into rough 3-inch pieces. Dip in batter, letting excess drip back into bowl. Fry in hot oil, turning once, until crust is crisp and deep golden brown and fish is opaque but still moist within, 4 to 5 minutes. Drain on paper towels. (Frying may need to be done in two batches.) Pass vinegar at table to sprinkle on fish.

227 HERB AND CITRUS BROILED TROUT
Prep: 7 minutes   Cook: 8 to 9 minutes   Serves: 4

4 whole boned trout (about 8 ounces each)	2 tablespoons chopped fresh dill
1½ tablespoons olive oil	1 lemon, thinly sliced
½ teaspoon salt	1 lime, thinly sliced
¼ teaspoon pepper	Parsley and dill sprigs, for garnish
½ cup chopped parsley	

1. Preheat broiler. Rub cavities of trout with olive oil and season with half of salt and pepper. Stuff with chopped parsley and dill. Place a slice each of lemon and lime in cavities.

2. Oil a broiler pan. Brush trout with oil and season with remaining salt and pepper. Broil about 5 inches from heat about 5 minutes, until skin is brown and blistered. Turn with a spatula and broil 3 to 4 minutes, until trout are browned on second side and opaque throughout. Garnish with remaining lemon and lime slices and herb sprigs.

228 CRISPY OVEN-FRIED FISH
Prep: 3 minutes   Cook: 10 to 12 minutes   Serves: 4

If you have seasoned Italian dry bread crumbs, omit the dried herbs in this recipe. Choose a shallow baking sheet, such as a jelly-roll pan, so heat can circulate around the fish to brown it evenly.

1 **cup fine dry bread crumbs**	1 **pound fish fillets, about**
½ **teaspoon Italian seasoning**	½ **inch thick**
¼ **teaspoon salt**	4 **tablespoons butter, melted**
¼ **teaspoon black pepper**	4 **lemon wedges**
¼ **teaspoon cayenne**	

1. Preheat oven to 500°F. On a plate, combine bread crumbs, Italian seasoning, salt, pepper, and cayenne. Brush fish on both sides with melted butter, then dip in seasoned crumbs to coat completely. Arrange fillets at least 1 inch apart on a large, shallow baking sheet.

2. Bake in upper third of oven 10 to 12 minutes, until fish is crusty and golden outside and opaque in center. Serve with lemon wedges.

229 SEAFOOD BROCHETTES
Prep: 10 minutes   Cook: 6 to 8 minutes   Serves: 6

¼ **cup canola oil**	¾ **pound swordfish**
3 **tablespoons lime juice**	¾ **pound sea scallops**
4 **teaspoons sugar**	¾ **pound shelled and deveined**
4 **teaspoons hot pepper sauce**	**raw shrimp**
1½ **teaspoons minced fresh**	1 **medium green pepper, cut**
ginger	**into ¾-inch squares**
2 **garlic cloves, minced**	12 **to 18 cherry tomatoes**
½ **teaspoon salt**	

1. Prepare a moderately hot fire in a charcoal or gas grill, or preheat broiler. In a small bowl, whisk together oil, lime juice, sugar, hot sauce, ginger, garlic, and salt. Divide mixture into 2 portions, reserving one half to serve with brochettes.

2. Cut swordfish into ¾-inch cubes. Cut scallops in half. Alternate shrimp, scallops, swordfish, green pepper, and tomatoes on long metal skewers.

3. Brush brochettes with one portion of ginger mixture and grill or broil 3 to 4 minutes per side, until shrimp is pink, scallops are white, and swordfish is flaky. Serve with reserved ginger sauce.

230   MONTEGO BAY SEAFOOD STEW

Prep: 7 minutes   Cook: 10 to 12 minutes   Serves: 6

Serve this wonderful sweet-hot-spicy stew as is, accompanied by Cuban bread, or with a cup of cooked white rice added to the soup bowl.

1 (14- to 16-ounce) can stewed tomatoes
1 cup clam juice
1 cup dry white wine
⅔ cup cream of coconut
1 tablespoon finely chopped jalapeño peppers, fresh or pickled
2 teaspoons curry powder
1 pound firm fish fillets, such as monkfish, halibut, or red snapper, cut into 2-inch chunks

1 pound raw medium shelled and deveined shrimp
1 cup thinly sliced scallions
¼ cup lime juice
¼ cup chopped cilantro
½ teaspoon salt
¼ teaspoon pepper

1. In a large nonreactive saucepan, combine tomatoes, clam juice, wine, cream of coconut, and 2 cups water. Bring to a boil over high heat, breaking up tomatoes into small pieces and stirring to dissolve cream of coconut. Stir in jalapeños and curry powder. Reduce heat to medium, partially cover, and simmer 8 minutes to blend flavors.

2. Add fish, shrimp, scallions, and lime juice. Cook uncovered until shrimp turn pink and fish is opaque throughout, 2 to 4 minutes. Stir in cilantro and season with salt and pepper.

231   SUPER SHRIMP COCKTAIL

Prep: 3 minutes   Cook: none   Serves: 2 to 3

½ cup ketchup
1 to 2 teaspoons prepared white horseradish
½ to 1 teaspoon Tabasco sauce
½ teaspoon lemon juice

¾ cup shredded iceberg lettuce
½ pound cooked shelled and deveined shrimp
2 to 3 lemon wedges
2 to 3 parsley sprigs

1. In a small bowl, combine ketchup, horseradish, Tabasco, and lemon juice. Blend well.

2. Place lettuce on 2 or 3 chilled luncheon plates. Arrange shrimp on lettuce beds and top with cocktail sauce.

3. Garnish with lemon wedges and parsley. Serve well chilled.

232   SHRIMP DIJON

Prep: 5 minutes   Cook: 4 to 5 minutes   Serves: 2

1 cup heavy cream
1 tablespoon Dijon mustard
1 tablespoon chopped parsley
¼ teaspoon grated nutmeg
⅛ teaspoon pepper

¼ teaspoon lemon juice
1 tablespoon butter
½ pound raw peeled and
   deveined shrimp
2 teaspoons Cognac or brandy

1. In a large saucepan, combine cream, mustard, parsley, nutmeg, pepper, and lemon juice. Cook over medium-high heat until reduced to about ½ cup, 4 to 5 minutes.

2. Meanwhile, in a medium skillet over medium-high heat, melt butter. When butter begins to bubble, add shrimp and sauté until pink, 3 to 4 minutes. Do not overcook. Stir Cognac into sauce.

3. Place shrimp on a warm platter and cover with sauce.

233   CREOLE SHRIMP SAUTÉ

Prep: 5 minutes   Cook: 8 to 10 minutes   Serves: 6

Bay leaves should always be removed before serving. Warming the serving dish in the microwave will help keep food hot. Serve the shrimp and sauce over white rice.

2 (14½-ounce) cans Cajun-
   style stewed tomatoes
1 garlic clove, minced
1 teaspoon sugar
1 small bay leaf
½ teaspoon salt
½ teaspoon dried thyme leaves

¼ teaspoon pepper
2 dashes of Tabasco sauce or
   more to taste
2 tablespoons butter or canola
   oil
1½ pounds large peeled and
   deveined shrimp

1. In a large skillet, combine tomatoes, garlic, sugar, bay leaf, salt, thyme, pepper, and Tabasco. Boil over medium-high heat, stirring occasionally, until most of liquid has evaporated and sauce is thick, 8 to 10 minutes.

2. Meanwhile, in another large skillet, melt butter over medium-high heat. Add shrimp and cook, tossing, until pink and curled, about 3 minutes.

3. Transfer shrimp to a serving platter and cover with sauce.

234   GREEK SHRIMP SAUTÉ
Prep: 6 minutes   Cook: 7 to 9 minutes   Serves: 4

2 tablespoons olive oil
1 small onion, coarsely
     chopped
1 pound large raw shelled and
     deveined shrimp
1 (14½-ounce) can pasta-ready
     tomatoes
1 teaspoon dried oregano

¾ teaspoon fennel seeds
⅛ teaspoon salt
⅛ teaspoon crushed hot red
     pepper
6 ounces feta cheese,
     crumbled
1 tablespoon chopped parsley

1. In a large skillet, heat oil over medium-high heat. Add onion and cook, stirring occasionally, until softened, about 3 minutes.

2. Add shrimp and cook, stirring, 1 minute. Stir in tomatoes with their liquid, oregano, fennel seed, salt, and hot pepper. Cook until shrimp are pink and sauce is slightly reduced, 3 to 5 minutes.

3. Transfer shrimp and sauce to a warm platter. Sprinkle feta and parsley on top and serve at once.

235   SHRIMP NEWBURG
Prep: 2 minutes   Cook: 5 to 6 minutes   Serves: 2

3 tablespoons butter
1 tablespoon flour
1 cup half-and-half or light
     cream
2 tablespoons dry sherry
½ teaspoon paprika

1 egg yolk, beaten
1 teaspoon Cognac
½ pound small cooked shelled
     shrimp
3 slices of white bread, lightly
     toasted

1. In a large skillet, melt butter over medium heat. Add flour and cook, stirring constantly, about 1 minute. Whisk in half-and-half, sherry, and paprika. Bring to a boil and cook, stirring, until mixture is smooth and thickened, about 3 minutes.

2. Remove from heat and whisk in egg yolk and Cognac. Stir in shrimp and return to low heat. Cook, stirring constantly, until heated through, 1 to 2 minutes; do not let mixture boil.

3. Serve shrimp and sauce over toast points.

236   SHRIMP SCAMPI
Prep: 5 minutes   Cook: 4 to 5 minutes   Serves: 4

If you are in a hurry, buying peeled, deveined, ready-to-cook shrimp is worth the extra cost.

4 tablespoons butter	**¼ teaspoon pepper**
1½ pounds large raw shelled	**3 garlic cloves, minced**
and deveined shrimp	**¼ cup chopped parsley**
¼ teaspoon salt	**Lemon wedges**

1. In a large skillet, melt butter over medium-high heat. Add shrimp and cook, stirring often, until pink and curled, about 3 minutes. With a slotted spoon, remove to a warm platter. Season shrimp with salt and pepper.

2. Add garlic and parsley to skillet and cook over medium heat 30 seconds. Pour garlic butter over shrimp and serve at once.

237   SHRIMP AND PASTA PIRI PIRI
Prep: 3 minutes   Cook: 6 to 7 minutes   Serves: 3 to 4

Shrimp Piri Piri is Portuguese in origin. Traditionally the shrimp are tossed with olive oil, garlic, hot peppers, and salt. Using Chinese chile paste with garlic produces similar results and avoids a lot of mincing.

1 pound large raw peeled and	**Juice of 1 lemon**
deveined shrimp	**1 (9-ounce) package fresh**
¼ cup olive oil	**linguine**
2 teaspoons Chinese chile	**1½ tablespoons butter**
paste with garlic	**3 tablespoons grated**
¾ teaspoon salt	**Parmesan cheese**

1. In a medium bowl, toss shrimp with 2 tablespoons olive oil, 1 teaspoon chile paste, and ½ teaspoon salt.

2. Place a large nonstick skillet over medium-high heat. Add shrimp with its marinade and sauté until they turn pink, about 3 minutes. Squeeze lemon over shrimp. Remove shrimp with a slotted spoon and set aside.

3. Meanwhile, cook pasta in a large pot of rapidly boiling lightly salted water until barely tender, 2 to 3 minutes. Drain well.

4. Add pasta, remaining oil, butter, chile paste, and Parmesan cheese to skillet. Top with shrimp and toss together over medium heat until heated through, about 1 minute.

238   QUICK SHRIMP CURRY
Prep: 5 minutes   Cook: 5 to 7 minutes   Serves: 4

1½ cups quick-cooking rice
 1 tablespoon butter
 1 tablespoon vegetable oil
 1 small onion, chopped
 1 tablespoon flour
 1 tablespoon minced fresh
    ginger

 2 teaspoons curry powder
 1 pound raw peeled and
    deveined shrimp
 1 (14½-ounce) can vegetable
    broth
 ¼ cup mango chutney
 2 tablespoons raisins

1. Bring 1½ cups water to a boil. Add rice and butter, cover, and remove from heat.

2. In a large skillet, heat oil. Add onion and cook over medium-high heat until slightly softened, about 2 minutes. Stir in flour, ginger, and curry. Add shrimp and cook, stirring, 2 to 3 minutes, until pink.

3. Stir in broth, chutney, and raisins. Bring to a boil and cook, stirring, until sauce is slightly thickened, 1 to 2 minutes.

239   PAN-FRIED SEA SCALLOPS WITH LEMON BUTTER
Prep: 3 minutes   Cook: 4 to 5 minutes   Serves: 2

The larger, meatier sea scallops are wonderful cooked this way. If using smaller bay scallops in the recipe, reduce the cooking time by a minute or two.

¼ cup flour
 ½ teaspoon salt
 ¼ teaspoon pepper
 4 tablespoons butter

 8 to 10 ounces sea scallops
 1 tablespoon lemon juice
 2 teaspoons chopped parsley
 4 lemon wedges

1. In a bowl, combine flour, salt, and pepper. Dredge scallops in flour mixture; shake off excess.

2. In a large heavy skillet, melt 2 tablespoons butter over medium-high heat. Add scallops and cook, turning occasionally, until golden brown outside and opaque inside, 3 to 4 minutes. Remove with tongs to a plate.

3. Reduce heat to low. Add remaining butter to pan and cook, stirring up browned bits, until melted, about 1 minute. Whisk in lemon juice and parsley. Spoon over scallops and garnish with lemon wedges.

240   LOBSTER THERMIDOR
Prep: 2 minutes   Cook: 5 minutes   Serves: 3 to 4

This recipe for Lobster Thermidor is the best I have found. With pre-cooked cut-up lobster meat, which is available in fish markets and in some supermarket fish sections, it's quick and easy to make. This recipe doubles perfectly. For cost-conscious cooks, substitute an equal weight of surimi, such as sealegs, for the lobster. Serve over toast points.

2 tablespoons butter
1 pound cooked cubed lobster
   meat
2 tablespoons flour
1 teaspoon powdered
   mustard

½ teaspoon salt
Dash of cayenne
1 cup light cream or half-and-
   half
⅓ cup dry sherry
1 tablespoon minced parsley

1. In a large skillet, melt butter over medium heat. Add lobster and cook, tossing, until heated through, about 2 minutes.

2. Add flour, powdered mustard, salt, and cayenne. Cook, stirring, for 1 minute.

3. Stir in cream, sherry, and parsley. Cook, stirring, until sauce is smooth and thickened, about 2 minutes.

241   HOT CRAB ON TOAST
Prep: 5 minutes   Cook: 3 to 4 minutes   Serves: 4

Because this dish is so rich, a mere 6 to 8 ounces of crabmeat will serve 4 adequately. Accompany with a Bibb lettuce salad.

1 (6-ounce) can fancy white
   crabmeat, or ½ pound
   fresh lump crabmeat
1 egg yolk
1 tablespoon dry sherry
3 tablespoons butter
2 tablespoons flour
1 tablespoon minced shallot

½ teaspoon paprika
¼ teaspoon salt
1 cup light cream or half-and-
   half
4 slices of white bread, lightly
   toasted
1 tablespoon chopped parsley

1. If using canned crab, drain and rinse lightly. In a small bowl, beat egg yolk with sherry.

2. Melt butter in a medium saucepan over medium heat. Stir in flour, shallot, paprika, and salt. Cook, stirring constantly, 1 minute. Slowly whisk in cream and bring to a boil, stirring constantly until thickened and smooth, 1 to 2 minutes. Add crabmeat and cook 30 to 60 seconds to heat through.

3. Remove from heat and whisk in egg mixture. Spoon crab over toast and garnish with parsley.

242   BALTIMORE CRAB CAKES
Prep: 10 minutes   Cook: 10 minutes   Serves: 3

Lump crabmeat from the Chesapeake Bay makes the very best crab cakes, but other types, including good-quality canned crab, work fine, too.

½ cup mayonnaise
1 teaspoon Old Bay or other seafood seasoning
1 teaspoon Worcestershire sauce
1 teaspoon lemon juice
¼ teaspoon cayenne

12 ounces crabmeat, picked over
2 cups fresh bread crumbs
⅓ cup finely chopped scallions
2 tablespoons vegetable oil
3 lemon wedges
½ cup tartar sauce

1. In a large bowl, whisk mayonnaise with seafood seasoning, Worcestershire sauce, lemon juice, and cayenne. Add crabmeat, 1 cup of bread crumbs, and scallions. Stir gently to avoid breaking up crabmeat. Form mixture into 6 (½-inch) patties. Place remaining bread crumbs on a plate. Press crab cakes into crumbs, turning to coat completely.

2. In a large heavy skillet, heat oil. Add crab cakes and cook over medium heat, turning once, until brown and crisp outside and hot in center, about 10 minutes total. Serve with lemon wedges and tartar sauce.

243   QUICK CRAB CIOPPINO
Prep: 7 minutes   Cook: 13 minutes   Serves: 6

Use any kind of firm-fleshed fish, such as sea bass, red snapper, or monkfish, for this San Francisco specialty.

¼ cup olive oil
1 large leek (white and pale green), thinly sliced
4 garlic cloves, chopped
2 (14½-ounce) cans Italian-style stewed tomatoes
1 cup clam juice
1 cup dry white wine
1½ teaspoons Italian seasoning

2 bay leaves
1 pound firm white fish, cut into 1-inch pieces
1 pound crabmeat, picked over
1 (10½-ounce) can baby clams with juice
½ teaspoon pepper
Salt

1. In a large saucepan or soup pot, heat oil. Add leek and cook over medium-high heat, stirring frequently, until it begins to soften, about 2 minutes. Add garlic and cook, stirring, until fragrant, 1 minute.

2. Add tomatoes, clam juice, wine, Italian seasoning, and bay leaves. Bring to a boil over high heat, reduce heat to medium-low, and simmer uncovered until slightly reduced and thickened, about 7 minutes.

3. Add fish, crabmeat, and clams and simmer until fish is opaque, about 3 minutes. If stew is too thick, add up to 1 cup water. Remove and discard bay leaves. Season with pepper and salt to taste. (Clam juice is salty, so no salt may be needed.) Serve stew in shallow soup bowls.

244   STIR-FRIED SCALLOPS AND SNOW PEAS

Prep: 8 minutes   Cook: 3 minutes   Serves: 2

If you can't get the small bay or calico scallops, use large sea scallops, but cut them in quarters before stir-frying. Serve with rice or Oriental noodles.

1 tablespoon dry sherry
2 teaspoons soy sauce
1 teaspoon Asian sesame oil
½ teaspoon sugar
½ pound bay scallops
2 teaspoons cornstarch
¼ teaspoon salt
1 tablespoon peanut or other
     vegetable oil

1 tablespoon minced fresh
     ginger
3 ounces snow peas, strings
     removed
5 scallions, cut into 1-inch
     lengths

1. In a small bowl, combine sherry with soy sauce, sesame oil, sugar, and 1 tablespoon water. Whisk until sugar is dissolved. Set sauce aside.

2. In a small bowl, sprinkle scallops with cornstarch and salt. Toss to coat scallops evenly.

3. In a large skillet or wok, heat oil over high heat. Add scallops and stir-fry until pale golden, about 1 minute. Add ginger, snow peas, and scallions and stir-fry until snow peas are bright green, about 1 minute longer.

4. Reduce heat to medium-low. Add reserved sauce and cook, stirring frequently, until sauce thickens slightly and scallops and vegetables are well coated, about 1 minute.

Chapter 8

Poultry Pronto

For quick cooking and versatility, nothing beats the skinless, boneless cuts of chicken and turkey that are so prominently featured in supermarkets today. Boneless chicken breasts, breast tenders and thighs, chicken and turkey breast cutlets, turkey tenderloins, and ground turkey and chicken are so popular that a good portion of most supermarket meat cases is devoted to them. In fancy butcher shops boneless duck breasts are also available. Even Cornish game hens can be prepared in 20 minutes or less.

Besides being easy to prepare and fast cooking, skinless chicken and turkey are lower in fat and cholesterol than most meats. They take well to quick-cooking methods, such as grilling, sautéing, and stir-frying. And they blend with other ingredients for either a delicate or robust effect.

The recipes in this chapter reflect the versatility of chicken and turkey. Chicken Seville, with its delicate orange-flavored cream sauce, is subtle and elegant, Grilled Chicken Fajitas are fiery, and Fried Chicken with Peppery Pan Gravy is comforting, perfect for a cozy family meal. Serve Quick Coq au Vin for a crowd and Duck Breast with Cherries for a small, elegant dinner party. Turkey and Wild Mushroom Hash makes leftover turkey a treat for two.

---

245   CAJUN GRILLED CHICKEN
Prep: 3 minutes   Cook: 8 to 12 minutes   Serves: 4

The popularity of Louisiana cooking has brought a number of Cajun and Creole seasoning mixtures to the market. I'm particularly fond of the line introduced by New Orleans super chef Paul Prudhomme.

4 skinless, boneless chicken breast halves (about 5 ounces each)
2 teaspoons canola oil

1½ to 2 teaspoons Cajun or Creole seasoning
1 tablespoon chopped parsley

1. Prepare a hot fire in a charcoal or gas grill or preheat broiler. Place chicken between sheets of lightly moistened plastic wrap and pound to an even thickness of about ½ inch.

2. Brush both sides of chicken with oil and sprinkle with Cajun seasoning. Grill 5 to 6 inches from heat, turning, until cooked through, 4 to 6 minutes per side. Serve sprinkled with parsley.

246　GRILLED CHICKEN FAJITAS
Prep: 5 minutes　　Cook: 8 to 10 minutes　　Serves: 6

2　tablespoons vegetable oil
2　tablespoons lime juice
¾　teaspoon ground cumin
½　teaspoon salt
¼　teaspoon pepper
1½　pounds skinless, boneless
　　chicken breasts or thighs

6　large (10-inch) flour tortillas
1　cup prepared guacamole
3　cups shredded romaine
　　lettuce
1½　cups chunky salsa

1. Prepare a hot fire in a charcoal or gas grill. In a shallow dish, combine oil, lime juice, cumin, salt, and pepper. Mix well. Place chicken in oil mixture and turn to coat. Let stand 5 minutes.

2. Grill chicken, turning once or twice, until browned outside and white but still moist within, about 8 minutes for breasts, 10 for thighs. Wrap tortillas in foil and place on edge of grill to warm while chicken cooks.

3. Cut chicken crosswise into thin slices. Spread some guacamole on each tortilla, place chicken in center, and top with shredded lettuce and salsa. Roll up and eat.

247　GRILLED BOMBAY CHICKEN WITH CUCUMBER-YOGURT SAUCE
Prep: 5 minutes　　Cook: 8 minutes　　Serves: 4

Butterflied and flattened boneless chicken thighs also work beautifully in this recipe.

2　tablespoons olive oil
4　teaspoons curry powder
4　skinless, boneless chicken
　　breast halves (about
　　5 ounces each)

1　cup plain yogurt
½　cup chopped cucumber
⅓　cup chopped scallions
⅛　teaspoon cayenne

1. Prepare a hot fire in a charcoal or gas grill. In a shallow dish, mix oil and curry powder. Add chicken and turn to coat completely. Let stand 5 minutes.

2. Meanwhile, in a medium bowl, combine yogurt with cucumber, scallions, and cayenne. Stir to mix well.

3. Place chicken on grill and cook about 8 minutes, turning once or twice, until browned outside and white but still moist inside. Pass yogurt sauce at the table to spoon over chicken.

248   BOURBON-BARBECUED CHICKEN
Prep: 5 minutes   Cook: 13 minutes   Serves: 6

Your favorite bottled barbecue sauce will taste fabulous doctored up this way with bourbon, chopped onion, and a little lemon juice.

2 tablespoons vegetable oil
1 medium onion, chopped
¼ cup bourbon
1¼ cups barbecue sauce
1 tablespoon lemon juice

6 skinless, boneless chicken
   breast halves (about
   5 ounces each)
½ teaspoon pepper

1. Prepare a moderately hot fire in a charcoal or gas grill.

2. In a nonreactive medium saucepan, heat 1 tablespoon oil over medium-high heat. Add onion and cook, stirring often, until it begins to soften, about 4 minutes. Stir in bourbon, raise heat to high, and boil until most of liquid is evaporated, about 1 minute. Stir in barbecue sauce and lemon juice. Divide sauce into 2 portions, reserving half for basting and remainder to serve with chicken.

3. Brush chicken breasts with remaining 1 tablespoon oil and season with pepper. Place on grill and cook about 2 minutes, until lightly browned on bottom. Turn, brush with sauce, and cook 2 minutes on second side. Continue to cook, turning once or twice more and brushing with sauce, until chicken is browned outside and white but still moist inside, about 8 minutes total. Serve chicken with remaining barbecue sauce alongside.

249   GRILLED JERK CHICKEN WITH AVOCADO AND LIME
Prep: 2 minutes   Cook: 8 minutes   Serves: 4

Jerk sauce, the fiery Jamaican meat marinade, is increasingly available on the spice shelf or gourmet section of the supermarket. In this recipe, the spicy chicken is garnished with slices of buttery rich avocado and lime wedges, which moderate the heat slightly.

½ cup purchased jerk sauce
4 skinless, boneless chicken
   breast halves (about
   5 ounces each)

1 ripe avocado, peeled and
   sliced
1 lime, cut into wedges

1. Prepare a hot fire in a charcoal or gas grill or preheat broiler. In a shallow dish, pour jerk sauce over chicken; turn to coat completely.

2. Grill or broil chicken, turning once or twice and brushing with any jerk sauce remaining in dish, until meat is nicely browned outside and white but still moist inside, about 8 minutes total.

3. Slice chicken crosswise into ¾-inch strips and fan out on a platter, alternating with avocado slices. Garnish with lime wedges.

250   HONEY MUSTARD GRILLED CHICKEN
Prep: 5 minutes   Cook: 8 minutes   Serves: 6

Try different brands of honey mustard until you find one with a good balance of sweet and sharp flavors.

⅓ **cup honey mustard**
5 **tablespoons olive oil**
1 **teaspoon dried tarragon**
6 **skinless, boneless chicken breast halves (about 5 ounces each)**

¼ **teaspoon pepper**
½ **cup finely chopped scallions**

1. Prepare a moderately hot fire in a charcoal or gas grill. In a small bowl, whisk mustard with ¼ cup olive oil and tarragon.

2. Brush chicken breasts with remaining 1 tablespoon oil and season with pepper. Place on grill and cook about 2 minutes, until lightly browned on bottom. Turn, brush with honey mustard sauce, and cook 2 minutes on second side. Continue to cook, turning once or twice more and brushing with sauce, until chicken is browned outside and white but still moist inside, about 8 minutes total.

3. Sprinkle scallions on top before serving.

251   GREEK CHICKEN KEBABS
Prep: 6 minutes   Cook: 12 to 14 minutes   Serves: 4

If you use wooden kebab skewers here, be sure to soak them in cold water for at least 30 minutes to prevent burning.

1 **pound skinless, boneless chicken breasts**
1 **medium zucchini, scrubbed**
1 **white onion**
1 **red bell pepper**
1 **tablespoon olive oil**
2 **tablespoons lemon juice**

1 **garlic clove, minced**
½ **teaspoon dried oregano**
¼ **teaspoon salt**
¼ **teaspoon pepper**
1 **cup plain yogurt**
2 **garlic cloves, minced**
1 **tablespoon chopped parsley**

1. Prepare a hot fire in a charcoal or gas grill or preheat broiler. Cut chicken and zucchini into ¾- to 1-inch squares. Cut onion into 8 wedges and red pepper into 1-inch squares.

2. In a small bowl, whisk together olive oil, lemon juice, garlic, oregano, salt, and pepper. Set marinade aside.

3. Thread alternating pieces of chicken, zucchini, onion, and pepper onto small metal or long wooden kebab skewers.

4. Brush generously with marinade and grill or broil kebabs, turning once or twice and basting several times with marinade, until chicken is lightly browned outside and white in center, 6 to 7 minutes per side.

5. While chicken is cooking, mix yogurt, garlic, and parsley. Season with additional salt to taste. Serve kebabs with yogurt sauce on the side.

---

252 ISLAND CHICKEN KEBABS
Prep: 6 minutes   Cook: 8 to 10 minutes   Serves: 4

Freshly cut pineapple, packaged in its own juices, is available in the produce section of most supermarkets. The flavor is wonderfully fresh, and buying it prepared eliminates the mess of cutting up a fresh pineapple as well as saving lots of time.

½ cup pineapple jam
2 tablespoons lemon juice
1 tablespoon canola oil
2 teaspoons soy sauce
2 teaspoons minced fresh
   ginger
1¼ pounds skinless, boneless
   chicken breasts, cut into
   1-inch pieces

1 green bell pepper, cut into
   1-inch pieces
1 white onion, cut into
   8 wedges
1 pound fresh pineapple
   chunks
Salt and pepper

1. Prepare a hot fire in a charcoal or gas grill or preheat broiler. In a microwave-safe cup, microwave jam 30 to 60 seconds on High, or until hot. Stir in lemon juice, oil, soy sauce, and ginger until well blended.

2. On 4 (12-inch) metal skewers, alternate pieces of chicken, bell pepper, white onion, and pineapple chunks. Season lightly with salt and pepper and brush generously with pineapple sauce.

3. Place on hot grill and cook, turning, until chicken is browned on the outside and white but still moist inside, about 8 to 10 minutes total.

253   GRILLED CHICKEN SATAY
Prep: 9 minutes   Cook: 4 to 6 minutes
Serves: 6 as appetizer, 4 as main course

Either short metal or long bamboo skewers work fine for this Indonesian-style satay. If you use bamboo, soak them in water for at least 30 minutes before using to help prevent them from burning on the grill.

¼ cup peanut butter (smooth or chunky)
3 tablespoons lime juice
3 tablespoons soy sauce
1½ tablespoons finely chopped fresh ginger
2 garlic cloves, finely chopped
½ teaspoon ground cumin
½ teaspoon crushed hot red pepper
1 pound thinly sliced chicken breast cutlets, cut lengthwise into 2-inch-wide strips
4 lime wedges

1. Prepare a moderately hot fire in a charcoal or gas grill. In a shallow dish, whisk peanut butter with lime juice, soy sauce, ginger, garlic, cumin, and hot red pepper until well blended. Dip chicken strips into peanut mixture, turning to coat thoroughly. Thread chicken onto skewers and let stand 5 minutes.

2. Grill skewers, turning once or twice, until chicken is lightly browned outside and white in center, 4 to 6 minutes total. Serve satays with lime wedges.

254   DIABLO CHICKEN BREASTS
Prep: 4 minutes   Cook: 12 to 15 minutes   Serves: 4

Grind two or three slices of firm white bread in a food processor to make the bread crumbs for this particularly delicious deviled chicken.

3 tablespoons grainy Dijon mustard
3 tablespoons olive oil
¼ cup finely chopped scallions
½ teaspoon dried thyme leaves
1 cup fresh bread crumbs
¼ teaspoon cayenne
4 skinless, boneless chicken breast halves (about 5 ounces each)

1. Preheat oven to 475°F. In a shallow dish, whisk mustard with oil, scallions, and thyme. In another dish, toss bread crumbs with cayenne until combined.

2. Use heel of your hand or a mallet to pound thicker part of chicken breasts slightly to flatten to even thickness. Dip both sides of chicken in mustard mixture, then roll in crumbs to coat completely. Place 1 inch apart on a greased, shallow baking sheet.

3. Bake until crumbs are golden brown and chicken is white but still moist in center, 12 to 14 minutes. If crumbs are not brown enough, run under broiler for 1 minute to crisp.

255   CHICKEN DIJON
Prep: 5 minutes   Cook: 8 to 10 minutes   Serves: 4

4 skinless, boneless chicken
    breast halves (about
    5 ounces each)
½ teaspoon salt
½ teaspoon coarsely ground
    pepper
1 tablespoon olive oil
¼ cup mayonnaise

1½ tablespoons Dijon mustard
1 tablespoon lemon juice
1 tablespoon minced fresh or
    frozen chives or thinly
    sliced scallion greens
2 teaspoons minced fresh
    tarragon, or ½ teaspoon
    dried

1. Prepare a hot fire in a charcoal or gas grill, or preheat broiler. Place chicken between lightly moistened sheets of plastic wrap and pound to an even ½-inch thickness. Season with salt and pepper and coat with olive oil.

2. In a small bowl, combine mayonnaise, mustard, lemon juice, chives, and tarragon. Stir to mix well.

3. Grill or broil about 6 inches from heat 4 to 5 minutes per side, until chicken is lightly browned outside and white but still moist inside. Serve chicken with mustard sauce.

256   STIR-FRIED GINGER CHICKEN AND BROCCOLI
Prep: 5 minutes   Cook: 5 to 6 minutes   Serves: 4

To save time, buy the broccoli florets for this dish already prepared. Serve this spicy stir-fry over a bed of oriental noodles or vermicelli.

½ cup reduced-sodium
    chicken broth
1 tablespoon soy sauce
1 teaspoon cornstarch
1 pound skinless, boneless
    chicken breasts
¼ teaspoon salt
⅛ teaspoon pepper

2 tablespoons peanut or other
    vegetable oil
4 cups broccoli florets (about
    12 ounces)
2 garlic cloves, finely chopped
1 tablespoon finely chopped
    fresh ginger

1. In a small bowl, stir together chicken broth with soy sauce and cornstarch until cornstarch dissolves. Set aside.

2. Cut chicken crosswise into ¼-inch slices and season with salt and pepper. In a wok or very large skillet, heat oil over high heat. Add chicken and broccoli and stir-fry until chicken is white throughout and broccoli is crisp-tender, 2 to 3 minutes. Add garlic and ginger and stir-fry until fragrant, 1 minute longer. Reduce heat to medium.

3. Stir sauce mixture again to mix, pour into pan, and cook, stirring, until sauce thickens and turns translucent, about 2 minutes.

257 LEMON CHICKEN AND ASPARAGUS STIR-FRY

Prep: 10 minutes   Cook: 5 to 6 minutes   Serves: 4

Make this lovely, lemony stir-fry in the spring when you can get tender, slim asparagus, and serve it over fluffy white rice.

1 cup reduced-sodium chicken broth
2 teaspoons cornstarch
1 teaspoon soy sauce
3 tablespoons lemon juice
1 tablespoon grated lemon zest
1 pound skinless, boneless chicken breasts
½ teaspoon salt

¼ teaspoon white pepper
2 tablespoons peanut or other vegetable oil
12 ounces slender asparagus, cut into 2-inch lengths
1 large celery rib, thinly sliced on diagonal (1 cup)
8 scallions, trimmed and cut into 2-inch lengths

1. In a small bowl, stir chicken broth with cornstarch and soy sauce until cornstarch dissolves. Stir in lemon juice and lemon zest. Set sauce aside.

2. Cut chicken crosswise into ¼-inch slices and season with salt and pepper. In a wok or very large skillet, heat oil over high heat. Add chicken, asparagus, and celery and stir-fry until chicken is white throughout and vegetables are crisp-tender, 2 to 3 minutes. Add scallions and stir-fry until slightly wilted, about 1 minute. Reduce heat to medium.

3. Stir sauce mixture again to mix, pour into pan, and cook, stirring, until sauce thickens and turns translucent, about 2 minutes.

258 BUFFALO WINGS

Prep: 8 minutes   Cook: 10 to 12 minutes
Serves: 4 to 5 as appetizers, 2 to 3 as main course

Invented at a bar in Buffalo, New York, these spicy chicken wings have become an American favorite. Tradition calls for serving the wings with celery sticks and creamy blue cheese dressing. To eat, you alternate dipping a wing and then a celery stick into the dressing.

12 chicken wings (about 2½ pounds)
Salt and pepper
Vegetable oil, for frying
3 tablespoons butter, melted
3 tablespoons Tabasco or other hot sauce

3 medium celery ribs, cut 3 inches long and ½ inch wide
1½ cups creamy, chunky blue cheese dressing

1. Use a cleaver or large knife to cut wings in half through joint; cut off and discard wing tips. Season chicken lightly with salt and pepper.

2. In a large heavy skillet, heat about ½ inch oil to 365°F. over medium-high heat. A cube of bread browns in 30 seconds when oil is correct temperature. Fry chicken in hot oil, turning once or twice, until skin is crisp and golden and meat is white but still moist within, 10 to 12 minutes. Remove with tongs and drain on paper towels.

3. Transfer wings to a platter. Combine melted butter and hot pepper sauce and pour over wings, tossing to coat. Serve wings with celery sticks and blue cheese dressing alongside for dipping.

259 CAJUN CHICKEN SAUCE PIQUANTE
Prep: 5 minutes   Cook: 13 to 15 minutes   Serves: 4

By using canned stewed tomatoes, which contain onion, green pepper, and other seasonings, this classic Cajun chicken dish can be brought in under the 20-minute time limit. True to Cajun tradition, the sauce is very spicy, so be forewarned! Serve the dish accompanied by plain steamed white rice.

½ teaspoon salt	1 (14½-ounce) can Cajun-style
⅛ teaspoon cayenne	or Mexican-style stewed
⅛ teaspoon white pepper	tomatoes
⅛ teaspoon black pepper	1 bay leaf
4 skinless, boneless chicken	1½ tablespoons red wine
thighs (about 5 ounces	vinegar
each), cut in half	¾ teaspoon Tabasco sauce
crosswise	½ teaspoon dried thyme
2 tablespoons vegetable oil	½ cup finely chopped scallions
2 tablespoons flour	
1 cup chicken broth,	
preferably reduced-	
sodium	

1. In a shallow dish, mix salt with cayenne, white pepper, and black pepper. Roll chicken in pepper mixture to coat all over.

2. In a large skillet, heat oil over medium-high heat. Add chicken and cook, turning once, until lightly browned on both sides, about 4 minutes total. With tongs, remove to a plate.

3. Reduce heat to medium and sprinkle flour over pan drippings and cook, stirring constantly, until medium-dark brown, 2 to 3 minutes. Add chicken broth, tomatoes, and bay leaf. Bring to a boil over high heat, stirring, until liquid is thickened and smooth.

4. Return chicken and any juices to sauce. Add vinegar, Tabasco, and thyme. Reduce heat to medium-low. Cook uncovered until sauce thickens and chicken is white but still moist in center, 7 to 8 minutes. Remove bay leaf. Sprinkle with chopped scallions before serving.

260   CHICKEN BREASTS WITH SAGE-CORNBREAD STUFFING

Prep: 3 minutes   Cook: 13 to 16 minutes   Serves: 4

Packaged cornbread stuffing (the crushed type, not bread cubes) makes a great topping for sautéed chicken breasts.

4 skinless, boneless chicken
   breast halves (about
   5 ounces each)
¼ teaspoon salt
¼ teaspoon pepper
1½ teaspoons dried sage

3 tablespoons butter
1 medium onion, chopped
1½ cups packaged cornbread
   stuffing mix
¾ cup reduced-sodium
   chicken broth

1. Preheat broiler. Season chicken breasts with salt, pepper, and ½ teaspoon sage.

2. In a large skillet, melt 2 tablespoons butter over medium-high heat. Add chicken breasts and cook, turning once, until golden brown outside and white but still moist within, 6 to 8 minutes. Remove with tongs to a broiler pan, leaving drippings in pan.

3. Add remaining 1 tablespoon butter to skillet. Add onion and remaining 1 teaspoon sage and cook, stirring frequently, until onion is lightly browned and softened, about 4 minutes. Stir in stuffing mix and broth. Reduce heat to medium and cook, stirring frequently, until liquid is absorbed but stuffing is still moist, about 2 minutes.

4. Spoon and pat stuffing atop each chicken breast. Broil about 5 inches from heat 1 to 2 minutes, until stuffing is crisp and golden brown.

261   MEXICAN CHICKEN STIR-FRY

Prep: 6 minutes   Cook: 6 to 8 minutes   Serves: 4

Stir-frying has become such a popular cooking method that it's being adapted to other ethnic cuisines. This Mexican version requires a minimum of chopping and is both quick and tasty. Serve over steamed rice.

1 pound chicken breast
   tenders
1 teaspoon chili powder
½ teaspoon ground cumin
¼ teaspoon dried oregano
2 tablespoons olive oil
1 garlic clove, minced
2 scallions, chopped

1 (15-ounce) can black beans,
   rinsed and drained
1 (11-ounce) can Mexicorn,
   with its liquid
1 (4-ounce) can chopped mild
   green chiles
¼ cup salsa
1 tablespoon minced cilantro

1. In a bowl, toss chicken with chili powder, cumin, oregano, and 1 tablespoon olive oil.

2. Heat a wok or large nonstick skillet over medium-high heat. When hot, coat with remaining 1 tablespoon oil. Add chicken tenders and stir-fry 4 to 5 minutes, until barely cooked through. Add the scallions, beans, corn, and chiles. Stir-fry 2 to 3 minutes, until heated through.

3. Stir in salsa and cilantro and serve.

262 QUICK CHICKEN CACCIATORE
Prep: 4 minutes   Cook: 12 minutes   Serves: 4

Domestic, or white button, mushrooms are just fine in this savory cacciatore (or "hunter-style" chicken), but if your supermarket produce department has fresh cremini or shiitake mushrooms, use them to turn the dish into something really very special.

4 skinless, boneless chicken thighs (about 5 ounces each), cut into 3-inch pieces	2 cups sliced fresh mushrooms (about 6 ounces)
¼ teaspoon salt	3 garlic cloves, minced
¼ teaspoon pepper	1 (28-ounce) can crushed tomatoes in puree
3 tablespoons olive oil	2 teaspoons Italian seasoning
	2 tablespoons lemon juice

1. Season chicken with salt and pepper. In a large skillet, heat 2 tablespoons oil over medium-high heat. Add chicken and cook, turning once, until brown on both sides, about 4 minutes total. Remove with tongs to a plate, leaving drippings in pan.

2. Reduce heat to medium and add remaining 1 tablespoon oil to skillet. Add mushrooms and garlic and cook, stirring often, until mushrooms wilt and begin to brown, about 3 minutes.

3. Add tomatoes and Italian seasoning and return chicken and any accumulated juices to pan. Bring to a boil over high heat, reduce heat to medium-low, and simmer uncovered until chicken is no longer pink in center, about 5 minutes. Stir in lemon juice.

263   QUICK COQ AU VIN

Prep: 3 minutes   Cook: 16 to 17 minutes   Serves: 6

Using packaged sliced fresh mushrooms, which are available in many supermarket produce departments, cuts preparation time for this French classic to a minimum. Serve with boiled red potatoes and a big green salad. It's a terrific dish for an informal dinner party.

8 slices of bacon, coarsely chopped	2 cups sliced mushrooms (about 6 ounces)
½ cup flour	1½ cups dry red wine
½ teaspoon pepper	1 cup reduced-sodium chicken broth
6 skinless, boneless chicken thighs (about 5 ounces each), cut into 3-inch pieces	2½ cups frozen pearl onions
	2 teaspoons dried thyme leaves

1. In a large skillet, cook bacon over medium-high heat, stirring frequently, until browned and crisp, 5 to 6 minutes. Remove with a slotted spoon and drain on paper towels. Pour off drippings, but leave 3 tablespoons in pan.

2. Meanwhile, combine flour and pepper on a plate. Coat chicken pieces with flour, shaking off excess. When bacon is removed, add chicken to drippings in pan and cook, turning, until browned, about 4 minutes total. Remove with tongs to a plate.

3. Add mushrooms to pan and cook, stirring, until lightly browned and beginning to wilt, about 2 minutes. Add wine, broth, pearl onions, and thyme and return chicken and any accumulated juices to sauce. Bring to a boil over high heat. Reduce heat to medium and cook uncovered until sauce is somewhat reduced, chicken is white in center, and onions are tender, about 5 minutes. Scatter reserved bacon over chicken and heat through before serving.

264   CHICKEN MARSALA

Prep: 5 minutes   Cook: 8 minutes   Serves: 2

1 pound chicken breast tenders	½ cup sliced fresh mushrooms
¼ teaspoon salt	⅓ cup Marsala
¼ teaspoon pepper	¼ cup heavy cream
1 tablespoon butter	½ teaspoon lemon juice
	1 tablespoon chopped parsley

1. Season chicken with salt and pepper. In a large nonstick skillet, melt butter over medium-high heat. Add mushrooms and chicken. Cook, stirring often, until golden brown, about 3 minutes.

2. Stir in Marsala, cream, and lemon juice. Lower heat to medium, partially cover with a lid, and cook until chicken is cooked through and sauce has thickened slightly, about 5 minutes. Sprinkle with parsley and serve.

265 GINGER CHICKEN SAUTÉ

Prep: 3 minutes   Cook: 10 to 14 minutes   Serves: 4

4 skinless, boneless chicken
    breast halves (about
    5 ounces each)
2 tablespoons soy sauce
¼ to ½ teaspoon hot sesame oil

1 tablespoon minced fresh
    ginger
1 garlic clove, minced
1 tablespoon peanut or
    canola oil

1. Place chicken in a shallow baking dish. Add soy sauce, sesame oil, ginger, and garlic. Turn chicken to coat well with seasonings.

2. In a large nonstick skillet, heat oil over medium-high heat. Remove chicken from marinade; reserve marinade. Add chicken to hot skillet and cook, turning, until lightly browned, 2 to 3 minutes per side.

3. Reduce heat to medium-low and stir in marinade. Cover and cook, turning 2 to 3 times, until chicken is white but still moist inside, 6 to 8 minutes.

266 GARLIC CHICKEN

Prep: 4 minutes   Cook: 10 to 12 minutes   Serves: 3 to 4

To impart flavor to a dish with less mincing and chopping, add slightly crushed fresh herb sprigs, garlic cloves, or hot chiles to the oil when heating it. The whole seasonings are easy to retrieve with a slotted spoon and discard.

6 skinless, boneless chicken
    thighs (about 5 ounces
    each)
¼ teaspoon salt
¼ teaspoon pepper

2 tablespoons olive oil
12 to 14 fresh rosemary sprigs
8 garlic cloves—6 smashed,
    2 minced

1. Place chicken between sheets of lightly moistened plastic wrap and pound to an even thickness of about ½ inch. Season with salt and pepper.

2. In a large heavy skillet, combine oil, 8 sprigs of rosemary, and smashed garlic. Cook over medium-low heat until garlic is golden, pressing rosemary sprigs and garlic cloves to release flavor, about 2 minutes. With a slotted spoon, remove and discard flavorings.

3. Place chicken in hot skillet and cook over medium-high heat, turning, until cooked through and golden brown on both sides, about 4 to 5 minutes per side. During last 2 minutes of cooking, add minced garlic and stir to cook and coat chicken pieces. Serve chicken, garnished with remaining rosemary sprigs.

267   CHICKEN PARISIAN
Prep: 5 minutes   Cook: 10 to 13 minutes   Serves: 4

1   tablespoon butter
4   skinless, boneless chicken
    breast halves (about
    5 ounces each)
4   teaspoons chopped shallots
¼   cup Cognac
½   cup heavy cream

4   teaspoons Parisian-style
    Dijon mustard
¼   cup chopped parsley
1   teaspoon chopped fresh
    thyme or ¼ teaspoon
    dried
¼   teaspoon salt
¼   teaspoon pepper

1. In a large nonstick skillet, melt butter over medium heat. Add chicken and cook, turning, until lightly browned outside and white in center, 4 to 5 minutes per side. Remove with tongs to a warm serving platter.

2. In same skillet, cook shallots until softened, 1 to 2 minutes. Remove from heat and pour in Cognac.

3. Return to heat and whisk in cream, mustard, parsley, thyme, salt, and pepper until well blended. Bring to a boil and cook until sauce thickens, about 1 minute. Spoon sauce over chicken and serve.

268   PECAN CHICKEN SAUTÉ
Prep: 5 minutes   Cook: 11 minutes   Serves: 4

The richness of pecans makes an unbelievably delicious crust for these sautéed chicken breasts.

¾   cup pecans
2   tablespoons flour
4   skinless, boneless chicken
    breast halves (about
    5 ounces each)
½   teaspoon salt
¼   teaspoon pepper

2½   tablespoons butter
3   tablespoons finely chopped
    shallots
1   teaspoon crumbled dried
    sage leaf
½   cup dry white wine

1. In a food processor, combine pecans and flour. Pulse until nuts are finely chopped but not oily. Transfer to a plate. Season chicken breasts with salt and pepper and dredge in pecan crumbs, pressing so coating adheres.

2. In a large skillet, melt 2 tablespoons butter over medium heat. Add chicken and cook, turning once, until crust is browned and meat is white but still moist inside, about 8 minutes total. Remove with tongs to a warm platter, leaving drippings in pan.

3. Melt remaining ½ tablespoon butter in skillet. Add shallots and sage and cook, stirring, until fragrant, about 30 seconds. Add wine, raise heat to high, and boil until slightly reduced, about 2 minutes. Pour sauce over chicken to serve.

269   CHICKEN SEVILLE

Prep: 5 minutes   Cook: 10 to 14 minutes   Serves: 4

The Spanish city of Seville is surrounded by fragrant orange groves and within reach of the vineyards of Jerez de la Frontera, where the world's best sherry is produced. These products, as well as the ground ginger that reflects the Moorish influence in Spanish cooking, come together in this easy, elegant dish. Serve it with hot fluffy rice and a green salad.

4 skinless, boneless chicken
   breast halves (about
   5 ounces each)
   Salt and pepper
½ cup orange juice
½ cup heavy cream

1 tablespoon medium-dry
   sherry
¼ teaspoon ground ginger
2 tablespoons butter
1 tablespoon chopped parsley

1. Place chicken between slightly moistened sheets of plastic wrap and pound to an even thickness of about ¾ inch. Pat chicken dry with paper towels and season with salt and pepper.

2. In a small bowl, combine orange juice, cream, sherry, and ginger. Blend well.

3. In a large skillet, melt butter over medium heat. When butter begins to bubble, add chicken and cook, turning, until lightly browned, 2 to 3 minutes on each side.

4. Reduce heat to medium-low and stir in orange juice mixture. Continue to cook, turning 2 to 3 times, until chicken is white inside but still moist, 6 to 8 minutes. Remove chicken to a platter. Spoon sauce in pan over chicken and garnish with parsley.

270 SOUTHWEST CHICKEN AND HOMINY STEW

Prep: 4 minutes   Cook: 12 minutes   Serves: 4

Hominy is hulled corn kernels. Although also available dried, it is readily found in cans in many regions of the country. In this recipe, if you cannot find hominy, substitute the same quantity of frozen corn kernels.

4 skinless, boneless chicken breast halves (about 5 ounces each), cut in half crosswise	2 (14½-ounce) cans Mexican-style stewed tomatoes
2 teaspoons ground cumin	1 (15-ounce) can hominy, drained
¼ teaspoon salt	¼ cup chopped canned green chiles
¼ teaspoon pepper	3 tablespoons chopped cilantro
2 tablespoons vegetable oil	
3 garlic cloves, minced	

1. Season chicken on both sides with cumin, salt, and pepper. In a large skillet, heat oil over medium-high heat. Add chicken and cook on both sides until lightly browned, about 4 minutes total.

2. Reduce heat to low, add garlic, and cook, stirring, 1 minute. Add tomatoes, hominy, and green chiles. Bring to a boil over high heat, reduce to medium-low, partially cover, and cook until sauce thickens somewhat and chicken is white in center but still moist, about 7 minutes. Stir in cilantro and serve.

271 CHICKEN AND VEGETABLE FRICASSEE

Prep: 3 minutes   Cook: 11 to 13 minutes   Serves: 4

Serve this quick country-style chicken and vegetable stew with mashed potatoes (the frozen ones are fine) and a tossed green salad.

¼ cup flour	1 cup chicken broth, preferably reduced-sodium
¼ teaspoon salt	
¼ teaspoon cayenne	1 (10-ounce) package frozen mixed vegetables
1 pound skinless, boneless chicken breasts or thighs, cut into 3-inch pieces	1½ teaspoons dried thyme leaves
2 tablespoons vegetable oil	1½ teaspoons Worcestershire sauce
1 large onion, sliced	
1 (14½-ounce) can stewed tomatoes	

1. In a shallow dish, combine flour, salt, and cayenne. Dredge chicken in flour, shaking off excess. Heat oil in a large skillet over medium-high heat. Add chicken pieces and sliced onion. Cook, turning and stirring frequently, until both are lightly browned, about 4 minutes.

2. Add tomatoes, chicken broth, and vegetables, breaking tomatoes up into smaller pieces with side of a spoon. Bring to a boil over high heat. Add thyme and Worcestershire.

3. Reduce heat to low and cook uncovered until sauce thickens somewhat, chicken is white but still moist in center, and vegetables are tender, 7 to 9 minutes.

---

272 SAUTÉED CHICKEN PROVENÇAL
Prep: 5 minutes   Cook: 10 to 14 minutes   Serves: 4

Oil-marinated sun-dried tomatoes and the new seasoned forms of stewed tomatoes are convenient, high-quality staples to have on hand. In this recipe, both are used.

4 skinless, boneless chicken breast halves (about 5 ounces each)	1 (14½-ounce) can pasta-ready tomatoes
2 teaspoons herbes de Provence or Italian seasoning	1 to 2 garlic cloves, minced
½ teaspoon salt	1½ tablespoons balsamic vinegar, or 1 tablespoon red wine vinegar
⅛ teaspoon pepper	1 teaspoon sugar
1½ tablespoons olive oil	1 tablespoon slivered fresh basil
¼ cup chopped dried tomatoes	

1. Pat chicken dry and season with herbes de Provence, salt, and pepper.

2. In a large nonstick skillet, heat olive oil over medium-high heat. Add chicken and cook, turning, until lightly browned, about 2 to 3 minutes per side.

3. Add sun-dried tomatoes, canned tomatoes, garlic, vinegar, and sugar to skillet. Reduce heat to medium-low and cook until chicken is no longer pink inside and sauce has thickened, 6 to 8 minutes. Sprinkle with basil and serve.

273   POACHED CHICKEN WITH GREEN SAUCE
Prep: 10 minutes   Cook: 7 minutes   Chill: 10 minutes   Serves: 4

This light and lovely poached chicken with green herb sauce is perfect for supper on a warm summer evening. The recipe can also be increased and served as part of a buffet for a large summertime party.

1 **pound skinless, boneless chicken breast halves**	¾ **cup fresh basil leaves**
½ **teaspoon salt**	1 **large garlic clove**
¼ **teaspoon pepper**	2 **teaspoons Dijon mustard**
1½ **cups parsley sprigs**	1 **teaspoon drained capers**
	¾ **cup mayonnaise**

1. Season chicken with salt and pepper. Place in a large saucepan or skillet, cover with water, and bring just to a boil over medium-high heat. Reduce heat to low, cover, and simmer until chicken is white but still moist throughout, about 7 minutes. Transfer to a plate and refrigerate until cool, about 10 minutes.

2. Meanwhile, in a food processor, finely chop parsley, basil, garlic, mustard, and capers. Add mayonnaise and process until almost smooth, stopping occasionally to scrape down bowl.

3. Cut chicken crosswise on the diagonal into ½-inch slices, fan out onto a plate, and coat lightly with sauce.

274   SICILIAN CHICKEN
Prep: 5 minutes   Cook: 10 to 13 minutes   Serves: 4

The sophisticated blending of sweet and savory flavors in this chicken sauté shows the influence of early Saracen invaders on the cooking of Sicily. Serve over couscous or rice.

4 **skinless, boneless chicken breast halves (about 5 ounces each)**	1 **(14½-ounce) can pasta-ready chopped tomatoes**
1 **teaspoon Italian seasoning**	½ **teaspoon cinnamon**
Salt and pepper	1 **tablespoon honey**
2 **tablespoons olive oil**	2 **tablespoons red wine vinegar**
1 **medium onion, chopped**	

1. Pat chicken dry with paper towels and sprinkle with ½ teaspoon Italian seasoning and salt and pepper to taste.

2. In a large nonreactive skillet, heat oil over medium-high heat. Add chicken and cook until brown on bottom, 2 to 3 minutes. Turn over and stir in onion and remaining Italian seasoning. Cook 2 minutes longer.

3. Add tomatoes and cinnamon. Dissolve honey in vinegar and pour into pan. Bring to a boil, reduce heat to medium-low, cover, and cook until chicken is no longer pink inside, 6 to 8 minutes.

275   FRIED CHICKEN WITH PEPPERY PAN GRAVY

Prep: 5 minutes   Cook: 13 minutes   Serves: 1 to 2

This is a quick way to make old-fashioned fried chicken for one to two people. Evaporated skim milk gives the gravy richness with fewer calories and less fat and cholesterol. Serve chicken with Garlic-Chive Mashed Potatoes (page 112) or Cheddar Cheese Drop Biscuits (page 99).

2 skinless, boneless chicken
    breast halves or thighs
    (about 5 ounces each)
1 (12-ounce) can evaporated
    skim milk
1 teaspoon lemon juice

⅓ cup flour
½ teaspoon salt
½ teaspoon coarsely ground
    pepper
¼ teaspoon cayenne
⅓ cup canola oil

1. Place chicken between sheets of lightly moistened plastic wrap and pound to an even thickness of about ½ inch. Trim off and discard any excess fat.

2. Place ⅓ cup evaporated milk in a shallow bowl and stir in lemon juice. On a plate, combine flour, salt, pepper, and cayenne. Dip chicken in milk and then in seasoned flour. Reserve remaining flour for gravy.

3. In a large skillet, heat oil over medium-high heat. When a little flour sizzles when dropped in oil, add chicken. Fry, turning, until golden brown and cooked through, about 5 minutes on each side. Remove chicken and keep warm.

4. Add remaining flour to about 3 tablespoons of pan drippings. Cook, stirring, over medium-high heat until flour has a golden tinge, about 1 minute. Gradually stir in remaining evaporated milk. Cook, stirring, until gravy is smooth and thickened, about 2 minutes. Spoon gravy over chicken and serve at once.

276   TENDERS PEPPERONATA

Prep: 5 minutes   Cook: 7 to 9 minutes   Serves: 2 to 3

Serve this quick dish with hot crusty garlic bread.

1 pound chicken breast tenders	1 medium red bell pepper, thinly sliced
1½ teaspoons Italian seasoning	1 small onion, thinly sliced
¼ teaspoon salt	⅓ cup olive-oil and balsamic
⅛ teaspoon crushed hot red pepper	vinegar vinaigrette salad dressing
1½ tablespoons olive oil	1½ tablespoons drained capers

1. Season chicken tenders with Italian seasoning, salt, and hot pepper. In a large skillet, preferably nonstick, heat oil over medium-high heat. Add tenders and cook, turning, until browned, about 1 minute on each side.

2. Add bell pepper and onion. Cook, stirring occasionally, until vegetables are slightly softened, 2 to 3 minutes.

3. Reduce heat to medium-low. Stir in salad dressing and capers. Cook until chicken is white but still moist inside and vegetables are crisp-tender, 3 to 4 minutes.

277   AUSTRIAN CHICKEN SCHNITZELS

Prep: 3 minutes   Cook: 4 to 6 minutes per batch   Serves: 3 to 4

This chicken variation on the traditional *Wiener schnitzel* is perhaps even more tender than veal and certainly less expensive. Already sliced or pounded chicken breast cutlets are widely available in many supermarkets. If you cannot find them, buy skinless, boneless chicken breast halves and pound as described below.

1¼ pounds thinly sliced chicken breast cutlets	2 teaspoons lemon-pepper seasoning
1 egg	¼ teaspoon paprika
1¼ cups bread crumbs	⅛ teaspoon salt
2 teaspoons minced fresh dill or ½ teaspoon dried	2 to 3 tablespoons butter or vegetable oil

1. Preheat oven to 250°F. If necessary, use a meat pounder or bottom of a heavy saucepan to pound chicken between lightly moistened sheets of plastic wrap to an even thickness of ¼ inch.

2. In a shallow bowl, beat egg with 1 tablespoon water. On a large plate, combine bread crumbs with dill, lemon-pepper, paprika, and salt. Dip cutlets in beaten egg, then dredge in seasoned crumbs to coat.

3. In a large skillet, melt 2 tablespoons butter over medium-high heat. When butter begins to bubble, add schnitzels in batches without crowding and cook, turning once, until golden brown and cooked through, 2 to 3 minutes per side. As schnitzels are cooked, remove them to a baking sheet and set in oven to keep warm. Add remaining butter to pan as needed.

278   BARCELONA CHICKEN WITH RICE AND SPANISH OLIVES

Prep: 6 minutes   Cook: 9 to 11 minutes   Serves: 4

Quick-cooking rice works beautifully in this recipe, which imbues it with the lusty flavors of garlic, onion, ham, olives, and well-flavored chicken broth.

1 pound skinless, boneless chicken breasts, cut into 2-inch pieces	3 garlic cloves, minced
¼ teaspoon pepper	2 cups quick-cooking rice
3 tablespoons olive oil	2 cups reduced-sodium chicken broth
1 large onion, coarsely chopped	1 cup sliced green pimiento-stuffed olives
1 cup diced smoked ham (about 4 ounces)	

1. Season chicken with pepper. In a large skillet, heat 2 tablespoons oil over medium-high heat. Add chicken and cook, turning once, until brown outside and white but still moist in center, 4 to 6 minutes total. Remove with tongs to a platter, leaving drippings in pan.

2. Reduce heat to medium and add remaining 1 tablespoon oil to skillet. Add onion and ham and cook, stirring frequently, until both are lightly browned and onion begins to soften, about 4 minutes. Add garlic and cook, stirring, until fragrant, about 1 minute.

3. Add rice and stir to coat with oil. Pour in chicken broth and bring to a boil over high heat. Distribute chicken over rice, cover, remove from heat, and let stand until rice is tender and liquid is absorbed, about 5 minutes. Stir in olives before serving.

279 HERBED CHICKEN WITH APRICOT WILD RICE

Prep: 6 minutes   Cook: 10 to 14 minutes   Serves: 4

¼ cup loosely packed cilantro
   leaves
¼ cup loosely packed fresh
   mint leaves
2 shallots, quartered
2 tablespoons lemon juice
¼ teaspoon salt
½ teaspoon pepper
4 tablespoons butter

4 skinless, boneless chicken
   breast halves (about
   5 ounces each)
1 (6¼-ounce) box fast-cooking
   seasoned long-grain and
   wild rice mix
½ cup chopped dried apricots
4 slices of lemon, for garnish

1. In a food processor or blender, combine cilantro, mint, shallots, lemon juice, salt, and pepper. Pulse to chop. Set herb mixture aside.

2. In a large nonstick skillet, melt 2 tablespoons butter over medium-high heat. Add chicken and cook, turning, until browned, 2 to 3 minutes per side.

3. Meanwhile, cook rice in 2 cups water with remaining 2 tablespoons butter and seasoning packet until liquid is absorbed, about 5 minutes. Stir in apricots.

4. When chicken is browned, stir in herb mixture. Cook over medium heat, turning 2 or 3 times, until chicken is coated with herbs and white inside but still moist, 6 to 8 minutes. Serve with rice and garnish with lemon slices.

280 GRILLED TURKEY TONNATO

Prep: 6 minutes   Cook: 12 minutes   Serves: 4

1 egg
1¼ pounds turkey breast cutlets
2 tablespoons olive oil
2 teaspoons Italian seasoning
¼ teaspoon salt
¼ teaspoon freshly ground
   pepper
1 (3½-ounce) can tuna packed
   in oil, drained
1 small red onion, thinly
   sliced into rings, plus 2
   teaspoons chopped red
   onion

1 anchovy fillet
1 tablespoon lemon juice
2 teaspoons drained capers
3 tablespoons plain low-fat
   yogurt
½ lemon, thinly sliced
1 tablespoon chopped parsley

1. Prepare a hot fire in a charcoal or gas grill. Place egg in saucepan and cover with water. Bring to boil over high heat, reduce heat to low, and cook for 12 minutes. Cool in a bowl of cold water, then set yolk aside and chop white.

2. While egg is cooking, rub turkey with 1 tablespoon oil, then sprinkle with Italian seasoning, salt, and pepper.

3. In a blender or food processor, combine tuna with hard-boiled egg yolk, chopped red onion, and anchovy fillet. Puree until smooth. With machine on, gradually add remaining 1 tablespoon olive oil, lemon juice, and ½ teaspoon capers. Scrape mixture into a bowl and stir in yogurt.

4. Grill turkey 5 to 6 minutes, turning 2 to 3 times, until lightly browned outside and white but still moist inside. Arrange cooked cutlets on a serving platter. Spoon tuna sauce over turkey and garnish with red onion rings, lemon slices, chopped egg white, parsley, and remaining capers.

281   TURKEY AND CRANBERRY SAUTÉ
Prep: 3 minutes   Cook: 8 to 10 minutes   Serves: 4

Turkey cutlets, cut from the breast, usually come sliced about ¼ inch thick. If they're a bit thicker, place between slightly moistened sheets of plastic wrap and pound with a mallet or the bottom of a pot so they'll cook evenly.

1 pound thinly sliced turkey cutlets	**1 teaspoon dried sage**
½ teaspoon salt	**½ cup reduced-sodium chicken broth**
¼ teaspoon pepper	**¾ cup whole-berry cranberry sauce**
3 tablespoons butter	
¼ cup chopped shallots	**1 tablespoon red wine vinegar**

1. Season turkey with salt and pepper. In a large nonreactive skillet, melt butter over medium heat. When butter begins to bubble, add turkey and cook, turning once, until golden brown outside and white but still moist within, 4 to 5 minutes. Remove to a plate, leaving drippings in pan.

2. Add shallots and sage to pan drippings and cook, stirring, until shallots are softened, 30 to 60 seconds. Add broth, raise heat to high, and cook, stirring up browned bits from bottom of pan, until liquid comes to a boil. Whisk in cranberry sauce and vinegar, reduce heat to medium, and cook until sauce thickens slightly, 2 to 3 minutes.

3. Return turkey and any juices to sauce and cook until meat is heated through, about 1 minute.

282   TURKEY MILANESAS

Prep: 3 minutes   Cook: 8 to 10 minutes   Serves: 4

Milanesas are the Latin American version of European *schnitzels*. Serve them with Havana Black Beans and Rice (page 116) or Mexican Risotto (page 117).

1¼ pounds turkey breast cutlets	½ teaspoon salt
1 egg	3 to 4 tablespoons olive or
1½ cups Italian seasoned bread	canola oil
crumbs	Tabasco or other hot sauce
1½ teaspoons chili powder	1 lime, cut into wedges

1. Preheat oven to 250°F. If necessary, pound cutlets between lightly moistened sheets of plastic wrap to an even thickness of about ¼ inch.

2. In a shallow bowl, beat egg with 1 tablespoon water. In a pie plate, combine bread crumbs with chili powder and salt. Dip cutlets in egg and dredge in seasoned crumbs to coat.

3. In a large skillet, heat 3 tablespoons oil over medium-high heat. Add cutlets in batches without crowding and cook, turning once, until crumbs are crisp and golden brown and turkey is white inside but still moist, about 2 minutes per side. As turkey is cooked, transfer to a baking sheet lined with paper towels and keep warm in oven. Add more oil to skillet as needed. Serve with hot sauce and lime wedges.

283   TURKEY TARRAGON

Prep: 3 minutes   Cook: 9 to 10 minutes   Serves: 4

4 to 8 thinly sliced turkey	3 tablespoons butter
cutlets (about 1¼ pounds)	¼ cup chopped shallots
½ teaspoon salt	1 cup dry white wine
¼ teaspoon pepper	½ cup heavy cream
1½ teaspoons dried tarragon	

1. Season turkey with salt and pepper and sprinkle with 1 teaspoon tarragon. In a large skillet, melt butter over medium heat. Add turkey and cook, turning once, until golden brown outside and white but still moist within, 4 to 5 minutes. Remove to a plate, leaving drippings in pan.

2. Add shallots to pan drippings and cook, stirring, until softened, about 1 minute. Add wine, raise heat to high, and cook, stirring up browned bits from bottom of pan, until reduced by one-third, about 2 minutes. Add cream and remaining ½ teaspoon tarragon and cook until sauce reduces slightly and thickens, about 2 minutes.

3. Return turkey and juices to sauce and cook until meat is heated through, about 1 minute.

284   QUICK TURKEY MOLE
Prep: 4 minutes   Cook: 11 minutes   Serves: 4

Serve this quick version of the popular Mexican dish with warm corn tortillas.

1 pound turkey breast cutlets, cut into 3-inch pieces	1 teaspoon ground cumin
5 teaspoons chili powder	½ teaspoon cinnamon
¼ teaspoon salt	2 (14½-ounce) cans Mexican-style stewed tomatoes
⅛ teaspoon pepper	½ ounce unsweetened chocolate
2 tablespoons olive oil	

1. Season turkey cutlets on both sides with 3 teaspoons chili powder, salt, and pepper. In a large skillet, heat oil over medium-high heat. Add turkey and cook, turning, until browned on both sides, about 4 minutes total. Remove with tongs to a plate, leaving drippings in pan.

2. Add cumin, cinnamon, and remaining 2 teaspoons chili powder to skillet and cook, stirring, until fragrant, about 30 seconds. Add tomatoes with juice and chocolate. Bring to a boil over high heat, breaking tomatoes into smaller pieces with side of a spoon.

3. Return turkey and any juices to sauce, reduce heat to medium-low, and cook uncovered until sauce thickens somewhat, chocolate melts, and turkey is white in center, about 6 minutes.

285   HAWAIIAN TURKEY CURRY
Prep: 5 minutes   Cook: 8 to 10 minutes   Serves: 4

If you don't have leftover roast turkey at home, buy a ¾- to 1-pound chunk of turkey breast at your supermarket deli.

1 tablespoon canola oil	1 (5½-ounce) can unsweetened pineapple chunks, with juice
3 cups diced cooked turkey	
½ cup chopped onion	Salt and cayenne
2 tablespoons curry powder	½ cup chopped macadamia nuts or dry roasted peanuts
1 (10¾-ounce) can cream of chicken soup diluted with ¾ can water	

1. In a large nonstick skillet, heat oil over medium heat. Add turkey, onion, and curry. Cook, stirring often, until onion begins to soften, 4 to 5 minutes.

2. Stir in soup with water and juice from pineapple. Cook, stirring occasionally, until hot and well blended, about 3 minutes.

3. Add pineapple chunks and season with salt and cayenne to taste. Simmer 1 to 2 minutes to heat through. Serve sprinkled with nuts.

286   TURKEY PATTIES DIJON
Prep: 5 minutes   Cook: 11 to 12 minutes   Serves: 4

Ground turkey is popular with health-conscious cooks. To make these patties even lower in cholesterol, use one beaten egg white instead of a whole egg.

1¼ pounds ground turkey	½ teaspoon dried tarragon
1 cup fresh bread crumbs	2 tablespoons butter
1 whole egg or 1 egg white	½ cup dry white wine
¼ cup finely chopped scallions	
1½ tablespoons grainy Dijon mustard	

1. In a large bowl, combine ground turkey, bread crumbs, egg, scallions, mustard, and tarragon. Use fingertips to mix gently but thoroughly. Shape into 4 patties ½ inch thick.

2. In a large skillet, melt butter over medium-low heat. Add patties and cook, turning once, until golden brown outside and white but still moist inside, about 10 minutes total. Remove to a plate, leaving drippings in pan.

3. Add wine to skillet, raise heat to high, and boil, stirring up browned bits, until slightly reduced, 1 to 2 minutes. Pour sauce over patties and serve.

287   TURKEY SAUSAGES WITH SWEET PEPPERS
Prep: 7 minutes   Cook: 13 minutes   Serves: 4

Lean turkey sausages flavored with Italian seasonings are an excellent reduced-fat alternative to regular fresh Italian sausages made with pork. Look for them either fresh or frozen in the supermarket.

1 pound fresh sweet or hot Italian turkey sausages	1 small yellow bell pepper, cut into 1-inch-wide strips
2 tablespoons olive oil	1 small red bell pepper, cut into 1-inch-wide strips
1 large onion, thickly sliced	¾ cup dry white wine
1 small green bell pepper, cut into 1-inch-wide strips	

1. If sausages are large, cut into 2-inch lengths. In a large skillet, heat 1 tablespoon oil over medium-high heat. Add sausages, cover, and cook, turning as necessary, until browned outside and no longer pink inside, about 8 minutes. Transfer to a plate, leaving drippings in pan.

2. Raise heat to high and add remaining 1 tablespoon oil to skillet. Add onion and peppers and cook, stirring often, until softened, about 3 minutes.

3. Return sausages and any juices to skillet and add wine. Bring to a boil and cook uncovered until juices thicken slightly, about 2 minutes.

288 TURKEY AND WILD MUSHROOM HASH

Prep: 10 minutes   Cook: 6 to 8 minutes   Serves: 2 to 3

Shiitake mushrooms add a wonderful depth of flavor to this simple yet savory hash. It's a great way to use up leftover turkey.

2 tablespoons butter
2 cups sliced shiitake
    mushrooms (about 5
    ounces)
3 tablespoons chopped
    shallots
¾ teaspoon dried tarragon
1 (10¾-ounce) can reduced-
    sodium condensed cream
    of mushroom soup

1 tablespoon dry sherry
2 cups diced cooked turkey
    (8 to 10 ounces)
½ cup fresh bread crumbs
2 tablespoons grated
    Parmesan cheese
⅛ teaspoon pepper

1. Preheat broiler. In an 8-inch ovenproof skillet, melt butter over medium-high heat. Add mushrooms and shallots and cook, stirring frequently, until mushrooms are somewhat wilted, pale golden, and fragrant, about 3 minutes. Add ½ teaspoon tarragon and cook, stirring, 1 minute.

2. Whisk in undiluted soup and sherry. Add turkey and cook, stirring, until sauce is bubbly and hot, about 1 minute.

3. In a bowl, toss bread crumbs with Parmesan cheese, pepper, and remaining ¼ teaspoon tarragon. Smooth top of turkey mixture in skillet and sprinkle crumb mixture evenly over top. Place skillet about 5 inches from heat and broil 1 to 3 minutes, until crumbs are deep golden brown and sauce is bubbly. Watch carefully to avoid scorching. Serve hash directly from skillet.

289   SMOKED TURKEY AND CHEESE ENCHILADAS

Prep: 5 minutes   Cook: 10 minutes   Serves: 4

If you can't get jalapeño pepper–studded Jack cheese, use plain Monterey Jack and add about 1 tablespoon minced jalapeño peppers.

1 (10-ounce) can mild enchilada sauce
1 (14½-ounce) can recipe-ready diced tomatoes
3 cups shredded Monterey Jack cheese with jalapeño peppers

1 cup diced smoked turkey
8 corn tortillas
2 cups shredded iceberg or romaine lettuce
½ cup sliced black olives

1. Preheat oven to 475°F. In a large skillet, heat enchilada sauce and tomatoes over medium-low heat until hot but not boiling. In a large bowl, toss 2 cups cheese with smoked turkey.

2. Spoon about 1 cup sauce in bottom of shallow 1½- to 2-quart baking dish. Dip a tortilla in warm sauce to soften, then place flat on a work surface and fill with ½ cup cheese and smoked turkey. Roll to enclose filling. Repeat with remaining tortillas and filling, placing enchiladas seam side down close together in a single layer in baking dish. Pour remaining sauce over enchiladas and sprinkle remaining 1 cup cheese on top.

3. Bake uncovered about 10 minutes, until cheese is melted and sauce is bubbly. Serve enchiladas topped with shredded lettuce and sliced olives.

290   DEVILISH GAME HENS

Prep: 3 minutes   Cook: 16 to 17 minutes   Serves: 2 to 4

To save time, ask your butcher to bone the hens for you.

2 (1-pound) Cornish game hens, backbones removed
1 tablespoon olive oil
1 teaspoon coarsely ground black pepper

¾ teaspoon crushed hot red pepper
¾ teaspoon white pepper
¾ teaspoon salt
1 tablespoon lemon juice

1. Preheat broiler. Rinse hens and pat dry with paper towels. Open hens out so they lay flat and press down on the breastbone to crack it.

2. Rub hens on both sides with oil. Mix black pepper, hot pepper, white pepper, and salt and rub over hens. Sprinkle with lemon juice.

3. Arrange on a broiler pan skin side up. Broil about 4 inches from heat 8 to 9 minutes, until skin is browned and crispy. Turn over and broil until hens are cooked through, about 8 minutes longer.

291   DUCK BREAST WITH CHERRIES
Prep: 8 minutes   Cook: 6 to 8 minutes   Serves: 4

Sautéed or grilled boneless duck breasts, usually cooked medium-rare, are a popular dish in trendy restaurants worldwide. Ready-to-cook duck breasts are now available at many butchers and fancy food stores in major U.S. cities. They may also be ordered from companies such as Game Sales International, Inc., in Loveland, Colorado; 1-800-729-2090. Duck breasts vary in weight depending on the variety and gender of the duck. For quick cooking, I suggest the smaller Muscovy hen breasts. The recipe that follows is also a good way to make use of wild ducks procured during hunting season.

4 skinless, boneless duck
    breast halves (about 5
    ounces each), or 4 large
    skinless, boneless
    chicken thighs
4 teaspoons cracked black
    pepper
½ teaspoon salt
3 tablespoons brown sugar
2 tablespoons butter

½ cup chopped onion
1 (21-ounce) can tart cherry pie
    filling
¼ cup golden raisins
2 tablespoons Cognac or
    brandy
1 tablespoon dry sherry
1 teaspoon Worcestershire
    sauce
1 tablespoon chopped parsley

1. Season duck breasts with coarse pepper and salt, cover with a piece of plastic wrap, and pound gently until breasts are about ⅜ inch thick. Coat both sides of duck breasts with brown sugar.

2. In a large nonstick skillet, melt butter over medium-high heat. When butter begins to bubble, add duck and cook, turning once, until lightly browned on the outside and pink inside, 1½ to 2 minutes per side.

3. Add onion to skillet and cook until slightly softened, 1 to 2 minutes. Pour in cherry pie filling, golden raisins, Cognac, sherry, and Worcestershire. Cook stirring gently, until sauce is hot and duck is medium-rare, about 2 minutes, or longer to desired doneness.

4. Place duck on warm individual plates. Spoon cherry sauce on top and garnish with parsley.

Chapter 9

Meat in Minutes

Steaks, lamb chops, and other small cuts of meat have always fit well into the repertoire of the cook on a quick time schedule. Other new convenience cuts, such as boneless beef for stir-fries and fajitas, boneless pork chops, and thinly sliced pork cutlets, have appeared in recent years in response to consumer demand. My favorite quick-cooking techniques for meat include grilling, broiling, stir-frying, and sauteing.

This chapter contains a variety of main-course meat recipes that are ready in minutes and are designed to fit most any occasion. For satisfying family dinners, try Peppery Bourbon Molasses-Glazed Pork Chops, Hamburger Stroganoff, or Quick Corned Beef Hash. Hot and spicy Grilled Jalapeño Beef Steaks will make your cookout memorable. Intimate dinners for two call for Steak Diane or Veal Piccata. And if special company is coming to dinner, either elegant Steak au Poivre or Rack of Lamb Dijonnaise will allow the cook to shine without camping out in the kitchen.

---

292 STEAK DIANE
Prep: 5 minutes   Cook: 8 to 10 minutes   Serves: 2

This flavorful classic is not difficult and would be perfect for a special meal. Serve with steamed asparagus and oven-roasted potatoes.

2 (6-ounce) ball tip or strip
  steaks
¼ teaspoon salt
⅛ teaspoon pepper
2 tablespoons butter
2 tablespoons minced shallots
1 tablespoon fresh lemon
  juice

1½ teaspoons Worcestershire
  sauce
1 teaspoon Dijon mustard
1 tablespoon minced fresh or
  frozen chives
1 tablespoon Cognac or
  brandy

1. Season steaks with salt and pepper. In a large skillet, melt butter. Add shallots and cook over medium-high heat 1 minute.

2. Add steaks and cook 3 to 4 minutes per side for medium-rare. Remove steaks to a warm serving platter.

3. Whisk lemon juice, Worcestershire, mustard, and chives into drippings in skillet. Cook 1 minute; stir in Cognac. Pour sauce over steaks and serve at once.

293   STEAK AU POIVRE

Prep: 5 minutes   Cook: 10 to 13 minutes   Serves: 6

This is an elegant recipe made with Cognac or a good brandy. Traditionally, this French dish is flambéed with Cognac. If the idea of flaming makes you nervous, add Cognac along with the broth and cream and cook down the sauce as directed in step 3.

2 tablespoons coarse ground
    black pepper
6 beef fillet steaks, ½ to ¾ inch
    thick
1 tablespoon vegetable oil
3 tablespoons Cognac or
    brandy

1 (14½-ounce) can reduced-
    sodium beef broth
¾ cup heavy cream
2 teaspoons Dijon mustard

1. Press ½ teaspoon pepper into each side of fillets. Heat oil in a 12-inch skillet over medium-high heat. Add steaks and cook 1 to 1½ minutes per side for rare or 1½ to 2 minutes per side for medium-rare. Remove skillet from heat.

2. Add Cognac to skillet. Remove from heat and ignite with a long fireplace match. As soon as flames subside, remove steaks to a plate.

3. Stir in broth, cream, and mustard and return pan to heat. Bring to a boil and let sauce reduce to about 1 cup, 8 to 10 minutes. Spoon sauce over steaks and serve immediately.

294   CHIMICHURRI STEAK

Prep: 7 minutes   Cook: 4 to 6 minutes   Serves: 4

4 boneless rib-eye steaks, ¾ to
    1 inch thick
½ teaspoon coarsely ground
    pepper
4 to 6 fresh jalapeño peppers,
    seeded and coarsely
    chopped

2 medium plum tomatoes
½ small onion
¼ cup balsamic vinegar
¼ cup olive oil
¼ cup parsley leaves
1 teaspoon sugar
⅛ teaspoon salt

1. Prepare fire in a charcoal or gas grill or preheat broiler. Season steaks with pepper. Grill or broil about 5 inches from heat 2 to 3 minutes per side until rare, or longer to desired doneness.

2. Meanwhile, in a food processor or blender, combine jalapeño peppers, tomatoes, onion, vinegar, olive oil, parsley, sugar, and salt. Pulse on and off until pureed. Serve sauce over steak.

295 STEAK IN RED WINE SAUCE
Prep: 5 minutes   Cook: 8 to 11 minutes   Serves: 2

1 tablespoon coarsely ground
   pepper
2 boneless rib-eye steaks, ¾ to
   1 inch thick
2 tablespoons olive or canola
   oil

½ cup thinly sliced red onion
2 tablespoons chopped
   parsley
1 teaspoon dried thyme leaves
⅓ cup dry red wine
2 tablespoons butter

1. Press pepper into both sides of steaks. Heat 1 tablespoon oil in a large skillet over medium-high heat. Add steaks and cook 2 to 3 minutes on each side for rare, or longer to desired degree of doneness. Remove steak and keep warm.

2. Add remaining 1 tablespoon oil, onion, parsley, and thyme to skillet. Cook until onion is soft and slightly glazed, 2 to 3 minutes.

3. Pour in wine and boil until reduced to about 2 tablespoons, about 2 minutes. Remove from heat and swirl in butter. Spoon sauce over steaks and serve at once.

296 STEAK WITH WILD MUSHROOMS
Prep: 7 minutes   Cook: 7 to 8 minutes   Serves: 2

Any variety of fresh mushrooms purchased from the supermarket can be used. Try a combination of shiitake, cremini, and wood ears for a flavorful combination.

3 tablespoons olive or canola
   oil
2 beef fillet steaks, ½ to ¾ inch
   thick
¼ teaspoon salt

½ cup sliced mushrooms
1 teaspoon dried thyme leaves
½ cup chopped scallions
⅓ cup chopped ham

1. Heat 1 tablespoon oil in a large skillet over medium heat. Add steaks and cook, turning, 1½ to 2 minutes on each side for rare and 2 to 3 minutes for medium. Lightly salt second side of steak. Remove to a warm platter.

2. Add remaining 2 tablespoons oil, mushrooms, and thyme to skillet. Cook 2 minutes. Add scallions and ham. Cook, stirring occasionally, until mushrooms are tender and scallions are just beginning to soften, about 2 minutes longer.

3. Spoon mushroom mixture over steak and serve at once.

297 BEEF FAJITAS

Prep: 10 minutes   Cook: 6 to 8 minutes   Serves: 4

It is important to cut beef strips thin to allow them to cook quickly. If a very large skillet is not available, use two smaller skillets because for best flavor and appearance, the meat needs to have room to cook without steaming in its own juices.

1 to 1¼ pounds ball tip or strip steak or steak of your choice
⅓ cup lime juice
¼ cup olive oil
2 garlic cloves, minced
¾ teaspoon Liquid Smoke
½ teaspoon cayenne
¼ teaspoon salt
1 red bell pepper, sliced into strips

1 green bell pepper, sliced into strips
1 medium onion, cut into 8 wedges
8 (10-inch) flour tortillas
½ cup shredded Monterey Jack cheese
½ cup salsa
¼ cup sour cream

1. With a sharp knife, slice steak into strips no more than ½ inch thick, ½ inch wide, and 4 inches in length. Whisk together lime juice, 2 tablespoons oil, garlic, Liquid Smoke, cayenne, and salt. Toss steak strips with lime mixture.

2. Place a very large nonreactive skillet over medium-high heat. Add steak and liquid to hot skillet and cook, tossing occasionally, until liquid has thickened to a glaze, 6 to 8 minutes.

3. While meat is cooking, place another large skillet with remaining 2 tablespoons oil over medium-high heat. Add peppers and onion and cook until crisp-tender, 6 to 8 minutes.

4. Meanwhile, wrap tortillas in aluminum foil and heat in 350°F. oven for 6 to 8 minutes. To serve, wrap meat, peppers, a spoonful of shredded cheese and salsa, and a dollop of sour cream in each tortilla and roll up.

298   GRILLED JALAPEÑO BEEF STEAK

Prep: 4 minutes   Cook: 10 to 12 minutes   Serves: 4

What a taste treat, jalapeños, cilantro, and steak—and such an easy meal.

¼ cup chopped cilantro	1 tablespoon canola oil
¼ cup sliced pickled jalapeño peppers, chopped	½ teaspoon ground cumin
4 ball tip or strip steaks, 1 inch thick (6 ounces each)	¼ teaspoon salt
	¼ teaspoon pepper

1. Prepare fire in a charcoal or gas grill or preheat broiler. Combine cilantro and jalapeños. Cut a pocket in side of each steak, leaving 3 sides intact. Stuff pockets with cilantro mixture. Secure edges with toothpicks. Rub outside of steaks with oil, cumin, salt, and pepper.

2. Grill or broil steaks 5 to 6 inches from heat 5 to 6 minutes per side for medium-rare, until they reach desired doneness.

299   CUBE STEAKS WITH CARAMELIZED ONIONS

Prep: 3 minutes   Cook: 14 to 15 minutes   Serves: 4

1 tablespoon olive oil	2 tablespoons butter
4 cube steaks (5 to 6 ounces each)	2 large onions, sliced
½ teaspoon salt	¾ teaspoon dried thyme
½ teaspoon pepper	½ cup dry red wine

1. In a large skillet, heat oil over medium-high heat until just beginning to smoke. Season cube steaks with salt and pepper and cook, turning once, until brown outside and medium-rare within, 2 to 3 minutes total. Remove to a plate and keep warm in a low oven, loosely covered with foil. Reduce heat to medium.

2. Add butter to pan drippings. As soon as it melts, add onions and cook, stirring frequently, until golden brown, about 10 minutes.

3. Stir in thyme and wine, raise heat to medium-high, and cook until most liquid is evaporated, about 2 minutes. To serve, spoon onions over cube steaks.

300   QUICK MIXED MEAT PICADILLO
Prep: 4 minutes   Cook: 15 to 16 minutes   Serves: 6 to 8

This sweet-sour Latin American ground meat stew, somewhat akin to a beanless chili, makes wonderful party fare for a crowd. Serve it with plain steamed white rice and a big leafy green salad.

2 pounds mixed ground meat (pork, beef, veal)	½ teaspoon cinnamon
1 large onion, chopped	½ teaspoon ground cumin
1 cup chopped sweet apple, such as Golden Delicious	1 teaspoon salt
½ cup sliced almonds	¼ teaspoon cayenne
1 tablespoon chili powder	1 (28-ounce) can crushed tomatoes
1 teaspoon dried oregano	½ cup raisins
	3 tablespoons cider vinegar

1. In a large heavy skillet or saucepan, cook meat, onion, apple, and almonds over medium-high heat, stirring frequently, until meat browns lightly and loses its pink color, 4 to 5 minutes. Spoon off excess fat.

2. Add chili powder, oregano, cinnamon, cumin, salt, and cayenne and cook, stirring, until chili powder is lightly toasted, 1 minute. Stir in tomatoes, raisins, and vinegar and bring to a boil over high heat. Reduce heat to medium and cook uncovered until picadillo is slightly thickened and flavors blend, about 10 minutes.

301   HAMBURGER STROGANOFF
Prep: 5 minutes   Cook: 13 to 15 minutes   Serves: 4

This rendition of stroganoff using hamburger is every bit as richly satisfying as the original made with beef fillet. Serve over cooked egg noodles with a steamed vegetable, such as green beans, on the side.

2 tablespoons butter	1¼ cups reduced-sodium beef broth
1 medium onion, chopped	1½ teaspoons Worcestershire sauce
2 cups sliced mushrooms (about 6 ounces)	⅔ cup sour cream
1 pound ground sirloin	2 tablespoons chopped fresh dill, or 1 teaspoon dried
½ teaspoon salt	
½ teaspoon pepper	
2 tablespoons flour	

1. In a large skillet, melt butter over medium heat. Add onion and mushrooms and cook, stirring frequently, until onion wilts and mushrooms give off liquid and are lightly browned, about 5 minutes.

2. Add ground beef, season with salt and pepper, and cook, stirring frequently, until meat loses its pink color, about 5 minutes. Sprinkle flour over meat mixture, raise heat to medium-high, and cook, stirring, 1 to 2 minutes to cook flour. Stir in broth and bring to a boil, stirring, until thickened, about 1 minute. Season with Worcestershire.

3. Remove from heat and stir in sour cream. Return pan to medium heat and cook, stirring, until sour cream is just warmed through, about 30 seconds. Do not boil or sauce may curdle. Sprinkle with dill before serving.

---

302   SPICY SESAME BEEF STIR-FRY
Prep: 5 minutes   Cook: 6 minutes   Serves: 2

Save time by buying sliced broccoli and carrots. Look for them in bags in the produce section or on a salad bar. This stir-fry is particularly nice over Oriental noodles or vermicelli.

2 tablespoons soy sauce
1 tablespoon minced fresh
  ginger
1 garlic clove, minced
1 teaspoon cornstarch
¼ teaspoon crushed hot red
  pepper
8 to 10 ounces tender boneless
  beef, such as sirloin

2 tablespoons sesame seeds
2 tablespoons peanut or other
  vegetable oil
3 cups broccoli florets (about
  10 ounces)
1 cup thinly sliced carrots

1. In a small bowl, combine soy sauce, ginger, garlic, cornstarch, and crushed red pepper with ½ cup water. Stir until cornstarch dissolves.

2. Cut beef crosswise into thin strips. Sprinkle beef with sesame seeds, tossing to coat evenly. In a wok or large skillet, heat 1 tablespoon oil over high heat. Add beef and stir-fry until brown, about 2 minutes. Remove with a slotted spoon to a plate.

3. Heat remaining 1 tablespoon oil in pan. Add broccoli and carrots and stir-fry until broccoli is bright green and carrots are crisp-tender, about 2 minutes. Reduce heat to medium.

4. Stir sauce mixture to blend and add to pan along with beef and any accumulated juices. Cook, stirring, until sauce thickens and becomes translucent, about 2 minutes. Serve at once.

303   GARLIC GINGER BEEF AND ASPARAGUS STIR-FRY

Prep: 6 minutes   Cook: 6 to 7 minutes   Serves: 4

When cutting meat for stir-fries, it's quite a bit easier to slice thin if it's partially frozen.

2 **teaspoons cornstarch**	1 **tablespoon peanut or other**
⅓ **cup dry sherry**	**vegetable oil**
1½ **tablespoons soy sauce**	1 **pound slender asparagus,**
1 **to 1¼ pounds tender**	**cut into 2-inch lengths**
boneless beef, such as	1 **tablespoon finely chopped**
sirloin	**fresh ginger**
¼ **teaspoon pepper**	2 **garlic cloves, finely chopped**

1. In a small bowl, dissolve cornstarch in ¾ cup water. Stir in sherry and soy sauce and set aside.

2. Cut beef crosswise into thin strips and season with pepper. In a wok or a very large skillet, heat oil over high heat. Add beef and stir-fry until it loses its pink color, about 2 minutes. Add asparagus and stir-fry until bright green, 1 to 2 minutes. Add ginger and garlic and stir-fry until fragrant, 1 minute. Reduce heat to medium.

3. Stir sauce mixture to combine, pour into pan, and cook, stirring, until sauce thickens and turns translucent, about 2 minutes.

304   QUICK CORNED BEEF HASH

Prep: 6 minutes   Cook: 12 to 14 minutes   Serves: 2

2 **cups cubed cooked potatoes**	½ **teaspoon Worcestershire**
or thawed frozen hash	**sauce**
browns	½ **teaspoon dried thyme leaves**
1½ **cups diced cooked corned**	¼ **teaspoon pepper**
beef (6 ounces)	2 **tablespoons olive oil**
1 **small onion, chopped**	3 **tablespoons cream or milk**
½ **cup chopped green bell**	
pepper	

1. In a mixing bowl, combine potatoes, corned beef, onion, bell pepper, Worcestershire, thyme, and pepper.

2. In a large skillet, preferably nonstick, heat oil over medium-high heat. Add hash mixture and press with a spatula to flatten to a cake. Cover partially and cook until bottom begins to get crusty and brown, 3 to 5 minutes. Use a wooden spatula to scrape up browned bits from bottom and cook, stirring twice, until hash is flecked with brown bits and onion and green pepper are soft, about 8 minutes.

3. Uncover, add cream, and cook until liquid is absorbed, about 1 minute.

305 GRILLED LEBANESE LAMB PATTIES
Prep: 6 minutes   Cook: 10 minutes   Serves: 4

If you like, sandwich the lamb patties inside split pita breads.

1¼ pounds lean ground lamb	1 teaspoon salt
1 small onion, chopped	¾ teaspoon freshly ground
½ cup dry bread crumbs	pepper
2 garlic cloves, finely chopped	½ teaspoon cayenne
1½ teaspoons ground cumin	1 large tomato, sliced
½ teaspoon ground coriander	½ cup alfalfa sprouts

1. Prepare a medium hot fire in a charcoal or gas grill.

2. In a large bowl, combine ground lamb, onion, bread crumbs, garlic, cumin, coriander, salt, pepper, and cayenne. Mix with your hands to blend well. Shape into 4 patties about ¾ inch thick.

3. Grill patties, turning, until meat is browned outside, with just a trace of pink within, about 10 minutes total. Top each patty with a tomato slice and about 2 tablespoons sprouts.

306 LAMB AND WHITE BEAN STEW
Prep: 4 minutes   Cook: 14 to 15 minutes   Serves: 5 to 6

1½ pounds lean boneless leg of lamb, cut into 1½-inch cubes	2 teaspoons dried rosemary, crumbled
½ teaspoon salt	2 (15-ounce) cans white beans, drained
¼ teaspoon pepper	2 (14-ounce) cans stewed tomatoes
3 tablespoons olive oil	
4 garlic cloves, chopped	
1 cup dry white wine or vermouth	

1. Season lamb with salt and pepper. In a large skillet, heat oil over medium-high heat. Add lamb and cook, turning so all sides brown lightly, 3 to 4 minutes. Add garlic and cook, stirring, until soft and fragrant, about 1 minute.

2. Add wine and rosemary and bring to a boil over high heat, stirring up browned bits from bottom of pan. Add beans and tomatoes. (If tomato pieces are large, snip with kitchen shears or break up with side of a spoon.) Bring to a boil again, reduce heat to medium-low, and cook uncovered until meat is no longer pink in center and sauce is somewhat reduced, about 10 minutes.

307 TUNISIAN BROILED LAMB CHOPS WITH MINT

Prep: 4 minutes   Cook: 8 to 10 minutes   Serves: 4

When fresh mint is in season, this Middle Eastern rub for lamb is a real treat. The chops are lovely served with a couscous and vegetable salad and warm pita bread.

1½ tablespoons olive oil	¼ teaspoon ground coriander
1 tablespoon chopped fresh mint, or 2 teaspoons dried	¼ teaspoon cayenne
1 garlic clove, minced	¼ teaspoon black pepper
½ teaspoon salt	4 loin lamb chops, about 6 ounces each
½ teaspoon ground cumin	Mint or parsley sprigs

1. Prepare a hot fire in a charcoal or gas grill or preheat broiler.

2. In a small bowl, combine oil, mint, garlic, salt, cumin, coriander, cayenne, and pepper. Stir to mix well. Spread spice paste over both sides of lamb chops and let stand 5 minutes.

3. Grill or broil chops 8 to 10 minutes, turning once or twice, until meat is browned outside and medium-rare to medium inside. Serve garnished with mint sprigs.

308 LAMB STEW PRINTEMPS

Prep: 4 minutes   Cook: 16 minutes   Serves: 4

In France, lamb stew was traditionally served in the spring, when both lamb and vegetables are young and tender. Thanks to modern freezing techniques, this delicacy is now available year-round.

1 to 1¼ pounds lean boneless leg of lamb, cut into 1½-inch cubes	3 garlic cloves, chopped
	2 teaspoons dried thyme
½ teaspoon salt	1 (14¾-ounce) reduced-sodium beef broth
¼ teaspoon pepper	1 (1-pound) package frozen stew vegetables
¼ cup flour	2 cups frozen baby peas
2 tablespoons olive oil	

1. Season lamb with salt and pepper and dredge in flour; shake off excess. Heat oil in a large skillet or Dutch oven. Add lamb and cook over high heat, turning, until lightly browned all over, about 3 minutes. Reduce heat to medium, add garlic and thyme, and cook, stirring, until fragrant, about 1 minute.

2. Add broth and frozen vegetables and bring to a boil over high heat, stirring up browned bits from bottom of pan. Reduce heat to medium and cook, covered, until vegetables are almost tender, about 10 minutes.

3. Add peas and cook until vegetables are completely tender, about 2 minutes. If gravy is too thick, thin with 2 to 3 tablespoons additional broth or water.

309   RACK OF LAMB DIJONNAISE
Prep: 2 minutes   Cook: 18 minutes   Serves: 4 to 5

Rack of lamb cooked in the French fashion with a coating of Dijon mustard and herbed bread crumbs is a quick, elegant entree. The recipe below calls for cooking the lamb rare. If you prefer your meat more well-done, additional cooking time will be needed.

2 **trimmed racks of lamb**	1 **tablespoon olive oil**
1½ **tablespoons Dijon mustard**	⅛ **teaspoon salt**
2 **slices of whole wheat bread**	⅛ **teaspoon pepper**
2 **garlic cloves**	
1 **tablespoon prepared pesto**	
sauce	

1. Preheat oven to 500°F. With a sharp knife, score cross-hatch marks through layer of fat on top of racks of lamb. Paint mustard over top and sides of meat. Wrap ends of rib bones with aluminum foil to prevent burning and place racks in shallow baking pan on upper-middle rack of oven. Roast 10 minutes.

2. Meanwhile, in a food processor, process bread, garlic, pesto, olive oil, salt, and pepper until bread forms fine crumbs.

3. Remove lamb from oven and pat crumbs over top of roast. Return to oven. Continue to roast 8 minutes, or until meat registers 130° for rosy rare. (If you prefer lamb cooked medium, add 5 minutes; for well-done, add 8 minutes.)

310   VEAL PICCATA
Prep: 3 minutes   Cook: 4 minutes   Serves: 4

When a recipe calls for a small amount of vegetable, beef, or chicken broth, rather than wasting the remainder of the can, freeze what's left in 1-tablespoon portions in an ice cube tray. To use, remember 16 tablespoons equals a cup, 8 tablespoons are ½ cup, and 4 tablespoons are ¼ cup. When cubes are frozen, pop them out and place in freezer in labeled sack.

1½ pounds veal or turkey breast, thinly sliced	2 garlic cloves, minced
¼ teaspoon salt	¼ cup vegetable broth
¼ teaspoon pepper	1 tablespoon drained capers
2 tablespoons butter	4 teaspoons pine nuts

1. Season veal slices with salt and pepper. In a large skillet, melt butter over medium-high heat. Add veal and cook, turning, until lightly browned outside and white throughout, 1½ to 2 minutes per side.

2. Remove veal to a serving platter. Add garlic to skillet and cook for a few seconds, until fragrant. Add vegetable broth, capers, and pine nuts. Cook 1 minute and pour over veal. Serve at once.

311   VEAL CHOPS WITH OLIVE AND PEPPER COMPOTE
Prep: 6 minutes   Cook: 11 to 13 minutes   Serves: 4

4 loin or rib veal chops, 1½ inches thick (about 8 ounces each)	1 (4-ounce) jar roasted peppers, drained and chopped
½ teaspoon salt	1 (2-ounce) can chopped black olives
¼ teaspoon pepper	
3 tablespoons olive oil	2 tablespoons chopped parsley
2 garlic cloves, minced	
⅓ cup vermouth or dry white wine	¼ teaspoon crushed hot red pepper

1. Prepare a medium-hot fire in a charcoal or gas grill or preheat broiler. Season chops with salt and pepper and rub with 1 tablespoon olive oil. Grill or broil chops, 8 to 10 minutes, turning once, until brown outside and white throughout but still juicy. Transfer to a platter and keep warm in a low oven, loosely covered with foil.

2. In a medium skillet, heat remaining 2 tablespoons oil over medium heat. Add garlic and cook, stirring, until soft and fragrant, about 1 minute. Add wine, raise heat to medium-high, and boil until reduced by half, about 1 minute. Stir in roasted peppers, olives, parsley, and hot pepper and cook until heated through, about 1 minute. Spoon compote over veal chops and serve.

312 SALTIMBOCCA ALLA ROMANA

Prep: 6 to 8 minutes   Cook: 4 to 6 minutes   Serves: 4 to 6

This typically Roman dish is so quick to prepare and tastes so good that it lives up to its name *saltimbocca*, which literally means "jumps in your mouth."

4 to 6 veal or turkey scallopini
   (about 1½ pounds)
Ground sage, salt, and
   pepper
4 to 6 thin slices of prosciutto
   or other ham

2 tablespoons butter
⅓ cup marsala or Madeira
   wine
1 tablespoon minced parsley

1. Season scallopini lightly with sage, salt, and pepper. Top each cutlet with a slice of prosciutto, pressing lightly so ham sticks to veal.

2. In a large nonstick skillet, melt 1 tablespoon butter over medium-high heat. Place veal ham side down in pan and cook, turning once, until lightly browned and cooked through, 1½ to 2 minutes per side. Remove to a warm serving platter.

3. Add marsala to skillet and boil, stirring, until liquid is reduced by about one-third, 1 to 2 minutes.

4. Swirl remaining 1 tablespoon butter into sauce and pour over cutlets. Sprinkle with parsley and serve.

313 SCALLOPINI WITH LEMON SAUCE

Prep: 5 minutes   Cook: 4 to 5 minutes   Serves: 4

The scallopini cook quickly, allowing the cook to prepare a special main dish with little time or work.

1½ pounds veal or turkey
   breast, thinly sliced
¼ teaspoon salt
¼ teaspoon pepper
2 tablespoons butter

⅓ cup lemon juice
¼ cup chopped parsley
4 teaspoons sugar
1 teaspoon grated lemon zest

1. Season veal slices with salt and pepper. In a large nonstick skillet, melt butter over medium-high heat. Add veal and cook, turning once, until cooked through, 1½ to 2 minutes per side.

2. Remove veal to a serving dish. Add lemon juice, parsley, sugar, and zest to skillet. Cook 1 minute and pour over veal.

314   SCALLOPINI ALLA PIZZAIOLA
Prep: 3 minutes   Cook: 5 to 6 minutes   Serves: 4

A less expensive version of this dish may be made with turkey scallopini.

1½ **pounds veal or turkey**
    breast, thinly sliced
¼ **teaspoon salt**
¼ **teaspoon pepper**
1 **tablespoon olive oil**

1 **cup prepared pasta sauce**
½ **teaspoon Italian seasoning**
2 **to 3 ounces shredded**
    mozzarella cheese

1. Season veal slices with salt and pepper. In a large nonstick skillet, heat oil over medium-high heat. Add veal and cook, turning once, until lightly browned outside and white in center, 1½ to 2 minutes per side.

2. Remove veal to a warm serving platter. Pour pasta sauce and Italian seasoning into pan and cook, stirring, until heated through, about 2 minutes. Pour sauce over veal. Top with shredded cheese and serve at once.

315   PORK CHOPS NORMANDE
Prep: 8 minutes   Cook: 11 minutes   Serves: 3 to 4

In France, when a dish is described as "Normande" it means that it contains cream and usually also apples or cider, which are both typical of Normandy.

4 **boneless pork loin chops,**
    ¾ to 1 inch thick
1 **teaspoon dried thyme leaves**
⅛ **teaspoon pepper**
2 **teaspoons butter**
2 **teaspoons canola oil**
1 **large Granny Smith apple,**
    peeled, cored, and thinly
    sliced

2 **large shallots, thinly sliced**
¼ **teaspoon salt**
½ **cup apple juice or cider**
½ **cup heavy cream**
2 **tablespoons Calvados,**
    applejack, or brandy

1. Pat chops dry and season with thyme and pepper. In a large nonstick skillet, melt butter in oil over medium-high heat. Add chops and cook 3 minutes.

2. Turn chops over and add apple and shallots to pan. Season with salt and continue to cook until chops are browned and apples and shallots are slightly softened, about 3 minutes longer.

3. Stir in apple juice, cream, and Calvados. Bring to a boil, reduce heat to medium-low, and cook until chops are tender and white throughout, apples are tender, and sauce has thickened, about 5 minutes.

316   SAUSAGE MAKER'S PORK CHOPS
Prep: 6 minutes   Cook: 8 to 13 minutes   Serves: 4

In France, pork chops cooked in this way are attributed to the *chacutière,* the maker of pâtés and sausages. The mustard and pickle in the recipe make additional salt unnecessary.

4 boneless pork loin chops,
   ¾ to 1 inch thick
2 teaspoons freshly ground
   pepper
2 teaspoons dried thyme
1 tablespoon vegetable oil
¼ cup chopped shallots
2 tablespoons chopped
   cornichons or dill pickle

2 tablespoons chopped
   parsley
¼ cup dry white wine
2 tablespoons butter
2 teaspoons spicy brown
   mustard

1. Season chops with pepper and thyme. In a large nonstick skillet over medium-high heat, heat oil. Add pork chops and cook, turning once, until browned outside and white but still moist inside, 3 to 5 minutes per side. Remove chops from skillet and keep warm.

2. Add shallots, pickle, and parsley to pan and cook until shallots are softened, 1 to 2 minutes.

3. Add wine and butter. Cook, stirring until butter is melted, about 1 minute. Whisk in mustard. Spoon sauce over chops and serve.

317   PEPPERY BOURBON MOLASSES-GLAZED PORK CHOPS
Prep: 3 minutes   Cook: 4 to 6 minutes   Serves: 4 to 6

6 pork loin blade chops, ½ to
   ¾ inch thick
2 teaspoons vegetable oil
2½ to 3 tablespoons coarsely
   ground pepper
2 tablespoons unsulphured
   molasses

2 tablespoons spicy brown
   mustard
2 tablespoons bourbon
1 teaspoon Worcestershire
   sauce

1. Prepare a hot fire in a charcoal or gas grill or preheat broiler. Coat pork chops lightly with oil and press pepper into both sides. In a small bowl, combine molasses and mustard. Stir in bourbon and Worcestershire until well blended.

2. Grill or broil chops 5 to 6 inches from heat 2 to 3 minutes, until nicely browned on one side. Brush with molasses mixture and turn over.

3. Cook, turning and basting often, 2 to 3 minutes, until chops are well glazed and cooked through.

318   HAM ON CREAMED GREENS
Prep: 6 minutes   Cook: 8 to 9 minutes   Serves: 2

1 (10-ounce) package frozen
   greens—collards, turnip,
   or dandelion—thawed
1 tablespoon butter
6 to 8 ounces smoked ham,
   cut into 4 slices

1 garlic clove, minced
¼ cup half-and-half or light
   cream
¼ teaspoon Tabasco sauce

1. Drain greens in a sieve. Press out as much excess liquid as possible.

2. In a medium skillet, melt butter over medium heat. Add ham and cook, turning, until tinged golden brown on both sides and heated through, 4 to 5 minutes total. Remove to a plate.

3. Add garlic to drippings and cook, stirring, until fragrant but not brown, about 1 minute. Add greens and half-and-half and cook, stirring occasionally, until most of liquid is absorbed, about 3 minutes. Season with Tabasco. Spoon greens onto plates and top with ham slices.

319   SAUTÉED PORK CUTLETS VALENCIA
Prep: 5 minutes   Cook: 9 minutes   Serves: 4

Pork cutlets, cut from the sirloin, generally come sliced about ¼ inch thick. If they're a bit thicker than that, cover with a sheet of plastic wrap and pound lightly with a mallet or the bottom of a small pot to flatten to an even thickness.

¼ cup orange juice
½ cup raisins
1 pound pork cutlets,
   pounded or cut ¼ inch
   thick
¼ teaspoon salt
¼ teaspoon pepper

2 tablespoons butter
½ cup sliced almonds
½ cup sliced scallions
1 cup reduced-sodium
   chicken broth
1½ teaspoons grated orange zest

1. In a small bowl, combine orange juice and raisins and set aside while meat is cooking.

2. Season pork with salt and pepper. In a large skillet, melt butter over medium-high heat. Add pork and cook, turning once, until browned outside and white in center, about 2 minutes per side. Remove to a plate.

3. Add almonds and scallions to pan drippings. Cook, stirring almost constantly, until almonds are golden and fragrant, about 2 minutes. Add chicken broth, orange zest, and orange juice–raisin mixture.

4. Bring to a boil over high heat, stirring up any browned bits from bottom of pan, and cook until sauce is somewhat reduced and syrupy, about 2 minutes. Return pork and any juices to sauce, spoon sauce over meat, and heat through, about 1 minute.

320 PORK SCALLOPS ON GREENS WITH WALNUT VINAIGRETTE

Prep: 5 minutes   Cook: 5 minutes   Serves: 4

Use lean boneless pork cut from the sirloin or the tenderloin for this sophisticated presentation. Mesclun, a combination of young, tender greens, is increasingly available packaged in plastic bags in the market. If you can't get it, substitute almost any tender lettuce, such as green leaf or Boston, torn into small pieces.

1 **pound pork cutlets or scallops, pounded or cut ¼ inch thick**	¼ **cup chopped shallots**
½ **teaspoon salt**	2 **tablespoons raspberry or other fruit vinegar**
¼ **teaspoon pepper**	2 **teaspoons Dijon mustard**
½ **teaspoon ground sage**	2 **teaspoons walnut oil**
¼ **cup olive oil**	8 **cups mesclun or other tender greens**

1. Season pork with salt, pepper, and sage. In a large nonstick skillet, heat 1 tablespoon oil over medium-high heat. Add pork and cook, turning once, until browned and cooked through, about 4 minutes total. Remove to a plate.

2. Add remaining 3 tablespoons oil to pan. Add shallots and cook, stirring, until softened and fragrant, about 1 minute. Remove pan from heat and whisk in vinegar, mustard, and walnut oil.

3. Divide greens among 4 plates. Spoon about two-thirds of dressing from skillet over greens. Top with pork scallops and spoon remaining dressing over meat.

321 STOVETOP BARBECUED PORK CHOPS

Prep: 2 minutes   Cook: 16 minutes   Serves: 4

Use your favorite bottled barbecue sauce here. They so vary in quality, so search for a brand that is not overly salty, with the degree of heat that you like.

1 **tablespoon vegetable oil**	1 **cup bottled hickory smoked barbecue sauce**
4 **boneless pork chops (5 to 6 ounces each)**	2 **teaspoons lemon juice**
½ **teaspoon pepper**	½ **teaspoon grated lemon zest**

1. In a large skillet or Dutch oven, heat oil over medium-high heat. Season pork chops with pepper. Add pork and cook, turning once, until browned, about 4 minutes.

2. Stir in barbecue sauce, lemon juice, lemon zest, and 1 cup water. Bring to a boil and reduce heat to low. Cook, covered, turning chops once or twice to coat with sauce, until pork is tender and no longer pink in center, about 12 minutes.

322 PORK MEDALLIONS WITH FRUIT VINEGAR

Prep: 3 minutes   Cook: 11 minutes   Serves: 4

This sweet and tangy sauce with sautéed pork is very popular. Use any type of fruit vinegar, such as raspberry or blueberry. Serve with wild rice and buttered broccoli.

1 **pound pork tenderloin, cut into medallions ½ inch thick**
¼ **teaspoon salt**
¼ **teaspoon pepper**
2 **tablespoons olive oil**
¼ **cup sliced shallots**

1 **cup reduced-sodium chicken broth**
2 **tablespoons raspberry, blueberry, or other fruit vinegar**
2 **teaspoons honey**

1. Flatten pork medallions with heel of hand or a mallet until about ⅜ inch thick. Season with salt and pepper.

2. In a large skillet, heat oil over medium-high heat. Add pork and cook, turning once, until meat is browned on both sides and white throughout, about 6 minutes. Remove with tongs to a plate, leaving drippings in pan.

3. Add shallots and cook, stirring, until lightly browned, about 1 minute. Add broth, raise heat to high, and cook, stirring up any browned bits from bottom of pan, until liquid is reduced by one-third, about 3 minutes. Stir in vinegar and honey. Return meat and any accumulated juices to sauce and cook until heated through, about 1 minute.

323 CANADIAN BACON ON WILTED CRESS

Prep: 4 minutes   Cook: 5 to 7 minutes   Serves: 2

2 **tablespoons butter**
6 **thin slices of Canadian bacon (about 3 ounces)**
⅛ **teaspoon coarsely ground pepper**
3 **tablespoons chopped shallots**

2 **tablespoons white wine vinegar**
1 **bunch of watercress, tough bottom stems removed**

1. In a large skillet, melt butter over medium heat. Season Canadian bacon with pepper and cook on both sides until edges are golden brown, 3 to 4 minutes total. Remove to a plate. Reduce heat to medium-low.

2. Add shallots to pan drippings and cook, stirring, until somewhat softened, 1 to 2 minutes. Add vinegar and cook, stirring, until brown bits clinging to skillet dissolve, about 30 seconds. Add watercress and cook, turning once, until just beginning to wilt, 15 to 30 seconds. Remove with tongs to plates and arrange Canadian bacon over cress.

324 SWEET-AND-SOUR PORK WITH APPLE
Prep: 8 minutes   Cook: 6 minutes   Serves: 4

Spoon this sweet-and-sour pork stir-fry over fluffy white rice.

1 pound well-trimmed
    boneless pork chops
¼ teaspoon pepper
2 tablespoons peanut or other
    vegetable oil
1 large red bell pepper, cut
    into 1-inch squares
8 scallions, trimmed and cut
    into 2-inch lengths

1 large tart apple, such as
    Granny Smith, sliced
    ½ inch thick
2 teaspoons finely chopped
    fresh ginger
1 garlic clove, finely chopped
1 cup sweet-and-sour sauce
2 teaspoons lemon juice

1. Cut pork crosswise into thin strips and season with pepper. In a wok or very large skillet, heat oil over high heat. Add pork and stir-fry until white throughout, about 2 minutes.

2. Add bell pepper, scallions, and apple slices. Stir-fry until scallion tops turn bright green, about 1 minute. Add ginger and garlic and stir-fry until fragrant, 1 minute. Reduce heat to medium.

3. Add sweet-and-sour sauce, lemon juice, and ½ cup water. Cook, stirring, until sauce is hot and coats meat and vegetables, about 2 minutes.

325 SMOTHERED PORK CHOPS
Prep: 3 minutes   Cook: 15 to 17 minutes   Serves: 4

Browned onions add such a marvelous depth of flavor to this sauce that no one will guess that it's made with canned soup.

4 bone-in pork loin chops,
    about ¾ inch thick
¼ teaspoon pepper
1 tablespoon vegetable oil
1 large onion, coarsely
    chopped

1 (10¾-ounce) can reduced-
    sodium condensed cream
    of mushroom soup
1 teaspoon dried thyme

1. Season pork chops with pepper. In a large skillet or Dutch oven, heat oil over medium-high heat. Add pork and cook, turning once, until browned on both sides, about 4 minutes total. Remove to a plate, leaving drippings in pan.

2. Add onion and cook, stirring frequently, until browned, 5 to 7 minutes. Whisk in condensed soup, thyme, and ½ cup water. Bring to a boil over high heat. Return pork and juices to sauce, cover, and cook over medium-low heat until pork is no longer pink in center, about 6 minutes.

326   PORK BRAISED WITH WINTER VEGETABLES

Prep: 3 minutes   Cook: 15 minutes   Serves: 4

If the frozen stew vegetable mix includes potatoes that are larger than about 2 inches in diameter, you may want to cut them in half to ensure that they cook through in the time allotted. Lean, buttery tender pork tenderloin cooks beautifully in this braised stew, which makes a fabulous meal on a cold winter night.

1 **pound pork tenderloin, cut into 8 slices**	1 **teaspoon dried thyme**
¼ **teaspoon pepper**	1 **(1-pound) package frozen stew vegetables**
⅛ **teaspoon salt**	1½ **cups chicken broth**
½ **cup flour**	2 **teaspoons grainy Dijon mustard**
2 **tablespoons olive oil**	
2 **garlic cloves, chopped**	

1. Season pork with pepper and salt and dredge in flour; shake off excess.

2. In a large skillet or Dutch oven, heat oil over medium-high heat. Add pork and cook until brown on one side, about 2 minutes. Turn meat over and cook 1 minute. Add garlic and thyme and cook, stirring, until garlic is fragrant and pork is lightly browned, about 1 minute longer.

3. Add frozen vegetables and chicken broth and bring to a boil over high heat, scraping up any browned bits from bottom of pan. Reduce heat to medium-low, cover, and cook, until vegetables are tender and pork is no longer pink in center, about 12 minutes. Whisk in mustard and season with additional salt and pepper to taste.

Chapter 10

Divine Desserts on the Dot

These days, more and more people are opting for a simple, unadorned piece of fresh fruit to eat as dessert after a family meal. Perfectly ripe fresh fruit—either raw or barely cooked—can also be the basis for any number of appealing desserts that are perfectly suitable to serve to guests as well. In spring, try Strawberries Romanoff or Mixed Melon Compote with Champagne. Summertime berries can be presented simply, as in Cherry-Berry Fruit Salad with Kirsch, or more elaborately, as in Blueberry Lemon Mousse or Raspberries with Rum Sabayon. In the autumn, Pears Belle Hélène or Spiced Applesauce take advantage of seasonal fruits at their peak, and wintertime spells the advent of tropical fruits, used here in such combinations as Tropical Fruits in Rum Sauce or the famous Bananas Foster.

Having a few special ingredients on hand ensures that a quick and elegant dessert can be produced at the drop of a hat. Good lemon curd is now available in jars, as are quite a number of excellent ice cream toppings, such as chocolate and butterscotch sauce. (I've given you recipes to make your own versions of some of these sauces as well.) In addition, an ever growing number of premium ice creams (both regular and low-fat) and frozen yogurts in a bewildering choice of flavors add variety and interest to the dessert smorgasbord. Ice cream or frozen yogurt is featured here in such sumptuous concoctions as Mile-High Mocha Ice Cream Pie, Crystallized Ginger Ice Cream, and Black and White Frozen Yogurt Sandwiches. And if you have some good semisweet chocolate on hand, a dessert such as Microwave Chocolate Fondue with Fresh Fruit can be ready in mere minutes.

327   SPICED APPLESAUCE
Prep: 6 minutes   Cook: 13 minutes   Serves: 2

2 large sweet apples, such as
  Golden Delicious,
  peeled, cored, and cut
  into ¾-inch-thick slices
2 tablespoons packed light
  brown sugar

¼ cup apple juice
1 teaspoon lemon juice
½ teaspoon cinnamon
1 teaspoon vanilla extract

1. In a heavy medium saucepan, combine apples with brown sugar and apple juice. Bring to a boil over high heat, reduce heat to medium, cover, and cook, stirring occasionally, until apples are tender, about 8 minutes.

2. Uncover, stir in lemon juice and cinnamon, and cook over medium heat until liquid is slightly reduced, about 5 minutes.

3. Scrape into bowl of food processor and pulse mixture to a chunky puree. Stir in vanilla. Serve warm or cold.

328   BANANAS FOSTER
Prep: 3 minutes   Cook: 5 to 6 minutes   Serves: 4

This signature dessert from Brennan's restaurant in New Orleans makes a fitting grand finale to one of their famous breakfasts or brunches.

3 large firm, ripe bananas
4 tablespoons butter
1 cup packed light brown
  sugar

¼ cup banana-flavored liqueur
¼ teaspoon cinnamon
¼ cup light rum
4 scoops of vanilla ice cream

1. Peel bananas, cut in half crosswise, and slice each half lengthwise. In a large skillet or chafing dish, melt butter over medium heat. Add brown sugar, banana liqueur, and cinnamon and cook, stirring almost constantly, until sugar dissolves and mixture is bubbly, about 2 minutes.

2. Add bananas and cook, turning once, until golden brown and slightly softened, about 2 minutes. Remove pan from heat.

3. In a small saucepan, heat rum over low heat. Remove pan from heat and, using a long match, ignite rum. Pour flaming rum over bananas and sauce. Swirl sauce gently, letting flame burn until it dies out, 1 to 2 minutes. Spoon bananas and warm sauce over ice cream to serve.

329   CARAMELIZED BANANAS
Prep: 3 minutes   Cook: 3 to 4 minutes   Serves: 4

3 large firm, ripe bananas
3 tablespoons butter
3 tablespoons packed light
    brown sugar

1 tablespoon rum or brandy
½ cup vanilla yogurt
½ teaspoon grated nutmeg

1. Peel bananas and cut on a sharp diagonal into slices ¾ inch thick.

2. In a large heavy skillet, cook butter and brown sugar over medium heat, stirring constantly, until sugar dissolves, about 1 minute. Add bananas and cook uncovered, carefully turning once, until bananas are richly browned and caramelized on both sides, 2 to 3 minutes.

3. Push bananas to one side of pan and add rum to sauce, stirring to blend. Spoon bananas onto dessert plates. Drizzle with sauce and top with a spoonful of yogurt. Dust with nutmeg and serve.

330   FROZEN COCONUTTY CHOCOLATE-DIPPED BANANAS
Prep: 5 minutes   Cook: none   Freeze: 15 minutes   Serves: 2 to 4

½ cup hot fudge sauce,
    homemade (page 202) or
    purchased
2 large bananas

½ cup purchased toasted
    coconut topping

1. Warm fudge sauce in a microwave or over low heat until thin enough to stir. Transfer to a small plate.

2. Peel bananas and cut in half crosswise. Spear each piece through cut end with a 7-inch bamboo skewer or popsicle stick.

3. Roll bananas in fudge sauce and then in coconut topping, turning to coat all sides. Place on a plate lined with plastic wrap and freeze until firm, at least 15 minutes.

331   BLUEBERRY LEMON MOUSSE
Prep: 5 minutes   Cook: none   Chill: 15 minutes   Serves: 4

This light and creamy mousse gets its intense lemon flavor from good-quality purchased lemon curd, which is increasingly available in grocery stores.

½ cup heavy cream   1 cup fresh blueberries
1 cup lemon curd

1. In a chilled medium bowl, whip cream with an electric mixer to soft peaks.

2. In another bowl, whisk one-third of cream into lemon curd to lighten. Fold in remaining cream and spoon mousse into 4 dessert dishes or stemmed goblets. Refrigerate until ready to serve, at least 15 minutes or up to 4 hours.

3. Just before serving, sprinkle berries over lemon mousse.

332   CHERRIES JUBILEE
Prep: 2 minutes   Cook: 5 minutes   Serves: 6

This classic restaurant dessert sauce is as simple to make as it is showy. Ideally, the cherries should be flamed at the table and spooned over the ice cream while still burning. Apricot or peach halves in heavy syrup can be served in the same manner.

1 (16½-ounce) can pitted Bing   ¼ cup Grand Marnier or other
   cherries in heavy syrup   orange-flavored liqueur
1 tablespoon cornstarch   1 pint French vanilla ice cream
½ cup rum

1. Place cherries and all but ¼ cup of syrup in a large skillet. In a small bowl, dissolve cornstarch in remaining ¼ cup syrup and add to skillet. Bring to a boil, stirring. Cook 1 to 2 minutes, until syrup thickens and clears.

2. In a small nonreactive saucepan, warm rum and Grand Marnier over low heat about 1 minute. Remove from heat, pour liqueur over cherries, and carefully ignite liqueur with a long fireplace match. Spoon flaming cherries and syrup over scoops of ice cream and serve at once.

333 CHERRY-BERRY FRUIT SALAD WITH KIRSCH

Prep: 5 minutes   Cook: none   Serves: 4 to 6

Three contrasting colors of fruit in a kirsch-flavored syrup combine to make a simple yet glamorous statement. You can pass softly whipped cream or vanilla yogurt to spoon on as a topping if you wish.

1 (19½-ounce) can Royal Anne cherries in heavy syrup, syrup reserved
1 pint strawberries, halved

1 pint black raspberries or blackberries
1½ tablespoons kirsch or cherry brandy

1. Measure out ½ cup of reserved syrup from cherries.

2. Place cherries, strawberries, and black raspberries in a large bowl.

3. Pour reserved syrup and kirsch over fruit and toss gently. Cover and refrigerate until ready to serve.

334 MIXED MELON COMPOTE WITH CHAMPAGNE

Prep: 2 minutes   Cook: none   Stand: 10 minutes   Serves: 6 to 8

Fresh melon balls are sold in many supermarket salad or produce sections.

8 cups fresh melon balls or 1 (40-ounce) package frozen, thawed
2 tablespoons sugar
2 tablespoons Cognac or brandy

2 cups chilled champagne or other sparkling wine
Mint sprigs

1. Use a melon baller to scoop out balls from each type of melon.

2. In a large bowl, toss fruit with sugar and Cognac. Set aside until sugar dissolves, at least 10 minutes.

3. Spoon fruit and syrup into stemmed goblets. Pour Champagne over all, decorate with mint sprigs, and serve.

335   GRATINÉED NECTARINES
Prep: 8 minutes   Cook: 3 minutes   Serves: 4

4 ripe nectarines, sliced about
   ¼ inch thick
2 tablespoons bourbon
2 teaspoons lemon juice
3 tablespoons brown sugar
2 tablespoons coarsely
   chopped walnuts

2 teaspoons flour
¼ teaspoon grated nutmeg
2 tablespoons cold butter
1 cup softly whipped cream
   (optional)

1. Preheat broiler. In a large (12- to 14-inch) shallow baking dish, toss nectarines with bourbon and lemon juice. Spread out evenly in bottom of dish.

2. In a food processor, combine brown sugar, walnuts, flour, and nutmeg. Process until nuts are finely chopped. Cut butter in several pieces and add to sugar mixture. Pulse until butter is size of tiny peas. Sprinkle topping evenly over nectarines.

3. Broil about 6 inches from heat about 3 minutes, until topping is bubbly and sugar is dark brown but not scorched. Serve warm, topped with whipped cream if desired.

336   RUM CARAMELIZED ORANGES
Prep: 8 minutes   Cook: 2 to 3 minutes   Serves: 3 to 4

These oranges are good served by themselves, and they make an unusual sundae when spooned over vanilla ice cream.

3 large navel oranges
2 tablespoons rum

3 tablespoons light brown
   sugar

1. With a sharp knife, peel oranges, removing all of white pith from outside. Slice oranges into rounds about ¼ inch thick.

2. Butter a 9 x 12-inch baking dish. Arrange overlapping orange slices in dish. Drizzle rum over oranges and sprinkle with an even layer of brown sugar.

3. Broil until sugar is caramelized, 2 to 3 minutes. Serve at once.

337   MINT JULEP PEACHES
Prep: 8 minutes   Cook: 1 minute   Chill: 10 minutes   Serves: 4

Make this dessert at the height of summer when peaches and mint are at their peak. If peaches are very ripe, they should peel easily. If not, drop in boiling water for 15 seconds, then remove skin with a sharp knife.

3 **tablespoons sugar**	¼ **cup bourbon**
2 **tablespoons chopped fresh**	4 **large ripe peaches, peeled**
mint leaves	**and sliced**
1 **tablespoon lemon juice**	8 **mint sprigs**

1. In a small saucepan, combine sugar, mint, and lemon juice with ¼ cup water. Bring to a boil over high heat, stirring to dissolve sugar, and cook 1 minute. Remove from heat, pour into a bowl, and stir in bourbon. Refrigerate or freeze until cool, at least 10 minutes. Strain to remove mint.

2. In a glass serving bowl or 4 dessert dishes or stemmed goblets, toss sliced peaches gently with syrup. Serve garnished with mint sprigs.

338   NECTARINES MELBA
Prep: 4 minutes   Cook: 3 to 5 minutes   Serves: 6

Nectarines Melba is a quick and easy relative of Peach Melba. The classic dessert was created in the late 1800s by the famous French chef Auguste Escoffier to honor Australian opera star Nellie Melba. I've called for whipping your own cream with powdered sugar and a hint of orange-flavored liqueur, because it tastes great and doesn't take long. In a pinch, aerosol whipped cream is even quicker.

1 **(10-ounce) package**	⅔ **cup heavy cream**
raspberries packed in	1 **tablespoon powdered sugar**
sugar, thawed	½ **teaspoon Grand Marnier**
¼ **cup granulated sugar**	1 **pint vanilla ice cream**
1 **tablespoon lemon juice**	3 **ripe nectarines, sliced**

1. If you wish to remove seeds, press thawed berries through a sieve.

2. In a small saucepan, over medium heat, combine raspberry puree and granulated sugar. Cook, stirring, until sauce starts to thicken, 3 to 5 minutes. Add lemon juice and mix well.

3. In a chilled bowl, using an electric mixer, beat cream, powdered sugar, and liqueur until cream holds soft peaks, 1 to 2 minutes.

4. Place scoops of ice cream in chilled, stemmed dessert dishes or wine glasses. Arrange nectarine slices over ice cream. Drizzle with raspberry sauce and top with whipped cream.

339   RASPBERRIES WITH RUM SABAYON
Prep: 2 minutes   Cook: 3 to 5 minutes   Serves: 4

This light and airy rum-spiked sauce should be served as soon as it is made, for it deflates as it cools.

3 egg yolks	2 tablespoons dark rum
⅓ cup sugar	2 cups fresh raspberries
⅓ cup dry white wine	

1. In a double boiler set over gently simmering water, whisk egg yolks with sugar, wine, and rum. Cook, whisking constantly, until mixture forms a soft, airy custard and triples in volume, 3 to 5 minutes.

2. Spoon warm sauce into stemmed goblets and scatter raspberries over sauce. Serve at once.

340   STRAWBERRIES ROMANOFF
Prep: 6 minutes   Cook: none   Stand: 10 minutes   Serves: 3 to 4

This simple, classic French treatment of fresh, ripe strawberries was originally done with Curaçao, but any orange-flavored liqueur will be just fine. For a modern touch, you could substitute crème fraîche or vanilla yogurt for the whipped cream.

1 pint strawberries, halved or quartered	1 teaspoon grated orange zest
1 to 2 tablespoons granulated sugar, or more to taste	2 tablespoons orange liqueur
	½ cup heavy cream
1 tablespoon orange juice	1 tablespoon powdered sugar

1. In a medium bowl, toss strawberries with 1 tablespoon granulated sugar, orange juice, orange zest, and orange liqueur. Taste, and if not sweet enough, add up to 1 tablespoon more sugar. Set aside at room temperature until sugar dissolves and a syrup forms, about 10 minutes.

2. Meanwhile, in a chilled bowl, using an electric mixer, whip cream with powdered sugar until cream holds soft peaks, 1 to 2 minutes.

3. To serve, spoon strawberries and syrup into dessert dishes or stemmed goblets and top with a large dollop of whipped cream.

341   GLAZED STRAWBERRY PIE
Prep: 2 minutes   Cook: 1 minute   Chill: 15 minutes   Serves: 4 to 6

The pleasantly bittersweet flavor of cassis, a black currant liqueur, adds sophistication to this spectacularly beautiful instant pie.

¾ cup strawberry jelly
2 tablespoons cassis or red wine
1½ pints (6 cups) strawberries, hulled

1 purchased 9-inch graham cracker pie crust
1 cup whipped cream

1. In a small saucepan, cook jelly with cassis over medium heat, stirring, until jelly melts, about 1 minute.

2. Arrange strawberries pointed ends up close together in pie shell. Brush berries with glaze.

3. Refrigerate until glaze begins to set, at least 15 minutes or up to 4 hours. Cut into slices and serve topped with whipped cream.

342   SUMMER STRAWBERRY SHORTCAKE
Prep: 2 minutes   Cook: 15 to 18 minutes   Serves: 2

Using these easy drop biscuits eliminates the rolling and cutting step of shortcake making, and they taste every bit as good.

½ cup buttermilk baking mix, such as Bisquick
¼ cup half-and-half or milk
1 pint strawberries, hulled

¼ cup sugar
1 teaspoon lemon juice
¼ cup heavy cream

1. Preheat oven to 425°F. In a medium bowl, stir baking mix and half-and-half together until a soft dough forms. Spoon dough onto an ungreased baking sheet, making 2 mounds 2 inches apart. Flatten mounds to roughly ¾ to 1 inch thick. Bake until rich golden brown outside, 15 to 18 minutes.

2. Meanwhile, place half of berries in a food processor with sugar and lemon juice. Pulse to a smooth puree and pour into a bowl. Slice remaining berries and stir into puree.

3. In a chilled bowl, using an electric mixer or whisk, whip cream to soft peaks.

4. Split hot shortcake biscuits in half horizontally. Place bottoms on plates and spoon half of strawberry sauce over biscuits. Replace tops, cover with remaining sauce, and top with a spoonful of whipped cream.

343   WHITE AND DARK CHOCOLATE-DIPPED STRAWBERRIES

Prep: 5 minutes   Cook: 1 minute   Chill: 10 minutes   Serves: 4 to 6

These chocolate-dipped strawberries are simple to prepare, and they make a spectacular presentation. The semisweet chocolate can be melted in a microwave, but the white chocolate should be melted over hot water, or it may separate.

⅓ **cup white chocolate chips**
⅓ **cup semisweet chocolate chips**

2 **teaspoons vegetable oil**
1 **pint strawberries, preferably long-stemmed**

1. Place chocolate chips in 2 small bowls. Microwave on High 1 minute. Stir until melted and smooth. Or melt over hot, but not simmering, water. Add 1 teaspoon oil to each bowl and stir until smooth.

2. Dip strawberries into melted chocolate, coming about halfway up sides of berries. Let excess drip back into bowl. Place on a plate lined with plastic wrap or wax paper and refrigerate until chocolate is firm, at least 10 minutes.

344   TROPICAL FRUITS IN RUM SAUCE

Prep: 6 minutes   Cook: 1 minute   Chill: 10 minutes   Serves: 4

A rum syrup flavored with grenadine, which is made from pomegranates, adds a subtly exotic taste to this dessert of tropical fruits.

3 **tablespoons sugar**
2 **tablespoons dark rum**
1 **teaspoon grenadine syrup (optional)**

1 **ripe medium papaya**
2 **ripe medium bananas**
4 **lime wedges**

1. In a small saucepan, combine sugar and ¼ cup water. Bring to a boil over high heat, stirring to dissolve sugar, and cook 1 minute. Remove from heat and stir in rum and grenadine. Pour into a bowl and refrigerate until cool, at least 10 minutes.

2. Cut papaya in half, scoop out seeds, and remove peel with a sharp knife. Slice about ½ inch thick and arrange on a platter. Peel bananas and cut in sharply diagonal slices. Arrange overlapping with papaya.

3. Spoon syrup over fruit and garnish with lime wedges to squeeze over fruit.

345   QUICK CRÈME BRÛLÉE
Prep: 2 minutes   Chill: 10 minutes   Cook: 4 to 8 minutes   Serves: 4

Since gas and electric ovens broil at different rates, be sure to watch the crème brûlée carefully until you know the time for your oven.

1 envelope (about 1¼ ounces) vanilla pudding, preferably Bird's Imported English Dessert Mix

3 tablespoons granulated sugar
2 cups half-and-half
¼ cup light brown sugar

1. In a medium saucepan, combine pudding mix, granulated sugar, and 2 tablespoons half-and-half. Whisk until smooth. Stir in remaining half-and-half and bring mixture to a full boil over medium heat, stirring constantly, 3 to 5 minutes.

2. Pour custard into a shallow 7 x 9-inch gratin dish or other shallow baking dish. Place dish in a larger flameproof dish filled with ice. Chill 10 minutes, until custard begins to chill and a skin has formed on top.

3. Keeping custard iced, sprinkle brown sugar over custard in an even layer. Place still on ice under broiler for 1 to 3 minutes to melt sugar. Watch carefully to avoid burning.

346   OLD-FASHIONED CHOCOLATE PUDDING
Prep: 3 minutes   Cook: 4 minutes   Chill: 10 minutes   Serves: 4

This chocolaty pudding is so much better than the packaged variety that it's not even a contest, and it cooks up in the same amount of time!

⅔ cup sugar
⅓ cup unsweetened cocoa powder
2½ tablespoons cornstarch

⅛ teaspoon salt
2 cups milk
1 tablespoon butter
1 teaspoon vanilla extract

1. In a heavy medium saucepan, whisk sugar with cocoa, cornstarch, and salt. Gradually add 1 cup milk, whisking until mixture is smooth. Stir in remaining milk.

2. Bring to a boil over medium-high heat, stirring constantly, about 2 minutes. Reduce heat to medium and cook, stirring, until mixture is smooth and thick, about 2 minutes. Remove from heat and add butter, stirring until melted, and stir in vanilla.

3. Pour pudding into 4 dessert dishes or custard cups, place plastic wrap directly on surface to prevent a skin from forming, and refrigerate until ready to serve, at least 10 minutes. Serve warm or chilled.

347   MICROWAVE CHOCOLATE FONDUE WITH FRESH FRUIT

Prep: 15 minutes   Cook: 4 minutes   Serves: 4

This sauce can also be made on top of the stove in a double boiler. For the fruits, use any combination of tropical or other ripe fruits to make a pretty presentation.

¾ cup heavy cream
6 ounces semisweet
   chocolate, coarsely
   chopped
1 teaspoon vanilla extract

1 pint strawberries, hulled
2 kiwifruit, peeled and sliced
1 medium banana, peeled
   and sliced
1 star fruit, sliced

1. In a large glass measuring cup, combine cream and chocolate. Cover loosely and microwave on High 2 minutes. Stir, return to microwave, and cook on High 2 minutes longer. Stir until chocolate is completely melted and smooth. Stir in vanilla.

2. Pour fondue sauce into 4 small ramekins and set ramekins on a large platter. Surround with fruit. Provide long forks for each person to spear fruit and dip in warm sauce.

348   MAINE BLUEBERRY COBBLER

Prep: 3 minutes   Cook: 13 to 15 minutes   Serves: 4

Serve this deliciously simple old-fashioned summer dessert with a scoop of vanilla ice cream if you like.

2¼ cups blueberries, fresh or
   frozen, thawed
¼ cup plus 2 teaspoons sugar
2 teaspoons lemon juice

1 tablespoon butter
1 cup buttermilk baking mix,
   such as Bisquick
½ cup half-and-half or milk

1. Preheat oven to 450°F. In a shallow 1-quart baking dish, toss blueberries with ¼ cup sugar and lemon juice. Cut butter in small pieces and scatter over berries. Place dish in oven to heat while preparing topping.

2. In a medium bowl, stir baking mix and half-and-half together until a soft dough forms. Spoon 8 rounded tablespoons of dough onto blueberry mixture, spacing them about ½ inch apart. Sprinkle remaining 2 teaspoons sugar over cobbler topping.

3. Return cobbler to oven and bake until topping is golden brown and fruit juices are bubbly, 13 to 15 minutes.

349 CREPES SUZETTE

Prep: 3 minutes   Cook: 10 to 15 minutes   Serves: 3 to 4

Crepes Suzette is a festive and spectacular dessert. Here's a shortcut version that's much easier to make than may appear.

1 egg
7 tablespoons butter, melted
1 (10-ounce) package Swedish
  pancake mix

¼ cup powdered sugar
  Juice of 1 orange
¼ cup Grand Marnier
¼ cup Cognac or brandy

1. In a mixing bowl, beat egg and 2 tablespoons butter with 1⅓ cups water. Add pancake mix and beat until smooth.

2. Heat a large nonstick skillet over medium-high heat and brush with melted butter. Use a 2-tablespoon coffee scoop to spoon out batter to make 2 or 3 small, thin crepes about 3 inches in diameter. When bubbles form on top, about 1 minute, turn and cook other side until lightly browned, about 1 minute. Fold in half, browned side out. Repeat with remaining batter, buttering pan as necessary.

3. Coat a chafing dish or large nonstick skillet with remaining butter. Arrange crepes in overlapping circle in pan. Sprinkle with powdered sugar. Place pan over medium heat until crepes are heated through, about 1 minute. Add orange juice and Grand Marnier and spoon over crepes until soaked.

4. In a small saucepan over low heat, warm Cognac until tepid. Remove chafing dish from heat, and pour Cognac over crepes. With a long match, carefully ignite Cognac. As soon as flames subside, return to medium-high heat and cook until sauce is reduced and slightly thickened, 2 to 3 minutes. Place pancakes on serving plates and spoon sauce on top.

350 INSTANT RASPBERRY SORBET

Prep: 5 minutes   Cook: none   Serves: 3 to 4

This sophisticated sorbet really is almost instant. It can be served as a soft sorbet directly from the food processor. If you prefer a firmer sorbet, make it before dinner and place in a metal bowl or ice tray in the freezer; it will be firm enough to scoop by the time you are ready for dessert.

1 (10-ounce) package
  sweetened frozen
  raspberries
2 tablespoons lemon juice

2 tablespoons framboise
  (raspberry eau-de-vie) or
  orange liqueur

1. Place frozen berries, lemon juice, and liqueur in a food processor. Pulse on and off until pureed.

2. Serve sorbet immediately or store in a covered metal bowl in freezer until ready to serve.

351   BANANA SPLIT

Prep: 6 to 8 minutes   Cook: none   Serves: 1

Less sweet than the 1950s soda-fountain giant, this updated version of the banana split nevertheless remains a glorious splurge.

Half a large banana
1 generous scoop vanilla ice
  cream
3 tablespoons hot fudge
  sauce, homemade (recipe
  follows) or purchased

3 tablespoons fresh
  raspberries or sliced
  strawberries
3 tablespoons whipped cream
2 tablespoons chopped
  toasted walnuts

1. Peel banana half, cut in 4 lengthwise slices, and arrange slices around side of sundae dish or stemmed goblet, placing pointed ends up.

2. Place scoop of ice cream in center and pour warm fudge sauce over and around ice cream. Reserve 1 raspberry for decorating top and sprinkle remaining raspberries evenly over ice cream. Spoon whipped cream over berries, sprinkle with walnuts, and top with a raspberry.

352   HOT FUDGE SAUCE

Prep: 3 minutes   Cook: 5 to 6 minutes   Serves: 6 to 8

Spoon this deeply fudgy, glossy sauce over ice cream or plain cake. If you want the sauce to harden when it hits the cold ice cream, cook it 2 minutes longer.

2 ounces unsweetened
  chocolate, coarsely
  chopped
2 tablespoons butter

1 cup plus 2 tablespoons
  sugar
2 tablespoons light corn syrup
2 teaspoons vanilla extract

1. In a heavy medium saucepan, combine chocolate, butter, and ½ cup water. Cook over medium heat, stirring constantly, until chocolate is melted and smooth, about 1 minute.

2. Add sugar and corn syrup and continue to cook, stirring, until sauce comes to a full boil. Reduce heat to low, cover, and cook without stirring so sugar crystals wash down sides of pan, 1 to 2 minutes. Uncover and cook over low heat without stirring until sauce is quite thick, about 3 minutes.

3. Let sauce cool 5 minutes. Stir in vanilla. Use immediately while hot or store in covered container in refrigerator for up to 3 weeks. Reheat gently over hot water or in a microwave before using.

353   RUM-RAISIN BUTTERSCOTCH SUNDAES
Prep: 2 minutes   Cook: 6 minutes   Serves: 4

3 tablespoons raisins
3 tablespoons rum
1 cup packed light brown
   sugar
½ cup heavy cream

2 tablespoons light corn syrup
2 tablespoons butter
1 teaspoon vanilla extract
1½ pints vanilla ice cream or
   frozen yogurt

1. In a small bowl, soak raisins in rum while making sauce.

2. In a heavy medium saucepan, combine brown sugar with cream, corn syrup, and butter. Bring to a boil over medium-high heat, stirring constantly, until sugar dissolves and butter melts. Reduce heat to low and cook uncovered, without stirring, until sauce is syrupy, about 4 minutes.

3. Remove from heat and let cool 2 minutes. Stir in vanilla and rum-raisin mixture. Scoop ice cream into dessert or sundae dishes and spoon warm sauce on top.

354   QUICK CASSATA
Prep: 10 minutes   Cook: none   Chill: 10 minutes   Serves: 10 to 12

The classic Sicilian sweetened ricotta cassata filling is made with candied fruit in addition to chopped chocolate. This one calls for grated orange zest, but if you have access to good, imported candied fruit, chop it medium-fine and add up to ½ cup to the cheese mixture.

1 pound ricotta cheese
¼ cup granulated sugar
2 ounces semisweet chocolate
   chips (⅓ cup), chopped
   medium-fine
1 teaspoon grated orange zest

⅓ cup Grand Marnier or other
   orange liqueur
2 tablespoons orange juice
1 (1-pound) pound cake
   Powdered sugar

1. In a food processor, pulse ricotta with granulated sugar until smooth. Transfer to a bowl and fold in chopped chocolate and grated orange zest.

2. In a small bowl, combine orange liqueur with orange juice.

3. With a long serrated knife, cut still-frozen cake horizontally into 4 layers. Place bottom layer on a serving plate and brush liberally with one-fourth of orange liqueur mixture. Spread with one-third of cheese filling. Top with next layer. Repeat brushing liqueur mixture and spreading filling twice and top with remaining cake layer. Use remaining liqueur mixture to brush over top of cake.

4. Wrap with plastic wrap and place in freezer for 10 minutes or refrigerate until serving time, up to 4 hours. To serve, dust top with powdered sugar and cut into thin slices with a serrated knife.

355 BLACK AND WHITE FROZEN YOGURT SANDWICHES

Prep: 5 minutes   Cook: 5 minutes   Freeze: 10 minutes   Serves: 4

½ cup chopped pecans
1 cup frozen vanilla yogurt, softened

16 chocolate wafer cookies

1. Preheat oven to 350°F. Spread nuts out on a shallow baking sheet and toast until fragrant and lightly browned, stirring once, about 5 minutes.

2. To make sandwiches, spread about 2 tablespoons frozen yogurt on 8 cookies and top with remaining 8 cookies. Roll edges in toasted pecans. Place on a plate lined with plastic wrap, cover loosely, and freeze until ready to serve, at least 10 minutes.

3. If sandwiches are solidly frozen, let stand at room temperature a few minutes before serving.

356 TIRAMISÚ

Prep: 10 minutes   Cook: 2 minutes   Serves: 4 to 5

The classic Italian tiramisú is made with mascarpone, a rich, concentrated sweet cream cheese. If you can get it, by all means use it here, but cut the sugar back to ¼ cup. For the strong coffee, use regular coffee or 1 teaspoon instant granules dissolved in ½ cup boiling water.

⅓ cup sugar
2 egg whites
6 ounces cream cheese, at room temperature
½ cup strong coffee

3 tablespoons dark rum
9 ladyfingers, split in halves
1 ounce semisweet chocolate, finely chopped or grated

1. In a small saucepan, combine sugar with 2 tablespoons water. Bring to a boil over high heat, stirring to dissolve sugar. Boil syrup uncovered 1 minute. Remove from heat.

2. With an electric mixer, beat egg whites in a large stainless-steel bowl to soft peaks. With machine on medium speed, slowly pour hot sugar syrup into egg whites; beat until whites are stiff and glossy. Continue beating until mixture is cool, about 2 minutes. Raise mixer speed to high. Beat in softened cream cheese 2 tablespoons at a time. Beat until smooth.

3. In a shallow bowl, combine coffee and rum. Dip cut sides of half the split ladyfingers into coffee-rum mixture and arrange rounded side up in a single layer in bottom of a glass serving bowl. Spread with half of cheese mixture and sprinkle with half of chopped chocolate. Dip remaining ladyfingers in coffee-rum mixture and arrange rounded side up over cheese layer. If any coffee-rum mixture remains, drizzle over ladyfingers. Spread remaining cheese mixture over ladyfingers and sprinkle with remaining chocolate. Serve immediately or cover and refrigerate up to 12 hours.

357 MERINGUE GLACÉ
Prep: 5 minutes   Cook: none   Serves: 4 to 6

Meringue glacé is a classic and always elegant dessert that can be assembled at the last minute with relative ease. Prepared meringue shells can be purchased at many supermarkets and bakeries.

½ cup heavy cream
¼ cup superfine sugar
1 pint fresh strawberries or frozen unsweetened, thawed
1 to 2 tablespoons lemon juice

2 teaspoons kirsch (optional)
4 to 6 individual meringue shells
1½ pints French vanilla ice cream

1. In a chilled bowl, with an electric mixer or whisk, whip cream until it begins to thicken. Gradually add 1 tablespoon sugar and continue to beat until cream holds soft peaks.

2. In a food processor or blender, puree strawberries with remaining 3 tablespoons sugar, lemon juice, and kirsch.

3. Place meringue shells on dessert plates and fill each with a scoop of ice cream. Drizzle with strawberry sauce and top with a dollop of whipped cream.

358 ANGEL FOOD CAKE WITH BERRY SAUCE
Prep: 4 minutes   Cook: 3 minutes   Freeze: 10 minutes   Serves: 10

When summer berries are in season, serve this fresh, colorful sauce with angel food cake. A bonus is that the dessert is virtually fat-free.

2 pints fresh strawberries
1 pint fresh blueberries
⅓ cup sugar
1 tablespoon lemon juice

¼ cup amaretto liqueur
¼ teaspoon almond extract
1 purchased 1-pound angel food cake

1. In a food processor, pulse 1 pint strawberries to a coarse puree. Pour into a large bowl. Slice remaining strawberries and add to bowl along with half of blueberries.

2. In a small nonreactive saucepan, combine remaining blueberries, sugar, and lemon juice. Bring to a boil over high heat, stirring and crushing some of berries with back of a spoon. Cook until sugar dissolves and juices become syrupy, about 3 minutes.

3. Pour blueberry sauce into bowl with strawberry mixture. Stir in amaretto and almond extract. Freeze sauce or stir over ice at least 10 minutes to cool to room temperature or cover and refrigerate up to 8 hours.

4. To serve, cut cake into slices and spoon berry sauce on top.

359   PEARS BELLE HÉLÈNE

Prep: 3 minutes   Cook: 3 to 5 minutes   Serves: 4

In classic cuisine, this dessert is garnished with candied violets. If you have any on hand, by all means use them.

½ cup half-and-half
3 ounces semisweet
   chocolate, coarsely
   chopped

1 teaspoon vanilla extract
8 small canned pear halves, in
   syrup
1 pint vanilla ice cream

1. In a double boiler set over simmering water, combine half-and-half and chocolate. Cook, stirring frequently, until chocolate is melted and sauce is smooth, 3 to 5 minutes. Remove from heat and stir in vanilla.

2. Remove pears from syrup. Scoop ice cream into dessert dishes or goblets. Place pear halves over ice cream and drizzle warm chocolate sauce on top.

360   INSTANT PEACH SORBET

Prep: 5 minutes   Cook: none   Serves: 4 to 6

When making sorbet with unsweetened fruit, superfine sugar works best. If you don't have superfine sugar, processing granulated sugar in a food processor with the steel blade for a few seconds will produce a superfine sugar.

1 (16-ounce) package frozen
   unsweetened peach slices
½ cup superfine sugar

¼ cup lemon juice
2 tablespoons amaretto
   liqueur

1. In a food processor, combine peaches, sugar, lemon juice, amaretto, and ¼ cup water.

2. Puree until smooth. Serve immediately or store in covered container in freezer.

361   CRYSTALLIZED GINGER ICE CREAM

Prep: 2 minutes   Cook: none   Freeze: 15 minutes   Serves: 2 to 3

The sweet bite of crystallized, or candied, ginger adds a surprisingly exotic twist to plain vanilla ice cream.

1 pint premium vanilla ice
   cream, softened
2 tablespoons finely chopped
   crystallized ginger

½ teaspoon cinnamon

1. In a large bowl, whisk ice cream with 1 tablespoon ginger and cinnamon until blended. Return to carton and refreeze until ready to use, at least 15 minutes.

2. Spoon scoops of ice cream into dessert glasses and sprinkle remaining chopped ginger on top.

---

362   THREE-BERRY COUPE
Prep: 8 minutes   Cook: none   Serves: 4

½ cup sliced strawberries
½ cup raspberries
½ cup blueberries
1 tablespoon kirsch
2½ tablespoons granulated
    sugar

½ cup heavy cream
1 tablespoon powdered sugar
¼ teaspoon vanilla extract
1 pint vanilla ice cream or
    sherbet

1. Place berries in a bowl and sprinkle with kirsch and granulated sugar.

2. In a chilled bowl, using an electric mixer or a whisk, whip cream with powdered sugar and vanilla until cream holds soft peaks, about 1 minute.

3. Place scoops of ice cream or sherbet in stemmed dessert dishes. Top with berries and whipped cream.

---

363   MILE-HIGH MOCHA ICE CREAM PIE
Prep: 5 minutes   Cook: none   Freeze: 15 minutes   Serves: 6 to 8

Customize this pie by using any combination of ice cream flavors that you like.

1 pint chocolate ice cream,
    slightly softened
1 purchased 9-inch graham
    cracker or chocolate wafer
    pie crust

1½ pints coffee ice cream
½ cup hot fudge sauce,
    homemade (page 202) or
    purchased

1. Spread softened chocolate ice cream in an even layer in bottom of prepared crust. Scoop ice cream balls from coffee ice cream and arrange close together on top of pie. Return to freezer for 15 minutes, or until ready to serve.

2. Just before serving, drizzle warm fudge sauce over pie.

364 CREAMY LEMON AND GRAND MARNIER TERRINE

Prep: 5 minutes   Cook: none   Chill: 10 minutes   Serves: 6 to 8

Look for a good-quality lemon curd in jars in the gourmet section of your supermarket or in specialty stores. Here the curd is sandwiched with orange liqueur–spiked whipped cream and pound cake to make a very elegant, quick dessert.

1 cup heavy cream
2 tablespoons powdered
   sugar
2 tablespoons Grand Marnier
   or other orange liqueur

1 (10¾-ounce) frozen pound
   cake, thawed
¾ cup lemon curd
5 thin slices of lemon

1. In a large chilled bowl, whip cream and powdered sugar with an electric mixer until soft peaks form, 1 to 2 minutes. Add Grand Marnier and beat until stiff peaks form, about 1 minute longer.

2. With a long serrated knife, cut cake horizontally into 4 even layers. Place bottom layer on a serving plate, spread ¼ cup lemon curd evenly over cake, then cover with ¼ cup whipped cream. Set next cake layer on top and repeat layering of lemon curd and cream twice more. Top with remaining cake layer.

3. Use remaining whipped cream to frost top and sides of cake. Decorate with lemon slices. Refrigerate until ready to serve, at least 10 minutes or up to 8 hours. To serve, cut terrine into slices with a serrated knife.

365 MOCHA GLACÉ

Prep: 2 minutes   Cook: none   Serves: 1 to 2

This sophisticated version of a milkshake is served as a light dessert, snack, or after-dinner drink. To make a Cafe Glacé, substitute coffee ice cream; for a Cappuccino Glacé, substitute vanilla ice cream. To save minutes, use whipped cream in a can.

2 scoops chocolate ice cream
1 tablespoon coffee liqueur,
   such as Kahlúa

1 cup cold coffee
   Whipped cream

1. In a blender or food processor, combine ice cream, liqueur, and coffee. Pulse on and off until mixture is slushy.

2. Pour into a tall glass or 2 smaller glasses. Top with whipped cream and serve immediately.

Index

Acknowledgments

I would like to express my appreciation to the following people, who made important contributions to this book: Many thanks to my friend Brooke Dojny, who helped enormously in the development of the recipes. And to Linda DeMartine, who lent invaluable help both cooking and being the computer whiz who pulled the manuscript together. I am also very grateful to Gretchen Barnes, Judy Day, and Jennifer Van Norman, the talented test cooks who made sure that these 365 recipes really work.

To order any of the
365 Ways Cookbooks
visit your local bookseller or call 1-800-331-3761

Our bestselling **365 Ways Cookbooks** are wire-bound to lie flat and have colorful, wipe-clean covers.

Each **365 Ways Cookbook** is $18.95 plus $3.50 per copy shipping and handling. Applicable sales tax will be billed to your account. No CODs. Please allow 4 – 6 weeks for delivery.

> **Please have your VISA, MASTERCARD, or AMERICAN EXPRESS card at hand when calling.**

• 365 •

Days of Gardening 0-06-017032-8
Easy Italian Recipes 0-06-016310-0
Easy Low-Calorie Recipes 0-06-016309-7
Easy Mexican Recipes 0-06-016963-X
Easy One-Dish Meals 0-06-016311-9
Great Barbecue & Grilling Recipes 0-06-016224-4
Great Cakes & Pies 0-06-016959-1
Great Chocolate Desserts 0-06-016537-5
Great Cookies and Brownies 0-06-016840-4
Great 20-Minute Recipes 0-06-016962-1
One-Minute Golf Lessons 0-06-017087-5
Quick & Easy Microwave Recipes 0-06-016026-8
Snacks, Hors D'Oeuvres & Appetizers 0-06-016536-7
Ways to Cook Chicken 0-06-015539-6
Ways to Cook Fish and Shellfish 0-06-016841-2
Ways to Cook Hamburger & Other Ground Meats
0-06-016535-9
Ways to Cook Chinese 0-06-016961-3
Ways to Cook Pasta 0-06-015865-4
Ways to Cook Vegetarian 0-06-016958-3
Ways to Prepare for Christmas 0-06-017048-4
Ways to Wok 0-06-016643-6

FORTHCOMING TITLES
Soups and Stews 0-06-016960-5
Low-Fat Recipes 0-06-017137-5
More Ways to Cook Chicken 0-06-017139-1
All-American Favorites 0-06-017294-0
Main-Dish Salads 0-06-017293-2
Jewish Recipes 0-06-017295-9
Asian Recipes 0-06-017292-4